COLLIER'S®

PHOTOGRAPHIC

HISTORY OF

WORLD WAR II

Action and Events in All Theaters
Recorded by Camera and Arranged in Sequence

BONANZA BOOKS
New York

FOREWORD

The camera played an important role in World War II, recording and documenting both major historic events and small but telling moments in the history of the conflict. By the late 1930s the camera had become an inexpensive, highly accessible item and its availability to both professional and amateur photographers made World War II the first major war to be heavily photographed. For both soldiers and civilians, pictures instilled the action with an immediacy never before experienced.

Collier's Photographic History of World War II is a faithful and fascinating account of the war, providing a clear chronology of events and ranging over all theatres of operation. From formal portraits of world leaders to intimate views of benumbed civilians, exhausted soldiers, and battle scenes, the pictures collected here serve as a complete and informative chronicle of World War II.

New York
1985

ANNE JAMES

Foreword copyright © 1985 by Crown Publishers, Inc.

All rights reserved.

This edition is published by Bonanza Books,
distributed by Crown Publishers, Inc.,
by arrangement with Macmillan Educational Company,
a division of Macmillan, Inc.

Collier's is a registered
trademark of Macmillan, Inc.
which is used with permission from Macmillan, Inc.

Manufactured in the United States of America

Library of Congress Cataloging in Publication Data
Main entry under title:
Collier's photographic history of World War II.
Reprint. Originally published: New York:
P. F. Collier, 1946.
1. World War, 1939-1945—Pictorial works.
I. P. F. Collier, Inc. II. Title: Photographic history
of World War II.
D743.2.C64   1985   940.53   84-24417

ISBN: 0-517-467852

h g f e d c

SUBJECT INDEX OF PICTURES

SUBJECT INDEX OF PICTURES

CHRONOLOGICAL HISTORY OF WORLD WAR II

The peace arrived at in the mirrored halls of Versailles unquestionably sowed the seeds of World War II. During the years which followed World War I, the terms of the Treaty of Versailles festered in the minds of the Germans, while political, social, and economic disorganization gave opportunity for the rise of Hitlerism. The League of Nations, formed solely as an advisory body, proved unable to halt the growth of aggression.

In Italy, Fasicism came into power less than four years after the Armistice, when Mussolini marched into Rome on October 28, 1922. The Austrian Adolf Hitler began his public career with his Beer Hall *Putsch* on November 8, 1923. His political ideology, manifesting itself in violent propaganda against communists, pacifists, Jews, and foreigners, gradually won him the support of the German electorate. When President von Hindenburg finally appointed him Chancellor of the Reich in 1933, Hitler set about ruthlessly transforming Germany into a totalitarian state.

Growth of Fascism

Meanwhile, Japanese militarists made pretext in 1931-1932 to attack and occupy Manchuria. The world protested this aggression, but took no action. In 1935 Mussolini, envisioning a Greater Italian Empire, invaded Abyssinia, which he conqered in May of the following year. Close accord between Italy, Germany, and Japan was reached in 1936 and 1937 when these nations joined in a pact against Communism.

On July 7, 1937, Japan started her war against China with what she termed the "China Incident." Her professed purpose henceforth was to do away with white domination of the Far East. The sinking of the gunboat *Panay* in the Yangtze River on December 13, 1937, was evidence of Japan's hostility toward the United States.

On July 17, 1936, Moroccan troops led by General Francisco Franco rebelled against the Republican Government of Spain and thus began the Spanish Civil War which lasted until March 28, 1939. Franco received aid from Italy and Germany, while the Republicans were helped by Russia. With Franco's victory Spain became a Fascist nation.

Hitler Absorbs Austria, Czechoslovakia

During these years Hitler was building up German military strength and extending Nazi control to the east. On March 12, 1938, he annexed Austria. Then, under the appeasement policy of France and Great Britain, he obtained the Sudetenland by the Pact of Munich, September 29, 1938. On March 15, 1939, he seized the rest of Czechoslovakia. Alarmed, England and France offered guarantees to any country menaced by Germany. Rumania and Poland accepted, causing German cries of "encirclement."

Next Italy launched an attack eastward, landing troops in Albania on Good Friday, April 7, 1939. On April 28, in a speech before the Reichstag, Hitler abrogated Germany's ten-year nonaggression pact with Poland, made in 1934, and denounced the 1935 Anglo-German Naval Agreement. He also made demands on Poland for Danzig and the Polish Corridor. A new treaty with Italy, signed in Berlin on May 22, 1939, changed the friendly arrangement between the two countries, known as the Rome-Berlin Axis, into a definite military alliance, offensive and defensive.

During the summer of 1939, Great Britain and France tried unsuccessfully to conclude a treaty with Russia. Instead, the Soviet Union, on August 24, 1939, signed a ten-year nonaggression pact with Nazi Germany. Immediately after Soviet ratification of this agreement, on August 31, Hitler launched his blitzkrieg against Poland.

World War II Begins

Early on the morning of September 1, 1939, German forces attacked Poland by land, sea, and air. The partly mobilized and ill-equipped Polish army proved unable to stop the mechanized Nazi divisions. Great Britain and France, fulfilling their pledge to Poland, on September 3, 1939, declared war upon Germany. Thus began World War II. On September 17 Russia invaded Poland from the east. Warsaw, the capital of Poland, fell on September 27. The partition of Poland followed. By an agreement signed with Germany on September 28, Russia took the Ukraine and White Russian parts of Poland, while Germany annexed the rich western portion. Italy remained neutral.

After the fall of Poland there began a period, popularly termed the "Phony War," in which land and air hostilities between Germany and the Allies remained relatively light. On the sea, however, German U-boats took a heavy toll of Allied and neutral merchant shipping. To avoid the possible sinking of United States vessels, Congress on November 4, 1939, amended the Neutrality Act to permit the sale of war supplies on a "cash and carry" basis.

Russia Invades Finland

In October, 1939, Turkey signed a pact of friendship and nonaggression with France and Great Britain. On November 30 Russia, having demanded but not received strategic bases from Finland, began an undeclared war against her small neighbor.

The first clash of naval units in World War II occurred off the coast of Uruguay on December 13, 1939, when three British cruisers fought a running battle with one of Germany's three pocket battleships, the *Graf Spee*. The German ship, badly damaged, took refuge in the harbor at Montevideo, but was forced to leave three days later in accordance with International Law. She was scuttled by her crew on December 17.

Russia, although greatly superior in equipment and manpower, encountered bitter resistance in her winter campaign against Finland. However, Soviet troops finally captured Viipuri, Finland's second largest city, and the strategic areas which Russia wanted in order to strengthen her borders. In a peace treaty signed on March 12, 1940, Finland was forced to accede to Russian demands.

Denmark and Norway Invaded
April 9, 1940

The entire character of the war changed with stunning suddenness when Germany, on April 9, 1940, invaded Denmark and Norway. Denmark made no resistance and was quickly overrun. Norway, although ill equipped and greatly outnumbered, tried to repel the highly organized blitzkrieg. British and French troops were sent to aid the Norwegians, while the British Navy attacked the invaders from the sea, but the Germans put 100,000 men in Norway and overwhelmed the Allies by the first week in May. On June 7, 1940, King Haakon and his Government fled to England. Three days later the last British units, holding out at Narvik, were evacuated.

Invasion of Low Countries, May 10, 1940

The conquest of Norway being virtually complete, Hitler on May 10, 1940, sent his troops into The Netherlands, Belgium, and Luxembourg. The next day Winston Churchill succeeded Neville Chamberlain as Prime Minister of England and British forces were rushed to the aid of the Low Countries. But the Dutch Army ceased resistance on May 14. Queen Wilhelmina and her Government crossed to England and the Dutch naval units joined the British Fleet. Luxembourg had been occupied in a few hours. France, having also hurried to assist the Low Countries, had thereby weakened her own defenses. On May 13, the Germans broke through at Sedan and swept on to outflank the Maginot Line. On May 21 they reached the French coast at Abbeville, effectively cutting off the Allied forces in Belgium. On May 28, 1940, King Leopold surrendered Belgium and himself became a prisoner of the Nazis.

The British, trapped and unable to stem the German onslaught, retreated to the beaches at Dunkirk. They escaped complete annihilation only through the epic evacuation of May 30 to June 4, 1940. Every vessel that could be pressed into service brought some 335,000 British and French troops back to England.

France Signs Armistice, June 22, 1940

On June 10, 1940, when France was all but defeated, Mussolini joined his Axis partner in the war against France and Great Britain. On June 13, French troops evacuated Paris, after it had been declared an open city, and the Germans occupied it the next day. The French Government was moved to Bordeaux and then to Vichy. On June 14 also, the Germans pierced the Maginot Line and captured Verdun. Marshal Pétain, the new Premier of France, on June 17 asked for honorable terms. An armistice was signed at Compiegne on June 22, 1940, in the same railway car in which the Germans had surrendered in 1918. Germany occupied more than two-thirds of France.

Russia, under her pact with Germany, demanded from Rumania the return of Bessarabia and Northern Bukovina. These were ceded to her on June 28, 1940. In the following August she incorporated the Baltic states—Estonia, Latvia, and Lithuania—into the Soviet Union.

On July 3, 1940, units of the British Navy confronted a portion of the French Fleet in the harbor of Oran, in North Africa, and gave it the choice of surrender or immobilization in the East Indies. When the French refused, the British sank or damaged several of the French warships.

The Battle for Britain

Soon after Dunkirk, on June 18, 1940, the Germans began their all-out bombing of Britain from the air. The attacks increased in force until on August 15 more than 1,000 German planes struck at London and neighboring cities. Thereafter wave after wave of planes were over England by day and by night, the air blitzkrieg reaching its greatest height of destruction and tragedy during September. In this month civilian casualties were officially reported as 6,954 persons killed and 10,615 injured. But in the end the price the British made the Nazis pay for the bombing of England was too high. In one London raid alone, on September 15, 1940, the Germans lost 185 planes. After the end of September the Nazis gave up mass bombing of Britain.

The Struggle for Libya Begins

Meanwhile, on August 6 to 19, 1940, Italy had occupied British Somaliland. On September 12 Italian armies under Marshal Graziani invaded Egypt from Libya in a drive toward the Suez Canal. However, the British held at Sidi Barrani, Egypt.

On September 27, 1940, Germany, Italy, and Japan signed the Tripartite Pact, pledging that each of the three nations would go to the aid of any one of the others which was attacked. Thus became official the Axis plan by which Germany was to dominate Europe; Italy, the Mediterranean area; and Japan, the Orient. Hungary joined the partnership on November 20 and Rumania followed suit on November 23, 1940.

On October 28, 1940, Mussolini sent an ultimatum to Greece, demanding territorial concessions, and three hours later invaded that country. But the Greeks resisted with such fury that by the end of December they had repulsed the Italians and even occupied strategic Italian bases in Albania. This was the first important defeat of Axis land forces in World War II.

The British from their base in Egypt on December 9, 1940, launched a surprise attack to recapture Sidi Barrani and smashed Graziani's divisions. Pressing the offensive, Wavell's forces took Bardia, Tobruk, Derna, and Bengasi, and reached El Agheila by February 9, 1941. This British victory, which cost Italy 170,000 men killed, wounded, and captured, virtually destroyed the Italian armies in Africa.

United States Arranges Lend-Lease Aid

The United States on September 14, 1940, passed the first Selective Service Act in this war. On November 3, 1940, our Government entered into an arrangement with Great Britain by which we turned over fifty World War I destroyers in return for permission to establish nine naval, air, and military bases on British possessions in the western hemisphere. President Roosevelt then proposed, as a further defense measure, the granting of lend-lease aid to those nations fighting the Axis. With the passage of the Lend-Lease Act on March 11, 1941, the United States became the "Arsenal of Democracy."

On January 20, 1941, the British invaded Italian East Africa. During the next four months they took Eritrea, Italian Somaliland, and then Abyssinia, re-establishing Haile Selassie on his throne. This campaign ended on May 20, 1941.

Hitler Invades Balkans, April 6, 1941

On March 1, 1941, Bulgaria joined the Axis and soon became a base for Hitler's next attack southward through the Balkans. With Greece endangered, Great Britain withdrew troops from Libya to support her Greek allies. On April 6 German armies struck simultaneously at Yugoslavia and Greece. In twelve days all organized resistance ceased in Yugoslavia. The Germans then moved down into Greece through Albania, thus coming to the rescue of Mussolini's forces. The Greek armies in Epirus and Macedonia surrendered on April 23, 1941. On April 25 the British made a last stand at the famed pass at Thermopylae. Two days later the Germans occupied Athens, and Greek and British troops were evacuated to Crete and North Africa. The Germans next staged an airborne invasion of Crete and by June 1, 1941, captured the island.

In the Near East the British seized control of Iraq in May and June of 1941. With the assistance of the Free French they took Syria in July. On August 25, with Russian cooperation, the Allies obtained control of Iran in order to speed Lend-Lease shipments to Russia.

Germans Invade Russia, June 22, 1941

By June, 1941, Hitler had conquered all of Western Europe with the exception of Great Britain and the neutral states. He then turned to the east and despite his treaty of nonaggression with Russia, on June 22, 1941, launched a powerful assault on the Soviet Union. On June 25 Finland, with Nazi support, joined in the fight against Russia.

The Nazi blitzkrieg drove across Russia and reached the outskirts of Moscow in late November of 1941. The Germans occupied Smolensk, Kiev, the rich food lands of the Ukraine west of the Dnieper. They encircled Leningrad, overran the vital industrial centers of the Donets basin, captured Kharkov and Rostov, and laid siege to Sevastopol. On November 18, they occupied Kerch, at the eastern tip of the Crimean Peninsula, and were poised for a crossing to the Caucasus. But as the Russian winter closed down, the Germans received their first serious setback before Moscow and were forced to retreat westward.

On July 7, 1941, by agreement with the Danish Minister in Washington, United States troops occupied Iceland. On August 14 Prime Minister Churchill and President Roosevelt announced a basis for common aims, known as the "Atlantic Charter." Congress on November 17, 1941, allowed American ships to be armed and to enter belligerent zones.

Attack on Pearl Harbor, December 7, 1941

The United States had meanwhile continued to permit the sale of materials to Japan for use in her war on China. On January 26, 1940, however, after six months' notice, America allowed her trade treaty with Japan to expire. In July, 1940, President Roosevelt banned shipments of aviation gasoline to Japan and followed this, in September, with an embargo on scrap metal. In July, 1941, Japanese assets in the United States were frozen by Executive Order. Undeterred by economic pressure, Japan continued her aggression in China while negotiating for American recognition of her "new order" in Asia. On November 14, 1941, Saburo Kurusu, special Japanese envoy, arrived in Washington to discuss peace. On November 26 Secretary of State Hull offered a plan for peace embodying America's principles. On December 6, President Roosevelt personally appealed to the Japanese Emperor for peace, and on December 7, 1941, a Japanese reply was transmitted to Mr. Hull. But several hours earlier Japanese planes had bombed Pearl Harbor. Great Britain on December 7 declared war against Japan.

The United States Declares War on Axis

On December 8, 1941, following an address by President Roosevelt, Congress declared that a state of war existed between the United States and Japan. On December 11 Germany and Italy declared war on the United States. The United States in turn declared war against these nations. On the same day Germany, Italy, and Japan signed a pact to conduct their war jointly, as a global conflict. Three Axis satellites then declared war on the United States—Rumania on December 12, Hungary and Bulgaria on December 13, 1941.

The attack on Pearl Harbor was costly for the United States. Of the eight battleships stationed at the base, the *Arizona* was a total loss, the *Oklahoma* capsized, and three others sank to the bottom of the harbor. The other three suffered minor damage. In all, nineteen of our warships were sunk or badly damaged, including three light cruisers and three destroyers. Personnel casualties were high. The Army, Navy, and Marine Corps lost 3,343 men killed or missing;

1,842 were wounded, some of whom later died. Destruction of Army and Navy planes, airfields, and installations was heavy. Japanese losses were about sixty planes shot down by anti-aircraft fire. A few hours later, in an attack on the Philippines, the Japanese destroyed practically our entire air force in the islands.

The United States, unified by the blow at Pearl Harbor, moved quickly to consolidate the democracies of the world in their fight against the Axis. On January 1, 1942, the United Nations was formed, an organization composed of twenty-six countries then at war with Germany or her allies. During January, 1942, nineteen Latin American nations united to aid the democracies in the war. Only Chile and Argentina continued friendly relations with the Axis. In the course of the next year Mexico and Brazil declared war against Germany and her allies. The first contingent of American troops arrived in Northern Ireland by the end of January, 1942, the vanguard of the vast army of invasion.

The Philippines Fall to the Japanese

The Japanese moved rapidly. On December 10, 1941, they invaded Luzon Island in the Philippines and by January 2, 1942, had captured Manila. Bataan surrendered on April 9; Corregidor, on May 6, 1942.

Striking simultaneously at British strongholds in the Far East, the Japanese captured Hong Kong on December 25, 1941, while other forces pushed down the Malay Peninsula toward Singapore. The British battleship *Prince of Wales* and the cruiser *Repulse*, in trying to prevent Japanese landings in Malaya, were sunk by Japanese aircraft on December 9, 1941. Singapore fell on February 15, 1942, after a two weeks' siege.

On January 15, 1942, the Japanese invaded Burma and by the first week in May had driven out the British, cutting China's vital supply route, the Burma Road. Thereafter, supplies had to be flown into China over the Himalaya Mountains. By March 8, 1942, Japanese forces had subdued the Netherlands East Indies.

On January 27, 1942, the Japanese landed troops on New Britain, New Ireland, and the Solomons. On March 8 they invaded the island of New Guinea, at Lae, Salamaua, and Finschhafen. An especially trained force then drove toward Port Moresby over the Owen Stanley Mountains, while a second spearhead pushed toward the British base by a coastal road to the south. American units, which had been arriving in Australia since March, were sent to reinforce Port Moresby on August 2. In September, 1942, the Japanese were stopped within thirty miles of the base. Later that month the Allies drove the enemy back across the Owen Stanley Mountains. On December 10, 1942, Australian troops seized Gona and with American help took Buna on December 15.

The Battle of Midway, June 3-6, 1942

This period of reverses for the United Nations was lightened somewhat on April 18, 1942, when sixteen American bombers led by Jimmie Doolittle took off from the carrier *Hornet* and bombed Tokyo. While of slight military value, the raid served as notice to Japan that her cordon of defenses was not impenetrable.

Then, on May 7 and 8, 1942, our Navy fought and won the Battle of the Coral Sea, turning back the Japanese thrust toward Australia. Our principal losses were the carrier *Lexington* and sixty-six planes. The Japanese lost seventeen ships sunk or damaged.

A month later the Japanese fleet swept toward Hawaii and met defeat in the Battle of Midway, on June 3-6, 1942. Our victory at Midway restored the balance of naval power in the Pacific, largely offsetting our losses at Pearl Harbor. From this point on the United States was increasingly on the offensive in the Pacific. On June 12, 1942, Japanese forces landed on Attu, Agattu, and Kiska, in the Aleutians.

Armies Shuttle To and Fro Across Libya

On the other side of the world, in North Africa, German forces under Marshal Erwin Rommel had been sent to oppose the British after the Italian defeat early in 1941. On March 30, 1941, Rommel attacked with his Afrika Korps and drove the British back to Sollum, Egypt, before being stopped on April 30. Under General Sir Claude Auchinleck, the British then launched a new offensive on November 18, 1941, which by January 2, 1942, had driven the Germans back to El Agheila. Rommel, getting reinforcements, attacked during the latter part of January, and by the first of July forced the British to El Alamein, Egypt, within seventy miles of Alexandria. Here the front remained stable until October 23, 1942, when the British under General Sir Bernard L. Montgomery launched their supreme offensive which was to carry them all the way to Tunisia.

Germans Lay Siege to Stalingrad

On the Eastern Front, the Germans began their 1942 offensive in April with a drive through Southern Russia, the Crimea, and the Ukraine. On July 3 they captured Sevastopol, which had held out since the previous summer. Hitler then sent his armies north and on August 23, 1942, laid siege to the great Russian city of Stalingrad. Another Nazi army tried to take the Caucasian oil fields but was stopped just short of success.

On May 30, 1942, Cologne in Germany was bombed by 1,000 British planes, marking the first mass air assault on the Continent.

On August 19, 1942, especially trained Allied forces made a cross-channel raid on Dieppe, which tested invasion techniques but proved costly in human lives.

Marines Land on Guadalcanal, August 7, 1942

Early in March, 1942, General MacArthur, on orders from President Roosevelt, had turned over the command in the Philippines to Major General Jonathan Wainwright. He reached Australia on March 17, 1942, and began operations as Commander in Chief of the Southwest Pacific Area. On August 7, 1942, United States Marines landed on Guadalcanal in our first invasion of Japanese-held territory. Months of bitter fighting followed, in which our men obtained their first taste of jungle warfare. The Japanese finally evacuated the island on February 8, 1943.

The struggle for Guadalcanal was accompanied by a series of naval engagements. The Bat-

tle of Savo Island occurred on the night of August 9, 1942, when the Japanese attacked our ships protecting our Guadalcanal beachheads. We lost the cruisers *Quincy*, *Vincennes*, and *Astoria*; the Australians, the cruiser *Canberra*. The Battle of the Eastern Solomons occurred on August 23-25. The carrier *Enterprise* was severely damaged. The Battle of Cape Esperance, resulting from a Japanese attempt to put reinforcements on Guadalcanal, was fought on October 11-12. We lost the destroyer *Duncan* and our cruisers *San Francisco* and *Boise* were badly damaged. The carrier *Hornet* and the destroyer *Porter* were sunk, and the *Enterprise* was again damaged. The Battle of Guadalcanal was fought on November 13, 14, and 15, and cost us seven destroyers and the cruisers *Atlanta* and *Juneau*. Seven other ships were damaged. In the Battle of Tassafaronga on November 30, we lost the cruiser *Northampton*.

Americans Invade North Africa, November 8, 1942

On November 8, 1942, United States troops aided by their British allies landed on the shores of North Africa. Although some resistance came from Vichy French forces, an armistice was signed on November 11. Admiral Darlan took charge of French affairs in North Africa until he was assassinated on Christmas Eve, 1942. On November 12 the Germans occupied all of France. The French scuttled their fleet at Toulon on November 27 to prevent its falling into the hands of the Nazis.

Meanwhile, the British, reinforced by fresh troops and American guns and tanks, started their surge westward from El Alamein on October 23, 1942, and drove the Germans across the coastal roads of North Africa until they dug in behind the Mareth Line on January 30, 1943.

Precedent-Setting Conferences

Five great conferences between United Nations leaders were held during the year 1943. The first, at Casablanca, held from January 14-24, 1943, planned particularly for the Tunisian, Sicilian, and Italian campaigns, and for increased aid to Russia. The Quebec Conference, held from August 11-24, formulated means for stepping-up the war in the Pacific and for greater aid to China. The Moscow Conference, attended by Hull, Eden, and Molotov, discussed unity between the three Powers in war and peace. The Cairo Conference, held from November 22-25, in which Generalissimo and Madame Chiang Kai-shek met with Roosevelt and Churchill, discussed Far Eastern affairs. The Teheran Conference, held from November 28 to December 1, 1943, the first which Marshal Stalin attended, set the agenda for the invasion. Later, at Cairo, President Inonu of Turkey met Roosevelt and Churchill and discussed his country's future course in the war.

Germans Turned Back at Stalingrad

The Germans, defeated in their five-month battle for Stalingrad, surrendered to the Russians on January 30, 1943. This marked the turning point in Hitler's war against the Soviet Union. Immediately Russian armies took the offensive and drove the Germans almost steadily westward. On January 18, 1943, the seventeen-month siege of Leningrad was finally broken.

Bombing by Royal Air Force planes was wreaking havoc upon military objectives in France, Italy, and Germany. On January 27, 1943, United States heavy bombers made their first all-American assault on Germany.

Axis Surrender in Tunisia, May 12, 1943

In February, 1943, the battle for Tunisia began in earnest. Two Allied armies, the British under Montgomery from the east and the Americans and British from the west, drew together gradually, squeezing Rommel's forces between them. The Germans attempted to break out of the trap and drove the Americans from the Kasserine Pass on February 21, but our troops reoccupied the pass four days later. On March 29 Rommel was dislodged from the Mareth Line. American and British units made a junction at Gabes on April 7. In full retreat, the Germans were driven northward into an ever-narrowing pocket. Bizerte and Tunis were captured on May 7, 1943, and all enemy resistance ended on May 12. Since El Alamein the Germans had lost 335,000 troops.

Allies Invade Sicily, July 10, 1943

After the surrender of the Germans in Tunisia, the Allies prepared for the invasion of Sicily. The Italian island of Pantelleria surrendered on June 11 and Lampedusa on June 12. On July 10, 1943, the Allies landed on the south and southwestern coasts of Sicily. American troops swung through the northern and western parts of the island, while Montgomery's Eighth Army pushed up the east coast. On August 17, 1943, the conquest of Sicily was completed.

Mussolini Ousted—Allies Land in Italy

On Sunday, July 25, 1943, the news was broadcast that Mussolini had been ousted and that King Victor Emmanuel had placed Marshal Pietro Badoglio at the head of the Italian government. On September 3, 1943, just four years after Britain's declaration of war against Hitler, Montgomery's Eighth Army crossed the Messina Strait and began the invasion of Southern Italy. On September 8 General Eisenhower announced the unconditional surrender of Italy, which had been signed on September 3.

On September 9, 1943, the Fifth Army, consisting of two divisions of British and one of American troops, landed at Salerno. The Allies met strong resistance from the entrenched Germans and the bridgehead was not secure until September 16. On October 1, 1943, General Clark's troops occupied Naples. The Fifth Army then continued to drive up the west side of the Italian Peninsula, while the Eighth Army pushed up the Adriatic coast. The Fifth Army arrived at the heights before Cassino on December 26, 1943, but the Germans, strongly dug in, were not dislodged until May of 1944.

Japanese Driven from Aleutian Islands

In the Pacific, American troops invaded Attu on May 11, 1943, and encountered fierce resistance from the Japanese. Of a garrison of some 2,300 men only twenty prisoners were taken. The rest either were killed or committed suicide. By May 30 the island passed entirely to United States control. On August 15 Allied units landed on Kiska, but found that the Japanese had already evacuated the island.

New Guinea and Central Solomons Campaigns

On New Guinea, General MacArthur's forces took Sanananda Point on January 22, 1943. On September 12 the Japanese were routed from Salamaua and on September 16, from Lae. Finschhafen fell on October 2, 1943.

On June 30, 1943, United States troops landed on Rendova Island in the Central Solomons. On July 2 and 3 landings were made at Empress Augusta Bay on New Georgia Island, and on Vanganu Island. Munda Airfield on New Georgia was captured on August 6. New Georgia was completely occupied by August 25, 1943.

On July 4-5, 1943, our forces invaded the island of Kolombangara, and on August 15 landed on Vella Lavella. The Central Solomons campaign ended on October 6 when the Japanese evacuated these islands. Incidental to these operations, three naval engagements took place. The first Battle of Kula Gulf, on July 6, 1943, cost us the cruiser *Helena*. In the second Battle of Kula Gulf, on July 13, two cruisers were damaged and a destroyer was sunk. The Battle of Vella Gulf was fought on August 6, 1943, with no damage to our ships.

On January 1, 1944, General MacArthur's forces made a surprise landing at Saidor, 110 miles north of Finschhafen on the New Guinea coast. In another "leapfrog" operation, he sent his troops ashore on April 22, 1944, between Aitape and Hollandia. On May 17 our infantry landed at Sarmi, 125 miles farther up the coast from Hollandia. The important airfield on Insumuar, largest of the Wakde Islands, was seized on May 19. On May 27 infantry and tanks were landed on Biak Island in the Schouten group. Its three airfields were secured by June 22, 1944. With the capture of the Sansapor region on July 30, 1944, our control of New Guinea was virtually complete. Morotai Island, lying northward in the Molucca group, was occupied on September 15-18, 1944, bringing MacArthur's forces within 300 miles of the Philippines.

Bougainville Invasion, November 1, 1943

On October 26 and 27, 1943, Mono and Stirling Islands in the Treasury group were occupied by our forces, and on October 28 a landing was made on Choiseul Island. On November 1, 1943, Marines invaded Bougainville Island, in the Solomons, reinforced by regular Army troops. Progress on Bougainville was slow due to the almost impenetrable jungle. On October 12-13, 1943, Allied air forces attacked Rabaul, strong Japanese base on New Britain, sinking 119 enemy vessels and destroying 177 planes. On December 15 Marines landed at Arawe and on December 26 at Cape Gloucester, at the western end of New Britain, to capture the vital airfield.

Tarawa and Makin, November 20-23, 1943

On November 20, 1943, United States forces poured ashore on the beaches of Tarawa and Makin Atolls, in the Gilbert Islands. Tarawa was taken after seventy-six hours of fighting in which the Marines paid a stiff price in human life. Makin was captured by men of the old "Fighting 69th Regiment." The entire Gilbert group of islands thus came under United States control.

Then our forces pressed on to the Marshall Islands which lie directly north of the Gilberts. On February 2, 1944, landings were made on Roi, Namur, and Kwajalein Atolls. Roi and Namur quickly fell into our hands, and on February 5 our troops had captured Kwajalein. On February 17 our forces landed on Eniwetok Atoll and in three days effected its capture. On February 18 our troops took Engebi Island. Thus we also obtained control of the Marshall Islands.

After a heavy attack by our naval and air forces on February 17-18, 1944, on the Japanese base at Truk, United States troops occupied the Admiralty Islands so as to cut the enemy supply lines from Truk to South Pacific bases.

Allies Capture Rome, June 4, 1944

The Italian battlefront suddenly came to life on May 11, 1944, with an Allied drive to take Rome and to destroy the German armies in Italy. By May 15 the first German defense line was broken. On May 25 the Fifth Army made contact with the forces which had been pinned since January on the Anzio beachhead. On June 4, 1944, the Fifth and Eighth Armies entered Rome. Without pausing, however, they pursued the fleeing Germans northward to Hitler's mountain defenses in the Gothic Line. With the capture of Florence on August 22 and Pisa on September 2, the Allies began their assault on this final Nazi barrier. The British broke into the Po Valley by taking Rimini on September 21, while the Americans battled their way through the Apennines. The coming of winter in the mountainous terrain then for many months reduced activity to relatively small-scale fighting.

On September 24, 1944, British troops landed in Greece. Meeting little opposition, as the Germans were evacuating the country, they liberated Athens on October 14. Soon all of Greece and most of the islands in the Aegean had been cleared of the Nazis.

Americans Return to the Philippines

On June 15, 1944, Marines landed on the island of Saipan, in the Marianas. On June 19 and 20, in support of this invasion, carrier planes from our Navy met and defeated the Japanese fleet with heavy losses in the Battle of the Philippine Sea. Saipan was taken by July 8 in bloody fighting. On June 16 Superfortresses raided the Japanese homeland for the first time, setting great fires in the steel plants at Yawata. Our Marines seized Guam between July 20 and August 10, 1944. On September 15, 1944, the Palau Islands were invaded. Control of the group passed to the United States on October 13, 1944, when Japanese resistance ended on Peleliu.

The recapture of the Philippines began with the invasion of Leyte Island on October 19, 1944. This goaded into action the Japanese fleet, which converged on the beachhead from three directions. In the ensuing Battle for Leyte Gulf, October 23-26, the Imperial Navy was decisively defeated. Final victory on Leyte was won by December 26. Landings were made on Mindoro on December 15, 1944, and on January 9, 1945, our forces went ashore on the main island of Luzon. American troops entered Manila on February 3, but did not control the city until February 25. Liberation of all of the Philippine Islands was announced on July 4, 1945.

Allies Sweep on Germany from the West

On June 6, 1944, began the greatest military operation of all history—the invasion of Hitler Europe by combined American and British forces. Landings were made in France on the beaches of Normandy, just east of the Cherbourg Peninsula. Within ten days our foothold on the Continent was secure. By June 27 American troops had driven up the Cherbourg Peninsula and captured Cherbourg, the third largest port of France.

On July 25, 1944, the Allies opened a powerful offensive which swept through France and Belgium and largely destroyed the German forces in both countries. Paris was liberated on August 23 and Brussels on September 3. Our armies battled into The Netherlands on September 4 and into Germany on September 11. Aachen, the first large German city to be taken, surrendered to American troops on October 21, 1944.

On December 16, while American forces were still trying to break the main Siegfried defenses, the Germans launched a sudden counteroffensive. Armored spearheads thrust fifty miles into Belgium before being stopped on December 28. Our armies then took the initiative. Through January and February they cleared the Nazis from the "Belgian Bulge" and resumed the drive into Germany.

German Debacle on the Eastern Front

From Stalingrad to Odessa and Sevastopol, Soviet troops surged forward on a 1,350-mile line almost without pause for fifteen months. Kiev was retaken on November 6, 1943. Odessa was recovered on April 10, 1944, and the Crimea was cleared of the Germans on May 10, 1944, with the fall of Sevastopol. Thus practically the whole vast territory that had been overrun by the Nazis was reconquered by the Russians.

On June 23, 1944, Soviet armies launched an offensive on their northern front to synchronize with the Anglo-American invasion in the west. German strongholds in White Russia fell as the Red Army drove on toward the Baltic and East Prussia. In late August the Russians opened an all-out attack along their entire Eastern Front. By November Soviet armies in the north were inside East Prussia and had invaded Norway through conquered Finland. In the south, Rumania yielded on August 30, and the Russians massed upon Hungary from Transylvania, Czechoslovakia, and northern Yugoslavia. Bulgaria signed a truce on October 28, 1944. Warsaw was finally liberated on January 17, 1945. On February 2 Marshal Zhukov's forces reached the Oder River, forty-six miles from Berlin. There they paused while Red armies to the north and south stormed forward to straighten Russian lines. An armistice with Hungary had been signed on January 22; Budapest, after a fifty-one day siege, was cleared of the Nazis on February 13. Danzig fell on March 30, Koenigsberg in East Prussia on April 9, and Vienna, capital of Austria, on April 11, 1945.

Nazi Germany Surrenders, May 7, 1945

On February 4-11, 1945, a conference of the Big Three was held at Yalta in the Crimea. Here major decisions were reached, including plans for the final blows against Germany.

On February 23, 1945, Allied armies began the assault on the Rhine. They took Cologne on the west bank on March 6 and one day later Remagen, with the Ludendorf railway bridge still intact. Streaming across, American troops quickly established a bridgehead on the east bank of the river. Other crossings were made by air, pontoon bridges, and invasion craft manned by Navy crews. By March 26 seven Allied armies were smashing forward, all east of the Rhine. Key Nazi cities fell in quick succession. Magdeburg on the Elbe River, only sixty-five miles from Berlin, was taken on April 11, while mobile forces to the south aimed for Hitler's "Bavarian Redoubt." On April 12, with victory in sight, President Roosevelt died suddenly and Vice President Truman became the new Commander in Chief.

On April 16, 1945, the Italian front burst into action. Allied forces, smashing through Nazi defenses, captured Bologna on April 21 and pursued the enemy across the Po River. On April 27 Genoa and Verona were taken. The German army in Italy was finished. On April 30 emissaries of the German general surrendered secretly to the Allies. On May 2, 1945, the war in Italy ended

officially. Mussolini, seized while trying to escape to Switzerland, was executed by Italian Partisans on April 28.

Meanwhile, on April 18, Soviet armies had opened their drive on Berlin. On April 20 Red troops entered the city's suburbs. To the south American and Russian units on April 25 made their first junction at the Elbe River, cutting the Reich in two. The death of Adolf Hitler in the ruins of Berlin was announced on May 1. On the same day Munich fell to the Americans. After bitter street fighting, the Berlin garrison finally surrendered to the Russians on May 2. German armies everywhere began to give up. On May 7 Germany surrendered unconditionally to the Allies at Rheims, in France. On May 8 the war in Europe officially ended.

Japan Defeated, September 2, 1945

In the Pacific at the start of 1945, American forces in Burma opened the Ledo Road to China on January 10, while the British advanced on Mandalay. Burma was finally liberated on May 3, 1945. The Chinese, after many reverses, took the offensive against the Japanese early in May and by May 20 had retaken the port of Foochow.

On February 19, 1945, our Marines stormed ashore on Iwo Jima, 750 miles from Tokyo. After a bloody struggle, the volcanic island was won on March 16. Strategic Okinawa, in the the Ryukyu Islands, was next invaded on April 1, 1945. The Japanese here made a suicide last stand and resisted for eighty-one days before surrendering on June 21.

Meanwhile, on April 25, the United Nations Conference opened at San Francisco. The outcome two months later was a World Charter designed to preserve the peace and security of all nations. On June 25, this Charter was signed by representatives of fifty countries.

The defeat of Germany on May 8 left the Japanese fighting alone. B-29's in ever-increasing tempo rained incendiary and explosive bombs on Japan and other enemy areas. Our Pacific Fleet shelled the Japanese homeland. The Potsdam Declaration, made public after a conference at Berlin of the three Major Powers, from July 17 to August 2, not only decided the future of Germany, but called upon Japan to surrender or be crushed. On August 6 the first atomic bomb destroyed the Japanese city of Hiroshima. Russia on August 8 declared war on Japan and invaded Manchuria. On August 9 Nagasaki was hit by the second atomic bomb. On August 10 the Japanese sued for peace. On September 2, 1945, the official surrender of Japan aboard the U.S.S. *Missouri* in Tokyo Bay ended World War II.

ACKNOWLEDGMENTS

The following tabulations show by pages the sources of the pictures in this volume. On those pages which contain more than one picture the credits are listed in order beginning with top left and running across the page from top to bottom.

11—EUROPEAN—EUROPEAN—INTERNATIONAL
12—EUROPEAN—INTERNATIONAL — INTERNATIONAL — WIDE WORLD
13—ACME—INTERNATIONAL
14— INTERNATIONAL — CZECHOSLOVAK INFORMATION SERVICE—INTERNATIONAL
15—INTERNATIONAL—ACME
16—ACME—POLISH INFORMATION CENTER—POLISH INFORMATION CENTER—EUROPEAN
17—BRITISH COMBINE—PATHÉ NEWS—SOVFOTO
18—WIDE WORLD — INTERNATIONAL — ACME — EUROPEAN
19—INTERNATIONAL—BLACK STAR
20—BRITISH COMBINE—BLACK STAR—WIDE WORLD
21—INTERNATIONAL—BELGIAN INFORMATION OFFICE
22—UNITED NATIONS INFORMATION OFFICE—BRITISH INFORMATION SERVICES
23—CANADIAN NATIONAL FILM BOARD — INTERNATIONAL—INTERNATIONAL—WIDE WORLD
24—BRITISH INFORMATION SERVICES—BRITISH COMBINE—BRITISH COMBINE
25—INTERNATIONAL
26—EUROPEAN—INTERNATIONAL—INTERNATIONAL
27—INTERNATIONAL
28—INTERNATIONAL—INTERNATIONAL—BRITISH COMBINE—BLACK STAR—BRITISH COMBINE
29—BRITISH COMBINE
30—INTERNATIONAL
31—ACME—GREEK OFFICE OF INFORMATION—BRITISH COMBINE—WIDE WORLD
32—UNITED YUGOSLAV RELIEF FUND—WIDE WORLD
33—INTERNATIONAL—GREEK WAR RELIEF ASSOCIATION—EUROPEAN
34—BRITISH PRESS SERVICE—BRITISH COMBINE—BRITISH COMBINE—BRITISH INFORMATION SERVICES
35-36—EUROPEAN
37—BLACK STAR—SOVFOTO—BLACK STAR—SOVFOTO
38—SOVFOTO — INTERNATIONAL — SOVFOTO — CANADIAN NATIONAL FILM BOARD
39—WIDE WORLD—SOVFOTO—INTERNATIONAL
40—PAUL GUILLUMETTE — INTERNATIONAL — UNITED CHINA RELIEF
41—PAUL GUILLUMETTE — UNITED CHINA RELIEF — WIDE WORLD—PAUL GUILLUMETTE
42—CANADIAN NATIONAL FILM BOARD—PAUL GUILLUMETTE—PAUL GUILLUMETTE
43—PRESS ASSOCIATION — WIDE WORLD — INTERNATIONAL
44-47—U.S. NAVY
48—U.S. NAVY—(*except bottom*) PRESS ASSOCIATION
49—INTERNATIONAL
50—U.S. MARITIME COMMISSION — ACME — LAWRENCE MONAHAN, *COLLIER'S* STAFF PHOTOGRAPHER — O.W.I.
51—CANADIAN NATIONAL FILM BOARD—U.S.O.—AMERICAN RED CROSS—O.W.I.
52—INTERNATIONAL — (*except center right*) U.S. ARMY SIGNAL CORPS
53—EUROPEAN—INTERNATIONAL—PRESS ASSOCIATION—AUSTRALIAN NEWS BUREAU
54—NETHERLANDS INFORMATION BUREAU — AUSTRALIAN NEWS BUREAU—INTERNATIONAL
55—U.S. ARMY SIGNAL CORPS—EUROPEAN—INTERNATIONAL—INTERNATIONAL
56—U.S. NAVY
57—U.S. NAVY—U.S. ARMY AIR FORCES—U.S. ARMY AIR FORCES
58—EUROPEAN—EUROPEAN—U.S. ARMY AIR FORCES—U.S. ARMY SIGNAL CORPS
59—INTERNATIONAL—(*except center right*) PRESS ASSOCIATION
60—INTERNATIONAL—(*except center right*) PRESS ASSOCIATION
61—U.S. ARMY SIGNAL CORPS
62—U. S. ARMY SIGNAL CORPS—(*except center left*) INTERNATIONAL
63—INTERNATIONAL—PRESS ASSOCIATION—EUROPEAN
64—U.S. ARMY SIGNAL CORPS—EUROPEAN—EUROPEAN—PRESS ASSOCIATION
65—Y.M.C.A.—INTERNATIONAL — PRESS ASSOCIATION — U.S. ARMY
66—ASSOCIATED PRESS — PRESS ASSOCIATION — WIDE WORLD
67-68—U.S. NAVY
69-70—INTERNATIONAL
71—INTERNATIONAL—(*except center right*) U.S. MARINE CORPS
72—INTERNATIONAL — PRESS ASSOCIATION — U.S. MARINE CORPS
73—U.S. NAVY—U.S. NAVY—INTERNATIONAL
74—U.S. NAVY—(*except center left*) INTERNATIONAL
75-76—U.S. NAVY
77—U.S. MARINE CORPS—U.S. NAVY—U.S. NAVY
78—UNITED SEAMEN'S SERVICE
79—UNITED NATIONS INFORMATION OFFICE—UNITED SEAMEN'S SERVICE—U.S. NAVY
80—BRITISH COMBINE—PRESS ASSOCIATION
81—UNITED NATIONS INFORMATION OFFICE—ROYAL CANADIAN NAVY—UNITED SEAMEN'S SERVICE
82—U.S. COAST GUARD—U.S. NAVY—BRITISH COMBINE
83—F.B.I.—F.B.I.—ACME
84—UNITED NATIONS INFORMATION OFFICE—PIX—NATIONAL WAR FUND—NORWEGIAN INFORMATION SERVICE
85—EUROPEAN—EUROPEAN—INTERNATIONAL— INTER-ALLIED INFORMATION OFFICE
86—BRITISH COMBINE
87—INTERNATIONAL — CANADIAN ARMY — INTERNATIONAL
88—INTERNATIONAL—WARTIME INFORMATION BOARD—CANADIAN ARMY
89—WIDE WORLD—INTERNATIONAL—BRITISH INFORMATION SERVICES
90—SOVFOTO—INTERNATIONAL—SOVFOTO
91—SOVFOTO
92—SOVFOTO—INTERNATIONAL—SOVFOTO
93—SOVFOTO—SOVFOTO—EUROPEAN
94—INTERNATIONAL—SOVFOTO—SOVFOTO—PIX
95—BRITISH INFORMATION SERVICES
96—POLISH INFORMATION CENTER—UNITED NATIONS INFORMATION SERVICE—BRITISH COMBINE—CANADIAN NATIONAL FILM BOARD
97—20TH CENTURY FOX
98—BRITISH INFORMATION SERVICES—20TH CENTURY FOX—AUSTRALIAN NEWS & INFORMATION BUREAU
99—BRITISH INFORMATION SERVICES—INTERNATIONAL—20TH CENTURY FOX—20TH CENTURY FOX
100—U.S. ARMY SIGNAL CORPS—U.S. NAVY
101—CANADIAN NATIONAL FILM BOARD—CANADIAN NATIONAL FILM BOARD—INTERNATIONAL—PRESS ASSOCIATION
102—INTERNATIONAL—BRITISH COMBINE—U.S. NAVY
103—INTERNATIONAL—INTERNATIONAL—U.S. ARMY SIGNAL CORPS—EUROPEAN
104—INTERNATIONAL
105—INTERNATIONAL—U.S. NAVY
106—ACME—INTERNATIONAL
107—U.S. ARMY SIGNAL CORPS—INTERNATIONAL—INTERNATIONAL
108—INTERNATIONAL—NEWS OF THE DAY NEWSREEL, INTERNATIONAL — BRITISH COMBINE — U.S. ARMY AIR FORCES
109—INTERNATIONAL
110—U.S. ARMY SIGNAL CORPS—U.S. ARMY AIR FORCES
111—BRITISH INFORMATION SERVICES—WOMEN'S ARMY CORPS—INTERNATIONAL—U.S. ARMY AIR FORCES
112—UNITED NATIONS INFORMATION OFFICE
113—AUSTRALIAN NEWS AND INFORMATION BUREAU—(*except bottom*) PRESS ASSOCIATION
114—AUSTRALIAN NEWS AND INFORMATION BUREAU—INTERNATIONAL—PRESS ASSOCIATION
115—U.S. ARMY SIGNAL CORPS—INTERNATIONAL—INTERNATIONAL
116—PRESS ASSOCIATION — ACME — INTERNATIONAL — PRESS ASSOCIATION
117—U.S. ARMY AIR FORCES—U.S. ARMY AIR FORCES—AUSTRALIAN NEWS & INFORMATION BUREAU—INTERNATIONAL
118—U.S. ARMY SIGNAL CORPS—U.S. NAVY
119—U.S. NAVY—PRESS ASSOCIATION from *YANK*—U.S. ARMY SIGNAL CORPS
120—U.S. ARMY SIGNAL CORPS—INTERNATIONAL
121—PRESS ASSOCIATION—(*except center left*) U.S. NAVY
122-126—U.S. NAVY
127—U.S. NAVY—U.S. ARMY SIGNAL CORPS—PRESS ASSOCIATION
128—U.S. NAVY—CANADIAN ARMY—U.S. NAVY
129—ROBERT LEAVITT—INTERNATIONAL
130—BRITISH COMBINE
131-132—U.S. NAVY
133—ROBERT LEAVITT
134—ACME
135—U.S. NAVY
136—U.S. ARMY
137—U.S. MARINE CORPS
138—U.S. ARMY
139—JOSEPH DEARING, *COLLIER'S* STAFF PHOTOGRAPHER
140—U.S. ARMY
141—U.S. NAVY—U.S. COAST GUARD—U.S. ARMY—U.S. MARINE CORPS
142—INTERNATIONAL
143-144—U.S. NAVY
145—U.S. ARMY AIR FORCES
146—U.S. ARMY SIGNAL CORPS — INTERNATIONAL — INTERNATIONAL—U.S. ARMY SIGNAL CORPS
147—U.S. ARMY SIGNAL CORPS—U.S. COAST GUARD—BRITISH INFORMATION SERVICES — U.S. COAST GUARD—INTERNATIONAL—U.S. COAST GUARD
148—U.S. ARMY SIGNAL CORPS—BRITISH INFORMATION SERVICES — INTERNATIONAL — BRITISH INFORMATION SERVICES
149—INTERNATIONAL—NEWS OF THE DAY NEWSREEL, INTERNATIONAL—U.S. ARMY SIGNAL CORPS—BRITISH INFORMATION SERVICES
150—INTERNATIONAL — INTERNATIONAL — UNITED NATIONS INFORMATION OFFICE
151—INTERNATIONAL
152—U.S. ARMY SIGNAL CORPS
153—U.S. ARMY SIGNAL CORPS—(*except top*) BRITISH INFORMATION SERVICES
154—WIDE WORLD—U.S. ARMY SIGNAL CORPS—PRESS ASSOCIATION
155—U.S. ARMY AIR FORCES
156—INTERNATIONAL—EUROPEAN—INTERNATIONAL
157—PRESS ASSOCIATION—INTERNATIONAL—EUROPEAN—INTERNATIONAL
158—INTERNATIONAL — CANADIAN NATIONAL FILM BOARD
159—U.S. ARMY AIR FORCES
160-161—U.S. COAST GUARD
162—INTERNATIONAL
163—INTERNATIONAL — U.S. ARMY AIR FORCES — U.S. ARMY AIR FORCES — INTERNATIONAL — CANADIAN ARMY
164—U.S. COAST GUARD — PRESS ASSOCIATION — U.S. NAVY—U.S. ARMY SIGNAL CORPS
165—U.S. NAVY
166—BRITISH INFORMATION SERVICES—INTERNATIONAL—PRESS ASSOCIATION—PRESS ASSOCIATION
167—PRESS ASSOCIATION—(*except bottom right*) U.S. ARMY SIGNAL CORPS
168—U.S. NAVY—PRESS ASSOCIATION—INTERNATIONAL—INTERNATIONAL
169—INTERNATIONAL—PRESS ASSOCIATION — INTERNATIONAL
170—PRESS ASSOCIATION — PRESS ASSOCIATION — U.S. ARMY SIGNAL CORPS
171—UNITED NATIONS INFORMATION OFFICE—INTERNATIONAL — INTERNATIONAL — U.S. ARMY AIR FORCES
172—UNITED NATIONS INFORMATION OFFICE—WIDE WORLD—INTERNATIONAL
173—U.S. ARMY SIGNAL CORPS — U.S. ARMY SIGNAL CORPS—INTERNATIONAL—CANADIAN ARMY
174—U.S. ARMY SIGNAL CORPS—PRESS ASSOCIATION—INTERNATIONAL
175—U.S. ARMY AIR FORCES—PRESS ASSOCIATION—CANADIAN ARMY
176—INTERNATIONAL—(*except bottom*) U.S. ARMY SIGNAL CORPS
177—INTERNATIONAL
178—CANADIAN ARMY — INTERNATIONAL — INTERNATIONAL—PRESS ASSOCIATION
179—U.S. ARMY
180—INTERNATIONAL—U.S. ARMY SIGNAL CORPS—U.S. AIR FORCES
181—AUSTRALIAN NEWS & INFORMATION BUREAU—INTERNATIONAL—INTERNATIONAL—U.S. NAVY
182—INTERNATIONAL—(*except bottom*) U.S. ARMY AIR FORCES
183—U.S. NAVY—ACME—U.S. NAVY—ACME
184—INTERNATIONAL — U.S. ARMY AIR FORCES — U.S. NAVY—U.S. ARMY SIGNAL CORPS
185—U.S. COAST GUARD—U.S. NAVY—U.S. NAVY—U.S. COAST GUARD
186—U.S. MARINE CORPS—(*except center left*) PRESS ASSOCIATION
187—U.S. NAVY—INTERNATIONAL—U.S. MARINE CORPS—U.S. MARINE CORPS
188—U.S. MARINE CORPS—U.S. ARMY SIGNAL CORPS
189—U.S. ARMY AIR FORCES—(*except center right*) U.S. NAVY
190—U.S. ARMY AIR FORCES—INTERNATIONAL—INTERNATIONAL
191—U.S. COAST GUARD
192—INTERNATIONAL—U.S. COAST GUARD
193—PRESS ASSOCIATION—INTERNATIONAL — INTERNATIONAL—INTERNATIONAL—U.S. MARINE CORPS—INTERNATIONAL
194—U.S. ARMY AIR FORCES—U.S. MARINE CORPS—INTERNATIONAL—U.S. COAST GUARD
195—PRESS ASSOCIATION—(*except bottom*) U.S. ARMY SIGNAL CORPS
196—WIDE WORLD
197—U.S. ARMY SIGNAL CORPS—ACME—INTERNATIONAL—INTERNATIONAL
198—INTERNATIONAL—(*except center left*) PRESS ASSOCIATION
199—INTERNATIONAL—U.S. ARMY SIGNAL CORPS—ACME
200—U.S. NAVY—PRESS ASSOCIATION—INTERNATIONAL
201—INTERNATIONAL—(*except top*) U.S. ARMY SIGNAL CORPS
202—U.S. ARMY SIGNAL CORPS
203—SOVFOTO—(*except center right*) INTERNATIONAL
204—PRESS ASSOCIATION — PRESS ASSOCIATION — SOVFOTO—SOVFOTO
205-206—SOVFOTO
207—WIDE WORLD—Y.M.C.A.—PRESS ASSOCIATION—INTERNATIONAL—INTERNATIONAL
208—U.S. ARMY SIGNAL CORPS—(*except center left*) INTERNATIONAL
209—INTERNATIONAL—(*except center left*) WIDE WORLD
210—PRESS ASSOCIATION
211—U.S. MARINE CORPS—(*except top left and center right*) INTERNATIONAL
212—U.S. MARINE CORPS—U.S. ARMY SIGNAL CORPS—U.S. NAVY—U.S. MARINE CORPS—U.S. MARINE CORPS
213—PRESS ASSOCIATION—U.S. ARMY—U.S. NAVY
214—PAUL GUILLUMETTE—(*except center right*) U.S. ARMY AIR FORCES
215—U.S. NAVY
216—U.S. NAVY — U.S. ARMY SIGNAL CORPS — JOSEPH DEARING, *COLLIER'S* STAFF PHOTOGRAPHER—U.S. NAVY—INTERNATIONAL
217—U.S. ARMY AIR FORCES
218—INTERNATIONAL—PRESS ASSOCIATION—ACME—U.S. COAST GUARD—U.S. ARMY SIGNAL CORPS
219—INTERNATIONAL—INTERNATIONAL—U.S. ARMY SIGNAL CORPS
220—SOVFOTO
221—SOVFOTO—(*except center right*) INTERNATIONAL
222—PRESS ASSOCIATION—U.S. ARMY SIGNAL CORPS
223—U.S. NAVY—PRESS ASSOCIATION—INTERNATIONAL—PRESS ASSOCIATION
224—INTERNATIONAL—U.S. NAVY—U.S. ARMY AIR FORCES PRESS ASSOCIATION—NEWS OF THE DAY, INTERNATIONAL
225—U. S. ARMY SIGNAL CORPS—INTERNATIONAL—INTERNATIONAL
226—BRITISH INFORMATION SERVICES—U.S. ARMY AIR FORCES—INTERNATIONAL — INTERNATIONAL — INTERNATIONAL
227—BRITISH INFORMATION SERVICES—U.S. ARMY SIGNAL CORPS
228—WIDE WORLD—INTERNATIONAL—U.S. ARMY SIGNAL CORPS—U.S. ARMY SIGNAL CORPS—PRESS ASSOCIATION
229—U.S. NAVY
230—U.S. MARINE CORPS — U.S. MARINE CORPS — U.S. ARMY AIR FORCES
231—U.S. COAST GUARD—ACME—INTERNATIONAL
232—INTERNATIONAL—U.S. MARINE CORPS—U.S. MARINE CORPS—U.S. ARMY AIR FORCES—U.S. MARINE CORPS
233—PRESS ASSOCIATION—U.S. NAVY—U.S. COAST GUARD
234—U.S. MARINE CORPS
235—PRESS ASSOCIATION—INTERNATIONAL—U.S. ARMY SIGNAL CORPS
236—U.S. NAVY—(*except bottom right*) INTERNATIONAL
237—U.S. NAVY
238—INTERNATIONAL—BRITISH INFORMATION SERVICES
239—INTERNATIONAL—INTERNATIONAL—U.S. ARMY SIGNAL CORPS
240—U.S. ARMY SIGNAL CORPS
241—U.S. ARMY—U.S. ARMY—U.S. ARMY SIGNAL CORPS
242—U.S. ARMY SIGNAL CORPS—INTERNATIONAL—U.S. ARMY SIGNAL CORPS
243—SOVFOTO—SOVFOTO—U.S. ARMY SIGNAL CORPS—U.S. ARMY SIGNAL CORPS
244—SOVFOTO—BRITISH INFORMATION SERVICES—U.S. ARMY SIGNAL CORPS—PRESS ASSOCIATION
245—INTERNATIONAL—U.S. ARMY SIGNAL CORPS—U.S. ARMY SIGNAL CORPS
246—U.S. ARMY SIGNAL CORPS — U.S. ARMY SIGNAL CORPS—U.S. NAVY—PRESS ASSOCIATION
247—PRESS ASSOCIATION—U.S. ARMY SIGNAL CORPS—INTERNATIONAL—SOVFOTO
248—U.S. ARMY SIGNAL CORPS—PRESS ASSOCIATION—SOVFOTO—SOVFOTO
249—U.S. ARMY SIGNAL CORPS
250—PRESS ASSOCIATION—U.S. ARMY SIGNAL CORPS—PRESS ASSOCIATION—WIDE WORLD
251—PRESS ASSOCIATION (*except center*) U.S. ARMY SIGNAL CORPS
252—SOVFOTO—U.S. ARMY SIGNAL CORPS—INTERNATIONAL—U.S. ARMY AIR FORCES
253—INTERNATIONAL — INTERNATIONAL — BRITISH INFORMATION SERVICES—PRESS ASSOCIATION
254—U.S. ARMY SIGNAL CORPS—U.S. ARMY SIGNAL CORPS—BRITISH INFORMATION SERVICES—SOVFOTO
255—PRESS ASSOCIATION—U.S. ARMY SIGNAL CORPS—U.S. ARMY AIR FORCES—PRESS ASSOCIATION
256—INTERNATIONAL—(*except center*) U.S. ARMY SIGNAL CORPS
257—U.S. ARMY SIGNAL CORPS
258—U.S. ARMY SIGNAL CORPS—U.S. NAVY
259—U.S. ARMY SIGNAL CORPS—(*except top*) U.S. COAST GUARD
260—U.S. ARMY SIGNAL CORPS
261—U.S. ARMY AIR FORCES—U.S. NAVY—PRESS ASSOCIATION—U.S. NAVY
262—U.S. NAVY — U.S. MARINE CORPS — U.S. MARINE CORPS
263—U.S. COAST GUARD—U.S. MARINE CORPS—PRESS ASSOCIATION—U.S. MARINE CORPS
264—U.S. NAVY—(*except bottom*) U.S. ARMY AIR FORCES
265—U.S. NAVY—U.S. ARMY SIGNAL CORPS—U.S. ARMY SIGNAL CORPS—U.S. NAVY
266-267—U.S. NAVY
268—U.S. NAVY—(*except bottom right*) U.S. ARMY AIR FORCES
269—U.S. ARMY SIGNAL CORPS—INTERNATIONAL—U.S. ARMY AIR FORCES
270—U.S. ARMY AIR FORCES—U.S. ARMY SIGNAL CORPS—U.S. ARMY SIGNAL CORPS
271—U.S. NAVY—U.S. NAVY—U.S. ARMY SIGNAL CORPS
272—U.S. NAVY—U.S. ARMY SIGNAL CORPS—U.S. NAVY—U.S. ARMY SIGNAL CORPS

WORLD WAR II

Prelude — Germans Invade Poland — The "Phony War" — Denmark and Norway Occupied — Netherlands, Belgium, France Fall

THE second World War began officially on September 3, 1939, two days after the Germans invaded Poland. But much had gone before which led up to this climax. Mussolini had brought Fascism to Italy in 1922, with his March on Rome. Hitler ten years later had ridden into power in the Reich on the dissatisfaction of the Germans with the Versailles Treaty. The former Allies of the first World War had fallen apart, with two of their principal members in the other camp of political ideology. In 1936 Spain had staged a prelude to the main event with the Spanish Civil War, and Fascism took root there. Hostilities between the factions ended only a few months before the curtain went up on the full-dress war. Mussolini had sought, in 1935–1936, to extend the boundaries of the greater Italian Empire by taking Ethiopia. Because the League of Nations tried to punish Mussolini for this adventure, with economic sanctions on Italy, he found solace in Hitler, and the Axis was born.

Hitler, feeling his growing strength and sensing the disunited front of the former Allies, withdrew Germany from the League of Nations in October, 1933, and speeded rearmament. The Saar, by plebiscite, was regained early in 1935; the Rhineland was militarized in 1936; and on January 30, 1937, Hitler declared that Germany was no longer bound in any way by the Treaty of Versailles. Next, he staged his *Anschluss* of Austria on March 11, 1938, announcing proudly that forever after Austria belonged to the Reich. Hitler than eyed Czechoslovakia, promising that if France and England would give him Sudetenland, he had no further ambitions for territory. The Munich and Berchtesgaden Conferences, espousing the cause of appeasement, were sad disillusions to Great Britain and her ally, who began now to take alarm. Mr. Chamberlain and Premier Daladier, by the Pact of Munich, on September 29, 1938, gave the Sudenland to *Der Führer*, but Hitler grabbed the rest of Czechoslovakia the next spring.

Meanwhile, Chamberlain and Daladier tried frantically to form an alliance with Russia to offset Hitler's aggression, but *Der Führer* checkmated them by signing an agreement with Russia in August, 1939. Hitler next turned his attention to the Polish Corridor, and challenged Poland, which he treated to his blitzkrieg on September 1, 1939. As Great Britain and France were obligated by treaty to defend Poland, they declared hostilities against Germany on September 3, 1939, and so was started the greatest war in all history.

Mussolini, in the heyday of his career, postures on his black-draped speakers' stand as he addresses huge crowds in the Piazza del Duomo, before the Cathedral in Milan.

Mussolini poses before the statue of Caesar. Mussolini's ambition was to build a new Roman Empire. The March on Rome, Oct. 28, 1922, brought Fascism into power in Italy. The Ethiopian conquest, completed in May 1936, fed his ambition. In April 1939 he seized Albania, and on Oct. 28, 1940, Italian forces invaded Greece, but were defeated by the Greeks who were conquered in 1941 by his allies, the Nazis. His house of cards fell July 25, 1943, when he was ousted from power.

Haile Selassie pleads before the League of Nations. In June 1936, the Emperor of Ethiopia protested Italy's invasion and plundering of his country and prophesied that Ethiopia's fate if unavenged was but the forerunner of other such violations against small nations by the dictatorships. The League applied economic sanctions against Italy to cripple her aggressions. Germany refused to abide by the sanctions and the basis was laid for the Rome-Berlin Axis partnership.

Early Nazi leaders pose after Munich Beer Hall *Putsch*, Nov. 8, 1923. Hitler's attempt to seize power miscarried when Bavarian officers failed to give support. The Nazi Party was formed by a handful of Army men, some of whom he purged from the organization in 1934, and unemployed Germans whom he encouraged in rioting and in anti-semitic demonstrations.

Adolph Hitler, new chancellor of the Reich, appears officially with President von Hindenburg (*left*). On Jan. 30, 1933, Hitler became Chancellor. After Hindenburg's death, Aug. 2, 1934, he consolidated the Presidency with the Chancellorship, and a plebiscite named him *Reichsfuehrer*. By inoculating Germany with his political ideology he rose from obscurity in World War I to head of the German Reich.

Fanatical members of the Nazi party, purging "non-Aryan" and "decadent" art, destroyed priceless treasures, a desecration which shocked the world (*right*). The first book-burning took place May 10, 1933. Many intellectuals, including musicians, painters and writers out of step with Hitler's New Order, had to flee the country.

Prisoners line up in a Nazi concentration camp (*right*). To stifle opposition, Hitler imprisoned thousands of German citizens throughout the Reich. Fanatical cruelty and torture, under the guise of racial superiority, snuffed out much of the finest manhood of Germany. Thus, the German people themselves were Adolf Hitler's first victims as thousands of them were starved, tortured to death, and murdered by the Nazis.

Hitler enters Austria on March 12, 1938. The lightning speed of Hitler's invasion checkmated international complications and stifled Austrian resistance. Mussolini, in exchange for Nazi support in his Ethiopian adventure, gave Hitler free rein in Austria. Austria's political-geographic union with the German Reich was a triumph for the Rome-Berlin axis. "Whatever happens," Hitler shouted exultantly when he reached Vienna, "the German Reich as it stands today shall never be torn apart."

Czechoslovakia is betrayed to the Nazis. This Czech woman weeps as she obediently salutes the Nazi forces invading her homeland. After the Berchtesgaden and Munich Conferences, with the acquiescence of Great Britain and France, the Nazis occupied Sudetenland on Oct. 5, 1938, and the whole of Czechoslovakia on March 15, 1939.

Munich conference showed the futility of appeasement. Left to right are Chamberlain, Daladier, Hitler, Mussolini, and Ciano. Chamberlain and Daladier, caught with their nations unprepared after years of semi-disarmament, were suddenly confronted by Hitler, who drove a hard bargain. By the Munich pact, signed Sept. 29, 1938, Hitler obtained Sudetenland, and the Allies abandoned pledges to Czechoslovakia. He at this time stated that he had no further territorial ambitions. Nevertheless, the next spring, Hitler, sensing his advantage, occupied Czechoslovakia and renewed his demand for the Polish Corridor.

Nazis occupied Prague on March 15, 1939, in violation of the terms of the Munich Conference (*left*). These troops have seized Hradcany Castle, residence of President Eduard Benes, who succeeded the revered Thomas G. Masaryk, first President of the country.

Franco salutes his Fascist troops as they parade through Madrid. On July 17, 1936, Moroccan troops led by Gen. Francisco Franco rebelled against the legally elected Republican Government of Spain and thus began the Civil War that devastated the country. Germany and Italy sent troops, planes and modern equipment to Franco, and Russia aided the Loyalists who finally were forced to give up the struggle on March 28, 1939. The Spanish Civil War thus became a rehearsal of military strategy used in World War II, which burst upon the world approximately five months after the fighting ceased in Spain.

THE NAZIS INVADE POLAND

As a Result of the Invasion of Poland, Great Britain and France Declared War on Germany, September 3, 1939

The heartbreaking days of the summer of 1939, for Great Britain and France, were climaxed by Hitler's invasion of Poland on September 1. He loosed his panzer divisions upon the ill-prepared and only partly mobilized Polish Army. The Poles tried to delay the advance of the Nazis by dynamiting bridges and tearing up roads, but to little avail. Warsaw had the distinction of receiving the first air *blitz* in the Hitler technique. The city fell on September 27, after a great part of the once beautiful capital lay in ruins and its water supply was destroyed. Hitler's troops had cap-

tured Danzig on September 7, and the hateful Corridor was no more. All organized resistance in Poland ceased by October 6. Hitler then turned upon Poland the full fury of his vengeance, executing its citizens by the hundreds of thousands, or putting them to work in German industries. Through the brutality of the German occupation, the Jews in Poland were reduced from more than 200,000 people to fewer than 50,000 souls herded into the ghettos of Poland's cities, especially Warsaw. After Poland fell, in accordance with Hitler's treaty with Stalin, the country was once more partitioned — a familiar pattern in Poland's history. The Russians occupied the eastern half of her territory, while the Germans took for their own the portion approximately from Warsaw westward. A few weeks later the Baltic states — Estonia, Latvia, and Lithuania, hitherto independent — signed mutual assistance pacts with Russia and in August of the following year these three small states were incorporated as part of the Soviet Union.

The signal given, World War II begins. German infantrymen, plunging through a smoke screen, go over the top in the all-out blitzkrieg on the fateful morning of Sept. 1, 1939. Crack troops, together with planes and tanks, streamed into Poland. The Polish Army put up a heroic resistance, but Nazi forces were infinitely stronger, and Poland soon lay at Hitler's mercy. The flat terrain proved ideal for mechanized warfare. Great Britain and France formally declared war against Germany on Sept. 3, 1939.

Polish troops rush to the defense of their homeland. Polish troops outside Warsaw offered stern resistance to the Nazi advance. However, the blitzkrieg moved so swiftly that the partly mobilized Polish Army was unable to bring its full weight against the invaders. Warsaw withstood heavy artillery attacks and dive-bomber raids for twenty-one days, but its surrender on September 27, 1939, signalized the collapse of Polish resistance. Their campaign in Poland cost the Germans 91,000 dead and 98,000 wounded.

Hitler triumphantly enters Danzig, on Sept. 19, 1939, after German troops quelled Polish resistance. Hitler's last attempt to win territory by threat came on Aug. 27, 1939, when he demanded return of the Free City of Danzig, administered by the Polish Customs Union. The Poles rejected Hitler's demands and, on Sept. 1, 1939, Germany invaded Poland.

Nazi firing squad executes Polish patriots, their bodies crumpling into ready-dug graves. Estimates place the Poles massacred by the Nazis as high as 3,200,000 persons.

Polish patriots are caught as saboteurs by the Gestapo. As guerrillas under the Polish government-in-exile, they derailed trains, wrecked bridges, and destroyed oil wells.

German conquerors brand Polish prisoner. Before Polish prisoners were put to work on farms, identification consisting of large violet and yellow markings was placed on each man's back. At the time of the invasion, Poland had only 300,000 men mobilized, and conscription was carried on in the face of Germany's Blitzkrieg. Polish losses were staggering, as the greater part of Poland's army was either killed, or captured and forced to labor for the German Reich; yet 75,000 soldiers escaped to France and, later, England.

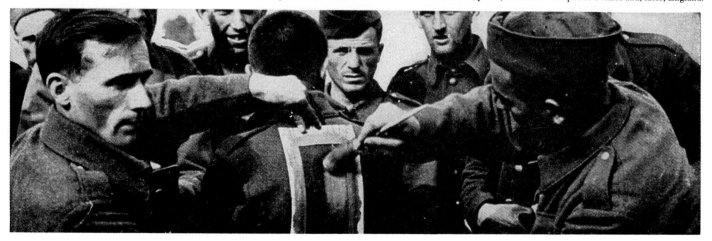

Finnish ski patrol keeps a sharp lookout for the Russian enemy. Patrols and snipers preyed relentlessly on Russian supply lines throughout the entire campaign. Their mobility out-manoeuvered Russian forces; their tactics often compensated for their scant numbers. Lack of modern military equipment, however, eventually led to Finnish defeat.

Grim tragedy stalks in bombing raid on Helsinki. The Russians invaded Finland by land, air, and sea on Nov. 30, 1939, after the Finnish refusal to cede strategic bases. The scene is typical of the terrors visited on Finnish cities in the four months of the war.

Arctic winter takes fearful toll of Russian soldiers in Russo-Finnish War of 1939–1940, when the temperature often ranged from 20° to 60° below zero. The weather was a powerful ally of the Finns in their attempt to check the invaders.

Troops massed on the French front during period of inactive war have lunch in the forest. Bringing the illusion of peace, the winter of 1939–40 proved to be the lull before a storm. Peace was sought, but German military preparations never ceased. In April, 1940, failure of the German peace feelers resulted in Hitler's decision to invade Norway.

London's children are evacuated to English countryside for safety. In 1939 thousands of London's women and children were removed from London to save them from possible bombing. Other thousands were sent to America to live until they could safely return.

French poilus in Maginot Line while away time during Phony War, in winter of 1939–40. The belligerents waged a propaganda battle while their armies stagnated. English leaflets were showered on Nazi troops while Germans broadcast opposite the Maginot Line.

Admiral Graf Spee is scuttled by her crew off the coast of Uruguay. After a running sea battle with the British cruisers *Ajax, Achilles* and *Exeter,* Dec. 13, 1939, the *Admiral Graf Spee,* one of Germany's three 10,000-ton pocket battleships, badly damaged, fled into the harbor of Montevideo. After three days she was ordered to leave, in accordance with international law. The crew took her out into the estuary, and blew up the *Graf Spee,* on orders from Berlin. Her crew was interned in Argentina, but her captain committed suicide.

NORWAY INVADED, APRIL, 1940

After a Winter of the "Phony War," the Germans Rushed Their Overpowering Forces into Norway Through Denmark

On April 9, 1940, after a winter of "phony war," the Germans in a surprise move simultaneously invaded Denmark and Norway. Nazi forces crossed the Danish border and German warships anchored in Copenhagen's harbor. By noon of that day the Nazis had occupied the whole of Denmark. Sailing up the narrow fjords, the Nazis landed at various strategic ports of Norway — in early morning at Oslo, in the southeast, on the Oslo Fjord, and before the day was over at the southern and western ports of Kristiansand, Stavanger, Bergen, and Trondheim; also at the northern port of Narvik. Norway had only about 30,000 troops, brave but ill-equipped for modern warfare. The British and French sent 12,000 troops to the country and warships to intercept the flow of German troops and supplies into Norway. But in spite of losing a number of troopships and warships, the Nazis placed 100,000 men in Norway within a few days, claiming that it was necessary to occupy the country as the British and French were planning to attack Germany from this quarter. In the first week of May, 1940, the Allies, defeated, withdrew the bulk of their forces, although they did not give up their toe-hold at Narvik until June 10, 1940. Thus the Germans secured themselves from Allied attacks through the Scandinavian countries, and protected the vital supplies of iron ore which came from northern Norway and Sweden. Hitler set up over the Norwegians a puppet government headed by Vidkun Quisling who betrayed his King and delivered his country into the hands of the Nazis. In the years of World War II this man's name became synonymous with traitor.

King Haakon of Norway and Crown Prince Olaf run for shelter from German bombs. After many narrow escapes, Haakon set up his government in London.

The Nazis invaded Norway, April 9, 1940, with crushing suddenness. They were opposed by the brave but inadequately equipped small Norwegian army and later by an expeditionary force of the Allies. Norwegian troops, however, capitulated on June 10, 1940, after Allied armies had been withdrawn, on May 2, in the face of superior German air power and land troops.

Nazi bicycle troops hug the ground as Norwegian troops fire upon them from the heights. Supported by the British and French armies and by the British navy which bombarded the coasts, the Norwegians fought tenaciously, but lack of men and air coverage eventually brought defeat. The British held out at Narvik until June 10, 1940.

German invasion forces disembark at Copenhagen, Denmark. On April 9, 1940, during the invasion of Norway, Denmark was overrun by Nazi troops. King Christian X ordered his people to give up the hopeless battle after a day of resistance.

Clouds of smoke rise over the port of Namsos after German bombardment. A week after the Nazis were established in Norway, the Anglo-French Allies landed forces near Namsos and defeated a German "death battalion" in their first engagement.

LOW COUNTRIES AND FRANCE

German Armies Sweep Through The Netherlands, Belgium, and France, Driving the Retreating British from the Continent

On May 10, 1940, after Hitler had settled the issue in Norway, his forces simultaneously invaded The Netherlands, Belgium, and Luxemburg. The brave little Dutch and Belgian armies were totally unable to stop the panzer divisions of the Nazis, with their umbrella of air power. The French and the British rushed to their assistance, but on May 14, only four days after the invasion, the Netherlands army capitulated. On May 28 King Leopold surrendered Belgium. Luxemburg had been overrun in a few hours. The French depended on their great Maginot Line for defense, but World War II, at Hitler's choosing, had become a mobile war. The Germans outflanked the Maginot Line, which they also broke through on June 14, and captured Verdun which the Germans could not pass in World War I. The capitulation of The Netherlands and Belgium left the British and French armies in a precarious situation. The British were pushed toward the seacoast along with a portion of the French forces, and were evacuated from France at Dunkirk from May 30 to June 4. Paris was declared an open city. French troops evacuated the capital on June 14. The Government of France was moved to Bordeaux and then to Vichy. Marshal Pétain, seeing the cause of France as hopeless and attempting to save a shred of her independence, appealed for honorable terms on June 17, 1940. France surrendered on June 22, 1940, — ironically, in the same car in the Compiègne forest in which Marshal Foch in 1918 had read the terms of armistice to the defeated Germans. The fall of France left Great Britain in desperate straits to face the Nazis alone.

Swastika waves over the Brussels City Hall. The Nazi juggernaut added another victim when King Leopold III surrendered all of Belgium on May 28, 1940. The surrender seriously undermined Allied strength and jeopardized Allied troops in the Low Countries, leading to the British rout at Dunkirk.

Belgian forts fall to the Nazi war machine (*below*). From the rubble of Fort Eben Emael come frightened Belgians to surrender to the Germans. Eben Emael and Fort Boucelles, key points in the vast Belgian defense system, were reduced by the Nazis in the first two days of fighting. Louvain, Antwerp, Brussels, and Ghent taken, the enemy turned towards Dunkirk.

Wartime spring comes to Belgium (*left*). Refugees wander homeless among the ruins of ruthlessly bombed cities, as this Belgian mother and her three young children. This has been considered one of the outstanding pictures of the war and has been shown in numerous exhibitions.

British tommies sit placidly at an anti-tank post in Louvain. When the Nazis invaded Belgium, May 10, 1940, British and French rushed to its aid. But the tragic experience of Louvain in the first World War was repeated, and the city was bombed into almost total ruin.

The ghost city of Rotterdam rises to haunt the Nazis. When the Nazis invaded the Low Countries in May 1940, they particularly punished Rotterdam, leaving, in one section, hardly a building standing and killing thousands of the inhabitants as a warning to other cities rash enough to resist. Picture shows bombed area after debris was cleared.

Nazis battle in the streets of a French town. Hitler's forces sped into France and kept the French army off balance. *Above*, a Nazi gun crew fires into a building.

General Henri Giraud falls into the hands of the Nazis, May 21, 1940, while directing his armies in northern France. He later escaped from a German prison camp.

Nazis seemed to spring from every siding and wheatfield in France's tragic month of June, 1940. After Belgium surrendered on May 28, 1940, and The Netherlands was crushed, the Germans pushed into France. The Battle of France began on June 5, 1940, and ended with a cessation of hostilities on June 25. Powerful mechanized troops broke the strong defense at the Somme. They commandeered railroads and overwhelmed faltering French armies. Picture shows Nazi troops battling French near a canal.

Transports, loaded to the gunwales with British and French troops, land in England from Dunkirk on May 30 to June 4, 1940 (*left*). History does not record any other military feat comparable to this magnificent rescue of more than 335,000 men, accomplished under almost impossible conditions. This disaster to Britain's armies, however, exposed Great Britain, inadequately prepared in every way, to the first invasion threat since Napoleon's.

British soldiers at Dunkirk fight off attacking German aircraft with rifles as the man at the right is hit. The Dunkirk nightmare lasted several days and nights. The capitulation of King Leopold on May 28, 1940, left the Allied Armies almost encircled.

The historic evacuation from Dunkirk, May 30 to June 4, 1940, was orderly. Queues of British and French troops waited on the dunes at Dunkirk for rescue. For three days and three nights vessels of every type transported some 335,000 weary men to England.

Nazis march though the heart of Paris. On June 14, 1940, the Place Vendôme resounded to the thud of hobnailed German boots. The day before, to preserve it from bombing, Paris was declared an open city and evacuated by French forces. The French Government was moved to Bordeaux and later to Vichy. Possibly no single event in the war symbolized so dramatically the disaster which had befallen France as the occupation of Paris by Germans.

France surrenders to the Nazis. An exact reversal of the scene of World War I is enacted in the forest at Compiègne. In the same railroad car in which, in 1918, the victorious Allies forced their terms upon Germany, German representatives present their terms to defeated France on June 22, 1940. The French government preferred to cease hostilities with Germany rather than to continue the struggle from Africa. Thus Marshal Pétain, head of the French government, asked for terms.

This weeping Frenchman tells a poignant story. Heartache and despair are written on his face as he watches the battle flags of French regiments taken away to Africa, where the French colonies were virtually untouched by the terms of the armistice.

Adolf Hitler gazes at tomb of Napoleon in Les Invalides, Paris. He ponders a moment at the foremost shrine of France. Napoleon, like Hitler, attempted to conquer all of Europe and invade Great Britain, but he failed. Hitler's visit to the tomb followed his triumphal entry into the city of Paris

BRITAIN BROUGHT TO BAY

Britain Prepares for Invasion—Italy Joins the War—Air Blitz—Hitler Attacks Russia

In the fall of 1940, The Netherlands, Belgium, and France lay prostrate before the Nazi conquerors. The British had succeeded in bringing back from Dunkirk some 335,000 men of their own and French troops. During the summer and fall of 1940, the British expected the Nazis to try to invade their island. Their forces were pitifully weak. Hitler was supposed to have set the date for sometime in September. But the invasion never came off. Goering's Luftwaffe chose to bomb England out of the war and sent great formations of airplanes over the capital day and night. In the month of September, 6,954 people were officially reported killed and 10,615 injured. Anti-aircraft devices and counter-measures in the air made the price too high for the Nazis. In one London air raid alone, on September 15, 1940, some 185 German planes were destroyed.

Meanwhile, Hitler was busy elsewhere. Japan joined the Axis on September 27, 1940; Rumania, on November 23, 1940. Italy declared war on Great Britain and France on June 10, 1940, "stabbing France in the back." On October 28, 1940, Italy invaded Greece through Albania, which she had grabbed in the spring of the previous year. But in Greece she had found a tartar who took the offensive away from her. In September, 1940, the campaigns in Libya began, with the Italians penetrating into Egypt. In December they were driven back by the British, who reached El Agheila in February, 1941. The Italians also invaded British Somaliland, but the following spring the British defeated the Italian forces in this region and in Ethiopia and put Haile Selassie back on his throne, May 5, 1941.

Hitler invaded Yugoslavia on April 6, 1941, and conquered the country in twelve days. He also invaded Greece, which surrendered seventeen days later. The British who had come to help their ally were too small a force successfully to oppose the Germans and were evacuated after severe losses, with a portion of the Greek army, to Crete and North Africa. Crete fell to the Germans in the last days of May. The Nazi armies turned eastward and attacked Russia on June 22, 1941; by December they had reached the suburbs of Moscow, where they were stopped.

Japan then launched her Greater Asia adventure with a smashing attack on the United States, on December 7, 1941, at Pearl Harbor.

Nazis prepared to invade Great Britain after the debacle at Dunkirk, concentrating invasion barges at many points along the French coast. Separated from Occupied France only by the narrow English Channel, Great Britain in 1940 faced her first invasion threat since the days of Napoleon Bonaparte. Nazi invasion fleets practiced daily maneuvers for the assault, which Hitler set for early autumn, but which was abandoned when the flotilla was dispersed and destroyed by the British Royal Air Force.

Unprepared Britain expected an invasion daily during the dark days following Dunkirk. The debacle at Dunkirk left Britain at the mercy of Hitler's Nazi hordes. With insufficient guns, ammunition, and aircraft, armies badly decimated and the island under constant air attack, the British set up every possible defense against invasion.

Queen Elizabeth comforts a newly made air-raid widow. The bomb that crashed through the roof of her tiny home took the lives of her husband, her sister, and her nephew. The King and Queen remained in London throughout the terrible raids during the fall of 1940. Fortunately Buckingham Palace, although hit, suffered but lightly from the bombing.

St. Paul's dome is silhouetted against burning London. London received its worst punishment during September, 1940, when 6,954 persons were killed and 10,615 injured, mainly in that city. British planes, however, took heavy toll, for on the 15th of that month the Germans lost 185 planes and on the 27th, 133 planes. Nazis decided price was too great.

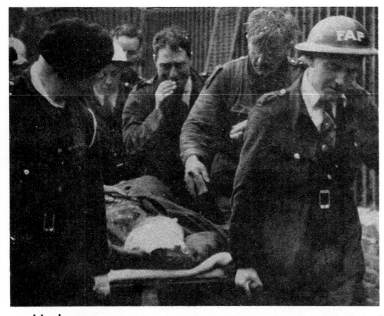

Injured woman is carried on a stretcher after bombing of London school. Trapped under debris and wreckage for seventeen hours and suffering intense pain, she was finally rescued. Picture shows her gratefully clasping the hand of her deliverer.

London's heart is gutted by fire from German bombings, September, 1940. These shells of buildings lie between St. Paul's Cathedral churchyard, in the foreground, and Newgate Street. German bombers left many blocks of ruins in widely separated sections.

English children in a trench, wide-eyed, watch sky battle over London. Plans for the evacuation of children to Canada and the United States were halted on Oct. 2, 1940, when a German submarine sank a vessel in which seventy-nine child evacuees were lost.

Coventry's fourteenth century cathedral was ruined by Nazi bombs. On two successive nights, November 14–15, 1940, more than 500 German planes attacked the city, dropping 60,000 pounds of incendiary bombs and 1,000,000 pounds of high explosives. Over 1,000 people were killed or injured. London, Plymouth, Bristol, and Coventry received the brunt of German blitzkriegs. Low flying planes dropped bombs for hours at a time bringing utter devastation to miles of city blocks. Civilian casualties in late 1940 were heavier than those of British fighting men in various war theatres.

Fuse is removed from a 1,200-pound time-bomb that fell on the grounds of a London hospital. Cleaning out unexploded bombs and duds after a Nazi raid was a dangerous job. Lieut. R. Davies saved St. Paul's by rendering harmless a bomb that fell near the famous cathedral. He later lost his life when another bomb exploded.

London's subways became homes for thousands nightly during bombing of London in September, 1940. Prepared shelters, inadequate to hold all that sought safety from the bombings, forced London civilians to seek protection wherever they could. Lack of ventilation and heat underground brought menace of disease to Britain.

Japan signs the Tripartite Pact with Germany and Italy, Sept. 27, 1940 (*above*). This economic, political, and military pact, running for ten years, pledged each of the three nations to go to the aid of any one of the others that was attacked. Thus officially began the "Axis" partnership in which Germany was to dominate Europe; Italy, the Mediterranean area; and Japan, the Orient. The scene is the Berlin Chancellery and shows Foreign Minister Joachim von Ribbentrop reading the terms of the agreement. Seated left to right are Saburo Kurusu, Japanese Ambassador to Germany, Italian Foreign Minister Galeazzo Ciano, and Adolf Hitler. On the same day a rescript approving the pact was issued by Emperor Hirohito. Hungary joined the German-Italo-Japanese partnership on Nov. 20, 1940, and Rumania followed suit on Nov. 23, 1940.

Adolf Hitler and Francisco Franco, two dictators with a common political ideology, smile warmly and clasp hands in friendship (*left*). Gen. Franco brazenly defied the United Nations by favoring Germany, sending much-needed war materials there.

Antonescu delivers Rumania to Axis, Nov. 23, 1940. Premier Ion Antonescu of Rumania stands at attention, as an aide, right, reads an address to which Hitler and his staff listen attentively. Directly behind Hitler stands Foreign Minister von Ribbentrop, while at Hitler's left is Rudolph Hess, who flew to England a year later. Then, from left to right, are Labor Leader Ley, Grand Admiral Raeder, Propaganda Minister Goebbels, and Field Marshal Keitel. Antonescu became dictator of Rumania on Sept. 5, 1940, following the abdication of King Carol. Rumania's inclusion among the Axis satellite nations gave Germany access to the rich Rumanian oil fields. In subsequent years Germany obtained from one-half to two-thirds of her total needs from these fields. Antonescu raised an army to fight with Germany on the Russian front.

Italian prisoners march past the ruins of Sidi Barrani during the African campaign late in 1940. After having been pushed back into Egypt earlier in the fall by the Italians, the British Army of the Nile, on Dec. 9, 1940, launched a surprise counter-offensive from Egypt, recaptured Sidi Barrani, smashed five Italian divisions, and took 40,000 prisoners. By Feb. 7, 1941, the British had retaken Bardia, Tobruk, Derna, and Bengasi, and two days later, on Feb. 9, 1941, El Agheila, Italian outpost in Libya. At this point their offensive stopped. British casualties during the Libyan campaign were comparatively light. However, total Italian losses were estimated at 170,000 in killed, wounded and captured. The British also took huge stores of supplies and motorized equipment. Remnants of the shattered Italian armies, estimated in December, 1940, to be 250,000 men, were withdrawn toward Tripoli. Thus, in less than two months, the British had all but destroyed Italian military power in North Africa.

Bearded Fascist prisoners are lined up by their Greek captors during the early Albanian campaign. Mussolini attacked Greece on Oct. 28, 1940. But for the German invasion of Greece in the spring of 1941, the Italians might have lost Albania.

British Infantrymen enter Bardia during an advance in the Libyan campaign of early 1941. The town fell on Jan. 5, 1941, after a twenty-day long-range bombardment by British field artillery and naval gunfire, and by the air force.

Italian patrol is attacked by Greek troops in Albanian mountains. One Italian infantryman has just been hit. The Greek armies, taking the initiative early in November, 1940, along a hundred-mile front, trapped and destroyed two Italian divisions. In astonishing advances, they pursued the heavily reinforced Italian troops deep into Albania, capturing the important bases as far inland as Palermo and Khimara. They had taken more than one fourth of Albania from the Italians before German aid arrived.

YUGOSLAVIA — GREECE — CRETE

Hitler's Time Schedule of Conquest Brought His Nazi Blitzkrieg Down Through the Balkans Early in April 1941

Nazis execute innocent women and children in Belgrade, Yugoslavia. Nazi divisions ruthlessly overran Yugoslavia, the thirteenth victim of Hitler's war machine. The nation was invaded by the *Wehrmacht* on April 6, 1941.

With France, the Low Countries, Denmark, and Norway prostrate before his panzer divisions, and with Hungary, Rumania, and Bulgaria his satellites, Hitler invaded Yugoslavia from Rumania, Hungary, and Bulgaria on April 6, 1941, with the purpose of separating the Greek and Yugoslav armies and joining Italian forces in Albania. After Yugoslavia had been overriden in twelve days, the Germans moved down through Albania and into Greece, thus coming to the rescue of Mussolini's armies which had been pushed back into Albania by the Greeks in the fall of 1940. The British tried to assist their allies, the Greeks, but it was another case of "too little and too late." The Greek armies in Epirus and Macedonia surrendered on April 23. At that time the British, including New Zealanders and Australians, were fighting near Thermopylae, but putting evacuation plans into effect. With Greek troops they embarked at Megara and other southern ports for North Africa and Crete, completing the operation by May 1, after the King and Cabinet had withdrawn to Crete on April 22. On the 27th of April, Nazi troops occupied Athens, and on the 29th a puppet government was formed. From May 20 to June 1, the Germans carried out a unique military operation against Crete, transporting parachute troops, mountain troops, and infantry by airplanes and gliders. The British defenders were no match for Hitler's airborne task force and by June 1 were either driven out of Crete or prisoners. The King and the Greek Government escaped from Crete to Cairo, Egypt, setting up a Government-in-Exile, which moved to London in September, 1941. Meantime Yugoslavian guerrillas continued to fight.

Nazi war machine rolls into Yugoslavia. On April 6, 1941, German mechanized forces invaded Yugoslavia from bases in Hungary, Rumania, and Bulgaria, sweeping through towns and cities not able to cope with blitzkrieg warfare. In twelve days the Yugoslav army was dispersed, and by April 18, 1941, German occupation was complete except for guerrilla resistance. Yugoslavia was dismembered by Germany, Italy, Bulgaria, and Hungary, but for the province of Croatia, which became independent under Nazi domination.

German mechanized forces occupy Salonika (*above*), the first big city in Greece to fall. The Nazis next attacked Larissa, Mt. Olympus, and Thermopylae. On April 23, 1941, the Greek army in the Epirus surrendered and on April 27 the Germans entered Athens, where they established a puppet government replacing the King, who narrowly escaped capture in his flight to Crete. Though Italians were in control, most of the airfields, chief ports, and other key points were occupied by the Nazis.

Greek civilians, like this mother and child, were famine-ridden after three years of German occupation of the country. In many sections of Greece twenty-five per cent of the children were found to be tubercular. Because of their condition all were easy prey to epidemics of malaria, typhoid, and dysentery. In Athens and other Greek cities civilians dropped from hunger in the streets, as Nazi agents requisitioned the country's meager food supplies for shipment to the German Reich. The little food remaining was consumed by occupational forces from Germany, Italy, and Bulgaria.

German Dorniers fly over the Acropolis in Athens (*below*). A tragic contrast are these couriers of destruction against a culture three thousand years old. In a period of twenty-two days, beginning on April 6, 1941, the British and Greek troops were forced to abandon Albania to the Italians and were routed from Greece by a superior Nazi army from Bulgaria. Between April 24 and May 1 the British were able to evacuate approximately 45,000 Australian and New Zealand troops to Crete and North Africa. However, the British losses in Greece were estimated at about 15,000 men.

Emperor Haile Selassie enters a beflagged Addis Ababa on May 5, 1941, in a triumphant return to his liberated country, five years to the day after he had been driven out by Mussolini's Fascists. He is shown receiving homage from his devoted native subjects after he attended church services in his capital. The East African campaign began on Jan. 17, 1941, when the British, in a combined operation, launched attacks on Eritrea and Ethiopia from several points along the Anglo-Egyptian Sudan border, and drove into Ethiopia and Italian Somaliland from Kenya. The campaign ended on May 20, 1941, with the surrender of the Duke d'Aosta, after the Italian forces had been driven into the mountains.

British occupy Palmyra in Syria. British and Free French armies crossed the Syrian frontier on June 8, 1941, to oust Vichy French forces suspected of allowing German infiltration and thus exposing Iranian and Iraqi oil fields to the Nazis.

British colonial troops on the Kenya-Italian Somaliland Frontier carry away the stones used to mark the boundaries of the Italian Empire, after the Italian surrender, May 20, 1941. This ceremony was symbolic of the crumbling of Mussolini's ambitions in North Africa.

Governor of Italian East Africa capitulates. Italian resistance ended in Ethiopia with the surrender of the Duke d'Aosta, Viceroy of Italian East Africa, to the British at Amba Alagi on May 20, 1941, with five other generals and 38,000 Italian and colonial troops. They had been trapped between British armies striking from Asmara, Eritrea, and from Addis Ababa. The British eliminated the Italian forces in East Africa and destroyed the Italian fleet in the Red Sea, and thus secured Suez from danger of attack from that area.

German Junkers-52 lands men and mechanized equipment on Crete. To capture Crete the Germans used 1,500 planes, including fighters, bombers, transports, and gliders. This was the first time in military history that an expeditionary force was transported and supplied almost entirely by air in combat against naval and land forces. Weapons were dropped in various-colored parachutes. Anti-tank guns were landed in parts, then reassembled by Nazi paratroopers, supported by ground attack planes and bombers.

Nazi paratroopers land outside the city of Heraklion, Crete (*right*). Parachute troops had their first real tryout in Crete. With the collapse of Greece, British forces in Crete were exposed to an air-borne invasion which began on May 20 and forced the defenders, after twelve days, to evacuate the island. Though 14,580 British troops were evacuated, 12,920 men were lost during the maneuver. Germany claimed 12,000 British prisoners. During the difficult evacuation, Nazi bombers successfully sank three British cruisers, four destroyers, and severely damaged two battleships and an aircraft carrier.

Fifth columnist welcomes German paratroop unit upon its arrival at Crete. Nazi "representatives of the populace" were a vital aid to the Germans in their occupation of Crete. Possession of the island, where resistance ceased on June 1, 1941, gave Germany a land base from which to attack Allied operations in the eastern Mediterranean and to supply her troops in North Africa. Part of Crete came under Italian control but the major portion went to the Nazis, who began extensive work on airfields and fortifications, some of which had been destroyed during the invasion.

THE NAZIS INVADE RUSSIA

Germany Attacked the Soviet Union, June 22, 1941, and Advanced 550 Miles into Russia in the First Year

At Moscow, on August 24, 1939, Nazi representatives signed a non-aggression treaty with Russia, thereby short-circuiting all efforts of Great Britain and France to bring Russia to their side. This ten-year pact was ratified by the Soviet Supreme Council on August 31, the day before Germany's attack on Poland. Warsaw fell on September 27; the next day Hitler and Stalin partitioned Poland. One year and ten months after the signing of the Moscow treaty, the Germans invaded Russia, June 22, 1941, and on the 26th Finland became a Nazi ally. German blitzkrieg was still at its peak of effectiveness. The former Baltic states and the Russian part of Poland were soon overrun, and the great cities of central and southern Russia — Smolensk (on July 16), Kiev (on September 19), Odessa (on October 16), Kharkov (on October 25), and Rostov (on November 22)—fell into the hands of the invaders. In the north the Germans besieged Leningrad. On the central front they were close to Moscow by late November. The population of Moscow heard the guns from the battle lines. Then the tide turned. In the Donets Basin, the Russians retook Rostov on November 29, and from December 3 to the end of the year they took the offensive on all fronts. As the Russian winter frustrated Napoleon in 1812, so winter and Russian might stopped Hitler in 1941. With the temperature at 13° below zero, the Moscow defenders counterattacked and forced the Germans to retreat to prepared winter lines they had not expected to occupy. This marked the first turning point against the Nazis in their war on Russia. Next spring they launched another offensive which ended with their defeat at Stalingrad in February, 1943.

Sorrow and hate grip the people as Nazi forces capture Lwow, Poland. In June, 1941, proceeding under Hitler's plan to seize Russia's richest areas and greatest cities, Nazi divisions drove toward Moscow while other German armies converged on Leningrad and struck through the Ukraine.

Nazis rejoice after hitting Russian farmhouse. The Germans made mass air attacks on Russian cities, smashing at Soviet troop concentrations, military arteries, and supply centers. Their mechanized forces scourged Russian villages. By July 22, 1941, they were four hundred miles inside Russia.

Soviet soldiers surrender to German Tank Corps driving through a captured Russian village. As the Russians retreated eastward, under their "scorched earth" policy they destroyed villages and granaries, so that nothing of value to the invader would fall into Nazi hands. Vast territories were laid waste, and industrial machinery from the cities was moved east of the Urals.

German shock troops lie in wait for the signal to begin the Russo-German war (*below*). On June 22, 1941, violating the nonaggression pact, German troops invaded Russia with an army of 150 divisions with 15,000 tanks and four fleets of the Luftwaffe. They were stopped at the outskirts of Moscow by Nov. 25, 1941.

People of Leningrad obtained their water from the streets when the city's reservoirs and water mains were destroyed by German bombing. Russian children supply water to the city's bakeries.

German prisoners, taken by Russian guerrillas during the siege of Leningrad, are woebegone and bedraggled (*below*). A symbol of Russian courage, Leningrad resisted the German siege for seventeen months until relieved in January, 1944, by their countrymen.

Soviet troops plunge through snow-covered fields in the dead of a Russian winter. After halting Hitler's armies before Moscow the Soviets launched a strong counter-offensive on Dec. 6, 1941, from Leningrad to the Sea of Azov. Rostov had fallen to the Russians on Nov. 29, 1941. Early in February, 1942, Russian armies threatened Smolensk and Kharkov and hammered the German forces besieging Leningrad. From the end of February to May, minor operations took place, opposing armies waiting for better weather to renew attacks.

Russian peasants in the Ukraine look upon all that remains of their home (*right*). In the summer of 1941, the Nazis struck deep into the southern Ukraine. Kiev, Russia's industrial city, surrendered on Sept. 20, 1941, with a Russian loss of about 400,000 men, and Kharkov fell on Oct. 26, 1941. By the year's end Russia had been forced to relinquish the greater part of the rich Ukraine to the invader.

Russian men, women, and children (*right below*), labored sixteen hours a day in building earthworks at Moscow to repel the Nazi invaders. The Nazis advanced to within a few miles of Moscow by Nov. 25, 1941. On Dec. 8, in the face of the Russian winter which had defeated Napoleon the century before, the German high command abandoned the drive on Moscow.

Russian mother collapses as she finds her son slaughtered by Nazis at Kerch, one of the most dastardly massacres of the war. On Oct. 30, 1941, the Nazis cracked the Russian wall at the Perekop Isthmus and invaded the Crimea taking Simferopol, the capital, on November 2. Stopped by the defense at Kerch, German troops were forced to hammer the city with all available forces for two weeks before winning it on November 16.

President Roosevelt and Prime Minister Churchill meet at sea off Newfoundland, in August, 1941, aboard the United States cruiser *Augusta* (*above*). Here the Eight Points for a just and lasting peace among nations were formulated and proclaimed on August 14 in what became known as "The Atlantic Charter." The principles expressed therein gave promise of a better world, in which all peoples might live out their lives secure from oppression and want.

Street fighting raged in Rostov as Soviet forces defended the city in hand-to-hand combat. It fell on Nov. 22, 1941, as the Germans pushed into the industrially rich Donets basin, but was recaptured in a determined counter-offensive on Nov. 29, 1941. The event was important since this was the first major Russian city recaptured from the Nazis. The Germans were forced to retreat along the north shore of the Sea of Azov.

Russian women weep as they watch their menfolk march off to a Nazi prison camp. On Nov. 20, 1941, after the first offensive had spent itself and the Germans were stopped before Moscow, the Russians admitted casualties reaching a total of 2,122,000 men killed, wounded, and missing. German losses to Dec. 11, 1941, were estimated by neutral sources at 1,300,000 killed and 2,600,000 wounded and missing, a fearful price to pay for failure. The habitations of more than fifty million Russian people had been overrun and devastated by German hordes during the invasion of Russian territories.

CHINA FIGHTS BRAVELY ON

China, Pitifully Unprepared, Fought the Japanese Invaders for More Than Four Years without Allies

On July 7, 1937, began what the Japanese termed "the China incident," with the clash between Japanese and Chinese troops outside of Peiping. In the weeks that followed, the Chinese lost Peiping and Shanghai, and were pushed back from their entire coast line farther into the interior of the country, moving their capital finally to Chungking. The full extent of Chinese casualties, civilian and military, will probably never be known, but some estimate that fifty million Chinese had been killed in the five years to January of 1942. The United States, particularly, and Great Britain sought to aid China with supplies through the Burma Road, which the Chinese, in one of the greatest engineering feats in all history, built to transport matériel to their hard-pressed forces. A small number of volunteer American fliers under Major General Claire L. Chennault — then Colonel — had gone to China in September, 1941, where they became known as the "Flying Tigers," and made a miraculous record in the Burma campaign in the spring of 1942. The Japanese had penetrated in late 1941 to Changsha in northern Hunan Province, China's rich "rice bowl." Here it was, early in 1942, that China scored her greatest victory against the Japanese. Meanwhile, on December 7, 1941, came the attack on Pearl Harbor, the Philippines, and on Hong Kong. These attacks immediately precipitated war with the United States and the British Empire. After the surrender of Hong Kong on Christmas Day, 1941, the Japanese launched their Malayan campaign which ended in the capture of Singapore on February 15, 1942. The Japanese, intent on stopping supplies reaching the Chinese through the Burma Road, invaded Burma on January 15, 1942, and won complete control by May 1. They then moved into China's Yunnan Province from the south.

China's president, Generalissimo Chiang Kai-shek, unified China's guerrilla armies and industrial resources into a solid front against the Japanese. Chiefly occupied with fighting China's Communist legions before 1937, he directed his armies at the Japanese threat after the clash at Peiping.

Chinese baby cries among ruins of Shanghai's north station during the bombing of Shanghai on Aug. 15, 1937, early in the Chino-Japanese war. By the end of 1938 an estimated 30,000,000 Chinese had been made destitute and homeless as nearly one fourth of China was overrun by the invaders.

Chungking was bombed almost daily by the Japanese during the summers of each year after it became China's war capital. So terrific were the bombings that three quarters of the city's dwellings were destroyed. The populace took shelter in some 400 caves blasted from the sandstone hills on which Chungking is built.

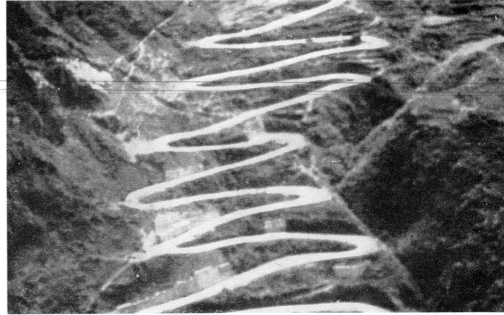

Chinese civilian stoically waits for the blade of the heavy sword to sever his head. With fanatical fury the Japanese tried to stamp out guerrilla bands, whose tactics caused continual harassment of the enemy.

The Burma Road, China's former supply line, twists among the mountains of Yunnan Province (*top, right*). It runs 726 miles from the railhead of Lashio in Burma to Kunming, Yunnan Province, China. The Japanese conquest of Burma in 1942 cut the road and the Allies resorted to the air to supply China.

Japanese bombers on a night raid hit a public air raid shelter in Chungking. Bodies of more than seven hundred women and children were piled up at the entrance of the tunnel in which they had suffocated to death.

Scoreboard in Chungking (*below*) signals the approach of enemy planes. The number of planes, their direction and distance from the city are indicated on these map boards by means of the small model planes pictured.

Major General Claire Chennault chats with an American pilot of the Flying Tigers. Identification on their jackets read: "A foreigner who came to assist China. All soldiers and civilians must give him protection." The Tigers shot down 286 Japanese planes in Burma.

Legless woman (*left*) makes her way with other refugees in the flight before the advancing Japanese. Tragedies of war laid a heavy hand on Chinese civilians. From the rubble of devastated homes, 50,000,000 people, sick and well, fled to safety in China's interior.

Chinese troops exhibit Japanese souvenirs from victory at Changsha. On Jan. 2–6, 1942, the Japanese launched a third drive to take Changsha, Chinese stronghold astride the important railway linking Hankow and Nanking. In this attempt, as in the two previous attacks on the city, the Japanese were badly defeated, losing more than 60,000 men.

Japanese struck at Pearl Harbor while their diplomats talked peace in Washington (*right*). Waiting outside of Secretary Hull's office are Japanese Ambassador Kichisaburo Nomura, right, who initiated the discussions late in August of 1941, and special Japanese Emissary Saburo Kurusu, who arrived in November, purportedly to further friendly talks aimed at achieving a Japanese-American understanding in the many critical Far-Eastern problems.

Premier Tojo, Japan's war leader, bows stiffly before Hirohito, 124th Emperor of Japan (*below, right*). Tojo assumed virtual dictatorship of Japan, Oct. 18, 1941. Ruthless and a stern disciplinarian, he succeeded in accentuating Japanese fanaticism, stemming from deism, with the Emperor occupying the central position of power.

Japanese records go up in smoke following Japan's Declaration of War on the United States (*below*). Diplomatic correspondence also was burned in the Embassy's gardens. The United States moved with equal speed following outbreak of hostilities. Japanese funds and assets in America were frozen and Japanese firms were closed. Within a short interval the FBI swooped down on Japanese aliens from New York to San Francisco, placed them in camps, and thus blocked any Fifth Column threat.

PEARL HARBOR ATTACKED

We Enter the War—Japanese Nearly See Their Dream Come True—Tokyo Raid

Pearl Harbor, the name and its significance, will be remembered as long as our country exists. In that treacherous Japanese attack, nineteen of our ships there (including all eight of the battleships) were wrecked or damaged; 177 planes were destroyed, 3,343 service men killed or missing, and 1,842 wounded. The Japanese lost some sixty airplanes. On the same day (December 7, 1941), the Japanese attacked the Philippines and wrecked most of our planes and airfields in the islands. This was a costly lesson for our nation, but it cleared the atmosphere of American opinion and united the people into a solid front. The record production of 1942 and 1943 in our war plants is eloquent testimony to what Pearl Harbor did for this country. On Monday, December 8, 1941, President Roosevelt appeared before Congress at noon to deliver a war message. The Congress declared war against Japan on the same day, and on Germany and Italy on December 11, after the declarations of those countries of the same date. Three Axis satellites then declared war on the United States — Rumania on December 12; Hungary and Bulgaria on December 13.

In the Pacific and Asiatic areas, the next few months after Pearl Harbor were not happy ones for the United States or Great Britain. Guam had fallen by December 13; Wake Island surrendered on December 22; Hong Kong was taken on Christmas Day of 1941. The Japanese speeded down both sides of Malay Peninsula, laid siege to Singapore on December 31, 1941, and took it on February 15, 1942. Manila and Cavite were entered on January 2; Bataan surrendered on April 9, and Corregidor fell on May 6, 1942. Netherlands East Indies had been largely subdued and occupied by March 8, 1942. Our little Asiatic squadron — one heavy cruiser, two light cruisers, thirteen overage destroyers, twenty-nine submarines, and some Catalina patrol bombers — together with the Dutch Navy opposed the powerful Japanese fleet. Within three months all our surface vessels were lost except two cruisers and four destroyers. A bright moment of this otherwise somber period was the Tokyo raid, led by Jimmy Doolittle on April 18, 1942.

By May 1, the Japanese had driven the British and Chinese out of Burma and cut china's southern supply route, the Burma Road. Supplies then had to be flown to China over the Himalaya Mountains.

U.S. destroyers Downes and Cassin, at the left and right in the foreground, were but a jumbled mass of wreckage after the Japanese air attack on Pearl Harbor, December 7, 1941. In the background is the *Pennsylvania*, 33,000-ton flagship of the Pacific fleet which suffered relatively light damage and after minor repairs rejoined the fleet. All three ships were in dry dock. The destroyers were almost a total loss but Navy salvage crews transferred their main and auxiliary machinery fittings to new hulls.

American planes were unable to rise to combat the Japanese attack on Pearl Harbor. In the background an oil tank has just exploded in a blast of white-hot flame. Of 202 Navy planes on Ford Island, 150 were destroyed or disabled, and of the remainder only thirty-eight were able to get off the ground to fight the invading enemy. The Japanese lost sixty planes, which was attributable largely to the anti-aircraft installations in the harbor.

U.S.S. Oklahoma rises from mud after seventeen months' immersion in the waters of Pearl Harbor. On February 13, 1944, the Navy announced that the *Oklahoma* had rejoined the United States fleet. The battleship capsized after being hit by bombs.

Two-man Japanese submarine is grounded on the beach during attack on Pearl Harbor. While Japanese bombers pounded the base, their submarines lurked in the harbor entrance or slipped past anti-submarine cables into the harbor itself where they spotted American ship positions.

Three civilians in this riddled car met death from fragments of a bomb dropped by a Japanese plane eight miles from Pearl Harbor, far from a military objective. Japanese planes, shuttling back and forth almost unopposed over their primary targets on Oahu Island, also bombed and strafed civilian areas, indiscriminately hitting residences, hospitals, and schools. In Waikiki they machine-gunned civilian centers and strafed streets.

Magazine of the U.S.S. Shaw explodes. This combat photograph, one of the most remarkable of all time, was taken at the exact moment when the destroyer's ammunition stores blew up during the attack on Pearl Harbor, Dec. 7, 1941. Hit in the bow by a Japanese bomb, the *Shaw* was set afire as she lay in drydock, and the flames spread until they reached the forward magazine. In the attack that day, 2,117 Navy and Marine personnel were killed, 960 were listed as missing, and 876 were wounded.

U.S.S. California settles into the mud and muck of Pearl Harbor. Black, oily smoke pouring from the *California* and her stricken sister ships conceal all but the hulk of the capsized *Oklahoma* shown at the extreme right of picture.

Hangar at the Naval Air Station, Pearl Harbor, is consumed by fire after it was smashed by Japanese bombs. Wreckage of planes littered aprons and runways, and the hangars collapsed. Most of the defending planes were destroyed on the ground.

U.S.S. Maryland almost entirely escaped damage at Pearl Harbor. To the right of the *Maryland* is the capsized *Oklahoma*. Smoke from burning ships and oil storage tanks rolls back. The *Maryland, Pennsylvania,* and *Tennessee* returned to the fleet soon after the attack, as did three cruisers, a seaplane tender, and a repair ship.

U.S.S. West Virginia, resting on the bottom of Pearl Harbor, burns fiercely. Disregarding the possibility of explosions, fire boats approach her while American sailors pump streams of water into the flames. Behind the *West* *Virginia* is the *Tennessee,* not so seriously damaged. Note the flag still flying against a background of smoke from the *Arizona* at the right. The *Tennessee* soon returned to action; the *West Virginia,* not until late 1942.

U.S.S. Arizona, afire and listing, sinks to bottom of Pearl Harbor. Of the eight battleships seriously disabled by the Japanese bombers, the *Arizona* was the only one that was a total loss. She was an old ship, having been commissioned in 1915. In all, nineteen of our ships lying at Pearl Harbor at the time were hit during the raid. In addition to the battleships there were seventy-eight other naval vessels at Pearl Harbor.

U.S.S. Shaw, superstructure ablaze after bombing, rests in the mud at Pearl Harbor (*below*). The destroyer suffered heavy damage when her bow was torn off by a magazine explosion. She was given a temporary bow and taken to the United States for repairs. Three destroyers in all were hit and badly damaged but all three were restored to service. The *Shaw* rejoined the fleet late in 1942.

Three of our first-line battleships are struck down at Pearl Harbor (*above*). Left to right are: the *West Virginia,* severely damaged; the *Tennessee,* damaged; and the *Arizona,* sunk. Despite the holocaust of exploding shells and burning oil, crews manned their guns until driven from their battle stations by the heat. Three of our battleships in all were so badly injured that they rested on the bottom of the harbor.

Battleship Row makes a perfect target for the enemy on Dec. 7, 1941. This aerial photograph, taken by one of the attacking Japanese planes, shows seven of our battleships moored in a double line off Ford Island, Naval Air Station in the center of Pearl Harbor. In background smoke rises from Hickam Field, Army base knocked out early in the assault when the Japanese blasted hangars, barracks, and grounded planes.

Japanese pilots on aircraft carrier run to their bombers for the attack on Pearl Harbor. From 7:55 in the early morning until 9:45 A.M., wave after wave of these planes attacked our warships, airfields, and shore defenses. The enemy lost about sixty planes.

Japanese aircraft carriers from which the attacks on Pearl Harbor were made came to within a few hundred miles of Hawaii without being detected. U.S. forces were too badly crippled to hunt them. This picture was taken from a captured Japanese newsreel.

President Roosevelt asks Congress to declare war on Japan. The President, on Dec. 8, 1941, delivered a war message to Congress. War was declared on Japan the same day; on Germany and Italy, Dec. 11, after their declarations. Three Axis satellites declared war on the United States—Rumania, Dec. 12; Hungary and Bulgaria, Dec. 13, 1941.

Liberty ships undergo their final outfitting at a West Coast shipyard. Mass assembly, prefabrication, welding, standardized design, and simplified construction, as well as the new "swing shift," all contributed to a building production of merchant-ship tonnage never before known in any country. By 1944 the United States Maritime Fleet was the largest in the world. The Liberty ship furnished the answer to the most acute problem confronting the United States in the early years of the conflict, namely, the need to deliver to the fighting forces and to the Allies, under lend-lease, implements of war. These vessels crossed the ocean despite U-boats.

First draft lottery of World War II was held in Washington, D.C., on October 29, 1940. Secretary of War Henry L. Stimson, blindfolded, drew the first capsule, numbered 158. The scene was reminiscent of 1917 when President Wilson officiated on a similar occasion.

The Robert J. Collier, christened by the widow of the famous publisher, slides down the ways. American yards produced 8,890,000 tons of cargo ships in 1942; the following year, 19,238,626 tons.

American youth take oath of allegiance at an induction center. Boys and men between the ages of eighteen and thirty-eight, by an elaborate but effective selective service system, were taken into the military services. The Conscription Bill was passed by Congress on September 14, 1940, long before the Pearl Harbor attack.

Alaska (originally "Alcan") Highway, from Dawson Creek, British Columbia, to Fairbanks, Alaska, was cut out of the wilderness at a cost of more than $25,000,000, in less than eight months, by 12,000 American and Canadian soldiers and civilians. This road is 1,671 miles long. Its importance in national defense became evident as the Japanese began operating in the Aleutians.

American soldiers dance at a USO center in Alaska. Aided by civilian funds and volunteer workers, USO centers established at home and abroad contributed much to the morale of America's fighting forces. Dances were considered the high lights of the entertainments.

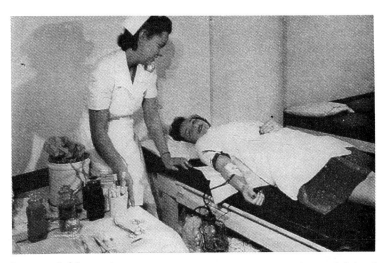

Donor at a Red Cross center gives a pint of blood destined for the veins of a wounded American boy on one of our battle fronts. Such transfusions greatly reduced deaths of the wounded in the various branches of the armed forces. By 1944, 5,300,000 pints had been donated.

"Big-Inch" Pipe Line, twenty-four inches in diameter, 1,362 miles long, brings oil from Texas to the Eastern seaboard. This pipe line helped to supply the East, and to speed much needed gasoline to our fighting zones, by saving thousands of miles of water transportation. As the war lengthened, and civilian rationing was instituted, the "big-inch" became an important war factor.

American infantrymen, with grim and determined faces, disembark on Australian soil. With them came war materials and supplies with which to organize Australia for immediate protection and future offensive operations against Japan. The first American contingent, an air unit, reached Australia late in December, 1941, and was sent almost immediately into action. These men, arriving at a critical time, augmented home forces and helped ward off possible invasion. They later participated in the Solomons and New Guinea campaigns.

American forces reach Australia. On March 16, 1942, Secretary of War Stimson announced that the first big American Expeditionary Force had landed without loss of life, after a 7,000-mile voyage through submarine-infested waters of the South Pacific.

American soldiers and army nurses crowd the rails as their ship reaches Ireland. This force arrived in February, 1942, following the first contingent which landed late in January. From this time on troop ships poured across the Atlantic to the British Isles.

American doughboys march through Ulster as Irish women and children keep step with them. The vanguard of the American Expeditionary Force arrived at an Ulster port on Jan. 26, 1942. Troops and completely equipped medical units which accompanied them were garrisoned at bases prepared by American construction companies working under U.S. Government contracts. For over a year American forces had been toughened by intensive training at home and were ready to embark for foreign soil soon after Pear Harbor.

SINGAPORE—INDIES—BURMA

Japanese Conquerors Sweep Swiftly Southward to Great Riches, Stopping Only Before Australia

After Pearl Harbor the Japanese wasted no time in bringing into being their conception of the Greater Japanese Empire. They landed at different points on the island of Luzon on December 10, 1941, pushed down toward Manila from the north and up from the south, and took the city on January 2, 1942, pressing the American and Philippine forces into Bataan Peninsula. They laid siege to the great base of Hong Kong and captured it on December 25, 1941. Two great ships of the British Navy, the *Repulse* and the *Prince of Wales,* were sunk on December 9. On February 15, sixty-nine days after they landed on the Malay Peninsula, Singapore, supposedly the strongest naval base in the world, surrendered, and Britain's greatest bastion in the Pacific, the symbol of her power in the East and the key to defense of the Southwest Pacific, was lost. With equal speed the Japanese had gone into the Netherlands East Indies, which they completely occupied by March 8, 1942. With these islands, in spite of the "scorched earth" policy of the defenders, they acquired great treasures of oil, rubber, quinine, and other strategic products. From January 15 to May 1, 1942, before the monsoon season set in, the Japanese had raced through Burma, had driven the British troops from the country, and had given Lieutenant General Stilwell's Chinese and American forces a beating. They thus blocked the Burma Road over which the Allies had supplied China. The Dutch Army garrisoned in the Netherlands Indies, the Dutch Navy, and our gallant little Asiatic Squadron were entirely inadequate to stop the onrush of the Japanese southward.

Japanese troops race through burning village in advance on Johore Bahru, Malaya. Japanese landing forces pushed ashore day and night from cruiser-escorted fleets of transports, overrunning beachheads and coastal areas on the Malay Peninsula. The power of the Japanese thrust is realized when we remember that between the fall of Hong Kong and the surrender of Singapore there were only 52 days. The enemy commander in Malaya, having studied military techniques in Germany in 1941, used coordinated land, sea, and air forces, together with infiltration tactics, to defeat the British.

Loss of Repulse and Prince of Wales was Great Britain's worst naval blow. These ships were caught without proper air cover and sunk on Dec. 9, 1941, while they were attempting to break up a Japanese landing at Kuala Lumpur. Here the crew is being rescued from *Prince of Wales.*

British surrendered Singapore on Feb. 15, 1942, to the Japanese. The man in right foreground is Lieut. Gen. A. E. Percival, British Commander of Singapore. Seated at left is the Japanese Commander, Lieut. Gen. Tomoyoki Yamashita who conducted the Malay campaign.

Singapore mother wails piteously for her dead child (*below*). The girl at left has been struck by a bomb splinter. Directly behind the twisted ricksha wheel, right center, the driver's body lies buried under bricks. Intensive daylight raids on Singapore began Jan. 12, 1942, and continued for four weeks, killing and wounding thousands of terror-stricken civilians in the British base.

Smashed B-17's burn on a runway of Andir aerodrome at Bandoeng, Java. This picture taken on Feb. 19, 1942, shows our planes caught and destroyed before they could take off. The Japanese held an almost complete mastery of the air and sea in the South Pacific until the late summer of 1942.

Docks at Soerabaja, Java, burn as Japanese drive out Dutch from the richest island of the Netherlands Indies, March 8, 1942. Retreating Dutch and British forces set fire to dock installations and oil refineries. It took Japan many months to rehabilitate these plants.

Burning petroleum fields delay advance of Japanese forces at Miri, Sarawak, British East Indies in December, 1941. The East Indies oil fields gave the Japanese the largest oil wells and refineries in the Far East. She also controlled huge supplies of rubber and quinine.

General Stilwell leads his column of troops to safety through Burma's jungles in May, 1942, after being beaten by the Japanese. Stilwell and his party were cut off from the main body of his army by Japanese forces, but he successfully threaded his way through 110 miles of jungle to India. On March 10, 1942, Lieut. Gen. Stilwell, who had much experience in the Far East, was appointed Chief of Staff under Generalissimo Chiang Kai-shek in the China theater of war. In the Burma campaign his Chinese forces as well as the British suffered a severe defeat.

Despair is eloquently written on this native's features after Japanese raid on Rangoon. Thousands of Burmese, crazed with fear, fled under the incessant Japanese bombing and were stampeded into rebellion. The evacuation of Rangoon thus became a catastrophe.

Japanese infantry follows in the path of dive bombers in cleaning up Burma. Opposing their invasion were two British imperial divisions, later bolstered by a division of the Indian Army and a combined R.A.F. and A.V.G. contingent which did not exceed 150 planes.

Japanese soldiers, heavily armed, cross a footbridge over a Burmese stream, as they move on Moulmein. The retreating British forces had destroyed the span to delay movement of troops and supplies. The Japanese invaded Burma on January 15, 1942, with ground forces numbering about four or five divisions and an air force of approximately 450 planes. By May 1, 1942, they had driven the numerically inferior British forces out of Burma and had stopped the flow of United Nations supplies over the Burma Road to China.

OUR PLANES BOMB TOKYO

Jimmie Doolittle's Sixteen Planes Shattered Much of the Japanese Confidence in Their Island Security

To counteract effects of disasters to Allied power in the early months of 1942, Americans were treated to the morale-building news that our fliers bombed Tokyo on the morning of April 18, a crushing blow to the confidence of the Japanese, who had felt safe behind the cordon of their fleet and outlying bases. The raid was led by Lieut.-Col. James H. Doolittle (later a Lieutenant-General), who was awarded the Congressional Medal of Honor for his leadership. Where the planes came from remained a military secret—"Shangri La," the President said.

Actually, the sixteen B-25 medium bombers, with eighty men aboard, took off from the deck of the carrier *Hornet* in early morning, 800 miles from Tokyo instead of the planned 400 miles from their destination. The change was due to the fear that a Japanese fishing boat had detected the carrier. Each crew had definite military installations in Tokyo, Yokohama, Kobe, Osaka, or Nagoya as targets, and every mission was carried out with precision. Then the planes flew on toward Chinese landing fields which storms and failing gasoline kept them from reaching. One plane came down in Russia and its crew were interned. The others crashed in Japanese-held areas on land or sea. Seven men were hurt; one was killed; eight were captured. Friendly Chinese helped the free survivors to safety. The Japanese, defying international law, executed some of the prisoners on the pretext that our pilots had been guilty of inhuman acts. The raid was unique in naval history, as it marked the first time that medium land bombers, transported across an ocean to their target, were launched from a carrier off enemy shores.

An army B-25 bomber speeds down the flight deck of the aircraft carrier *Hornet*, as plane takes off for the bombing mission over Tokyo, April 18, 1942. Carefully selected pilots had practiced lifting the big planes within the limits of a flight deck outlined on the ground, to perfect the quick take-off necessary.

American fliers gather on the deck of the carrier *Hornet* to receive last-minute instructions before they take off to bomb Japan, April 18, 1942. Lieut.-Col. Doolittle stands at the left foreground, chatting with Captain Mitscher, skipper of the *Hornet*. The attack was carried out ten hours ahead of schedule because they feared the carrier had been detected by a Japanese fishing vessel.

B-25 North American medium bomber soars off the flight deck of the *Hornet* en route to Tokyo. Additional planes are waiting, crowded at the stern of the *Hornet's* flight deck, and will follow in turn. On April 18, 1942, Tokyo, the capital of Japan, was bombed by Army planes which took off from the carrier *Hornet,* amid strong naval units that had steamed to within 800 miles of the target. The American raiders appeared over Tokyo at midday, dropping high explosives and incendiary bombs which started fires that raged for hours. In addition, harbor installations at Yokohama were bombed, as were factories and other industrial units in Kobe and Nagoya, two of Japan's principal cities. This attack on the Japanese homeland was particularly stimulating to American morale which was at low ebb after the surrender of Bataan, April 9, 1942.

Fifteen of our planes landed in enemy-held territory (*left*). Japanese searching parties were sent out to capture the fliers, but Chinese guerrillas found our men, and guided them to safety. Later they made their way back to the United States.

General Doolittle sits beside his wrecked plane, forced down in China after the Tokyo raid. The first to leave from the *Hornet,* he was the last man to crash, stepping out of his plane on the night of April 18 into the darkness over occupied China. He later received the Congressional Medal of Honor from President Roosevelt.

American officer from one of our planes that came down in Japanese-held territory following the Tokyo raid of April 18, 1942, is landed blindfolded at a Japanese airport. Eight of the crew members were taken prisoners by the Japanese. Two of the men who were forced to bail out of their plane when their fuel became exhausted have never been accounted for. Medium land bombers were used in the 800-mile flight from the carrier *Hornet* to the Japanese home island. Our fliers hoped to land in China.

Captured Doolittle fliers pose for Japanese cameraman. A year later the Japanese announced that they had executed some of the prisoners, claiming that fliers had intentionally bombed non-military objectives and had fired on civilians. The remaining fliers were imprisoned.

Major General Doolittle's Tokyo raiders group themselves outside a shelter carved from the mountainside. They were rescued by Chinese guerrillas and hidden here for ten days. Thus the crews that had landed in enemy-controlled territory or in free China escaped capture.

General Doolittle is decorated at Chungking by Madame Chiang Kai-shek for a job well done in the Tokyo raid. The American officer is Colonel Hilger, Doolittle's second in command. Our planes flew over Emperor Hirohito's palace, but dropped their bombs only over military installations north of Tokyo, the navy yard at Yokohama, the Mitsubishi aircraft factory at Nagoya, and shipyards, fuel and storage tanks, and ammunition dumps at Yokesuke, Kenagawa, Kobe, and Osaki. The Japanese sent out feelers as to where American planes had been based. President Roosevelt answered at a press conference, a few days later, that our raiders had come from Shangri-La.

Smiling faces of American prisoners belie real conditions in Japanese camps (*right*). The majority of these men are civilian construction workers who were engaged in fortifying Wake Island when the attack came. The engineers from this group were sent into Japanese factories and others to Manchuria to work on roads and canals. Naval officer in dark uniform has been identified as Commander Winfield Scott Cunningham, who was garrison chief at Wake. At the lower left a camera records the scene for the benefit of Japanese at home and relatives and friends of the prisoners.

Allied prisoners—Dutch, English, and American—exercise in a Japanese prison camp in Java. Jutting ribs and drawn faces of the men contradict claims of good treatment. Japanese blocked efforts of the Red Cross to inspect conditions in concentration camps. Perhaps here, as elsewhere, exercise was prescribed by prison officials instead of food. In the prison camp at Cabanatuan, in the Philippines, numbers died from starvation or beri beri, dysentery, scurvy, dengue fever, and others caused by meager diet.

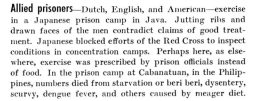

American internees (*above*) in Nipponese prison camp at Shanghai stoically receive news of the fall of Singapore. Matsuda, a Japanese press officer, is shown reading the news bulletin to the Americans. Pictures on Singapore's fall carried the caption "Freedom" in a Japanese propaganda magazine.

American prisoners at Woosung, China, are photographed for propaganda purposes. Prisoners were not allowed to shave or cut their hair, and they wore Japanese uniforms instead of their own clothes. They made phonograph records to relay messages to the United States. Other American prisoners were less fortunate. Gloating Japanese treated the soldiers and civilians who surrendered on Bataan to exhaustion, torture, and often death. The story of their six-day "march of death" was told officially by three American officers who escaped— Lieut. Col. William E. Dyess (later killed in an airplane crash), Commander Melvyn H. McCoy, and Lieut. Col. S. M. Mellnik. Prison camps to which the Corregidor captives were taken provided little water, food, and medical treatment.

Americans and British play volley ball in a Japanese prison camp. Japanese released this picture of a scene in a Shanghai internment camp in an effort to counteract eyewitness stories of Japanese brutality. Note the guard with his bayoneted gun ready for any eventuality should there be the least infraction of the rules. The atrocities committed by the Japanese, in direct violation of international agreements, have startled and shocked Allied peoples.

Marines from Wake Island, prisoners in Zentsuji camp, wash in common sink. Japanese claimed that sanitary washrooms guaranteed good health and that doctors visited camps regularly. Actually our men received only neglect and brutal treatment in enemy camps.

Poker-faced Major James P. Deveraux, commander of Marines on Wake Island, and Raymond R. Rutledge, of San Francisco, receive "prop" radios from grining Japanese. Picture appeared in Japan's English-language magazine *Freedom*, in Shanghai.

Captured American nurses are interviewed by a Japanese newspaper woman at the Zentsuji internment camp in 1942. They were later sent to a civilian internment camp in Kobe, Japan. The Japanese quoted them as stating "all was well," but this was doubted in face of the reports of inhuman treatment.

THE PHILIPPINES INVASION

Our Troops, Outnumbered, Waged an Epic Struggle on Bataan and Corregidor

A few hours after the holocaust at Pearl Harbor, the Japanese attacked the Philippines, bombing airfields and communication centers and destroying the greater portion of our aircraft in the islands. Damage to our shipping, however, did not compare with that at Pearl Harbor. The Japanese landed on December 10, 1941, at Aparri on the north coast and Vigan on the northwest coast of Luzon. They then came ashore at Legaspi on the southwest coast on the 12th, and before the month ended at various other points. These armies converged toward Manila. It was near Aparri that heroic Captain Colin Kelly bombed the Japanese battleship *Haruna;* he later perished with his plane, after saving his crew. The enemy soon had some 200,000 troops on Luzon. MacArthur may have had 30,000 American soldiers in addition to Philippine troops. The Cavite naval base had to be abandoned, and on January 2, 1942, Manila was taken by the Japanese. MacArthur withdrew his forces into Bataan Peninsula, where they held off the invaders for more than three months, from January 3 to April 9, 1942, before the overwhelming strength of the enemy and their own lack of food and munitions compelled surrender. In March, General MacArthur, on instructions from President Roosevelt, had escaped by PT boat and submarine to Australia, where he took command of the United Nations' Southwest Pacific forces. General Wainwright with 10,000 Americans and Filipinos crossed the two-mile-wide channel from Bataan to the fortress of Corregidor. Bombed unmercifully by Japanese airplanes and shelled by their naval guns, the little garrison, after supplies and ammunition had given out, surrendered, on May 6, 1942. Our men were marched to prison camps and brutally treated by their captors.

During the same week that marked the fall of Corregidor, our Navy fought and won the Battle of the Coral Sea, May 7–8, 1942, turning back the two-headed Japanese drive toward Port Moresby. We lost the carrier *Lexington,* the destroyer *Sims,* and sixty-six airplanes. A month later the Japanese made a feint toward the Aleutians while their powerful fleet swept toward Hawaii. The result was the Battle of Midway, June 3-6, 1942, in which the Japanese Navy was decisively defeated for the first time in 350 years. Our victory restored the balance of naval power in the Pacific, offsetting our losses at Pearl Harbor. We then took the offensive.

Harbor installations at Cavite naval base, near Manila, go up in flames after a raid by Japanese bombers. Barge at the right, center, is loaded with burning torpedoes, those at the left with exploding small-arms ammunition. Admiral Hart was able to evacuate most of the Pacific Fleet at the base, losing only one submarine. The Japanese captured Manila on January 2, 1942, General MacArthur ordering his troops to withdraw to Bataan.

Exhausted American dispatch rider on Bataan sleeps beside his motorcycle, using an ammunition drum for a pillow. He keeps his weapons ready for instant use. Note that his helmet was badly dented, probably from shrapnel bursts. The Americans were not easily dislodged from Bataan, their tenacity causing the suicide of the Japanese commander, Lieut. Gen. Masaharu Homma, who failed to overcome American resistance on schedule.

Lightly constructed houses of a Bataan village burn fiercely during one of the many Japanese bombing attacks (*below*). The villagers sought safety in air-raid shelters and in the surrounding jungle, usually leaving the streets entirely deserted while enemy planes did their deadly work.

Under fire from American artillery, Japanese barges advance on Luzon, main island of the Philippines (*left center*). Although at a tremendous cost, the Japanese were able to land 200,000 troops by Christmas of 1941 and seize most of the eighty large airfields in the islands. The enemy had almost complete air superiority since nearly all American planes had been destroyed a few hours after the bombing of Pearl Harbor.

Forty-three thousand Americans and Filipinos, in the foxholes of Bataan, held up 200,000 troops, the flower of the Japanese army, and seriously disrupted the Japanese timetable. Despite the lack of food, medicines, heavy guns, and air support, they tenaciously held out for four months.

Japanese troops, captured when they tried to outflank the American lines by swimming through Manila Bay, are fed before being questioned at U.S. field headquarters. Even though supplies were insufficient for our own forces, enemy prisoners received food and medical treatment. The hundreds of captured Japanese became a problem for General MacArthur.

Three army nurses stand before the rough canvas walls of their quarters, wearing air corps coveralls, the only clothes left for them after they were driven from their hospitals. The sixty-eight nurses on Bataan faced same perils as the soldiers. When the peninsula fell they were evacuated to Corregidor.

First American prisoners claimed by the Japanese in the Philippines line up for inspection at an enemy base. Apparently they are American sailors, survivors from a torpedoed merchant ship or small naval vessel.

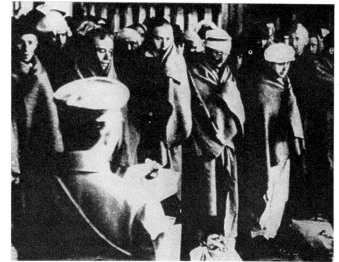

Bataan was shelled and bombed unmercifully (*left*) for four months by artillery and planes hammering at American-Filipino positions in the narrow confines of the peninsula. This panoramic view of the battle-scarred district reveals the horror and fury of the Japanese attack which American forces endured until April 9, 1942, when they surrendered.

Major General Edward P. King, last U.S. Commander on Bataan, waits with his aides to discuss terms of surrender with the Japanese on April 9, 1942 (*below*). The enemy captured 35,000 American and Filipino troops, several thousand noncombatant troops, and 20,000 civilians. A number of troops were able to escape across the two-mile-wide channel to Corregidor.

Filipino troops surrender to the Japanese (*below*). The fall of Bataan came after fifteen days of constant battering, night and day, by Japanese artillery and crack Japanese troops. Weakened by hunger, disease, with shortage of ammunition, the defending army capitulated. The men ate horses, pack mules, pigs, water buffalo, and monkeys. In the last days 10,000 patients crowded the peninsula's two field hospitals. As many more had malaria, but had to go without hospitalization or even quinine.

"A bunch of guys named Joe" was the American description of the tough Filipino troops who fought side by side with MacArthur's men. Some 20,000 Filipino soldiers died in attempting to stop the Japanese. The men pictured here hold a Japanese officer's sword and other booty captured while they repelled an attempted enemy landing on Bataan.

Major General Jonathan M. Wainwright, commander of United States forces in the Philippines, still wearing his steel helmet, faces a Japanese camera after the surrender of Corregidor. General Wainwright had assumed command of the American forces on March 17, 1942. When General Douglas MacArthur, on order from the President, left the Philippines for Australia, the task of directing the desperate resistance on Bataan Peninsula and in Corregidor fell to General Wainwright, who shared the fate of his men as a prisoner.

Picture taken by Japanese shows a tunnel of Corregidor, used as a hospital (*below*). Tunnels were not so extensive as was popularly supposed, and were used chiefly for casualties and as ammunition depots. Most of the defenders endured Japanese bombs in the open.

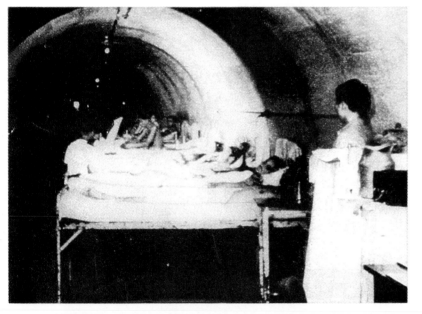

American sailors escaped from Corregidor in this 36-foot motor launch at whose stern waves a home-made American flag (*above*). These men were part of the crew of the U.S.S. *Quail* on duty in the Philippines at the time. Despite the many hazards they reached Australia safely.

Island fortress of Corregidor, which was held by 10,000 weary men, became an epic of bravery and courage in Army annals. Bataan, where the Japanese set up heavy artillery to shell the island, is two miles to the right. The open patch of ground is Kindley Field, Army balloon base.

The exhausted defenders of Corregidor surrendered to the Japanese after thirty-three hours of hand-to-hand combat. The enemy bombed and shelled the island for twenty-eight days, then made a landing shortly before midnight of May 4, 1942. All through the next day and the following dawn, the battle raged fiercely over the two square miles of rock. Thousands of fresh enemy troops finally sealed the fate of the brave men who fought as long as human endurance could sustain them and then were marched off to Japanese prison camps.

General Douglas MacArthur (*right*) is greeted in Melbourne by Brig. Gen. Patrick A. Hurley, then minister to New Zealand. MacArthur escaped by PT boat, submarine, and airplane to Australia, March, 1942, to command United Nations forces in the South Pacific.

Corregidor's sick and disabled were shrouded in blankets, suspended between the shoulders of their comrades, and thus transported to the prison camps (*below*). This picture, taken by the Japanese, was uncovered after American invasion of the Philippines in early 1945.

The crew scrambles down ropes from the sinking *Lexington*. The 33,000-ton carrier was hit on May 8, 1942, last day of the Battle of the Coral Sea, by two torpedoes and at least three bombs, but was not fatally stricken until five hours later when an explosion brought orders to "abandon ship." Destroyer at right evacuates wounded.

Japanese carrier Ryukaku burns furiously from torpedo attack, as two U.S. Navy torpedo planes close in for the kill during the Battle of the Coral Sea. One plane is just below the bow of the ship, the other is seen silhouetted against the smoke.

Japanese heavy cruiser is battered by American bombers into a flaming mass of twisted steel at the Battle of Midway, June 3–6, 1942. Four Japanese cruisers were sunk. The Battle of Midway, in which the fighting was carried on by torpedo and dive bombers, equalized naval power in Pacific.

U.S.S. Yorktown suffers direct hit during Battle of Midway. Despite her fighter-plane and anti-aircraft screen, three Japanese dive bombers got through to bomb the carrier on June 4. The same day enemy torpedo planes scored two hits. The *Yorktown*, badly damaged and afire, was taken in tow in an effort to save the ship, but salvage failed. On June 6 she was struck by two torpedoes from an enemy submarine. Next morning the *Yorktown* sank.

Only one man of Air Torpedo Squadron 8 is living today of the fifteen pilots who destroyed three Japanese aircraft carriers at the Battle of Midway. Kneeling, fourth from left, is Ensign George H. Gay, the sole survivor, who was picked up at sea, hidden in floating wreckage. Gay gave a graphic account of the battle he watched from the water.

Burning oil tanks, damaged by Japanese bombings of Midway Island, send up billows of smoke, unnoticed by the "goonie" birds. The Japanese defeat at Midway removed the threat to Hawaii and the West Coast of the United States and ended the enemy offensive.

United States Marines wait for Japanese attacks on Dutch Harbor, Alaska, June 3–4, 1942. Flaming oil tank in background was struck by first wave of Japanese bombers. The attacks on Dutch Harbor were apparently feints.

Crew of aircraft carrier Yorktown examine damage caused by Japanese raiders in Midway Battle. The *Yorktown* was torpedoed on June 6, 1942, and sank the following day. Her escorting destroyer, the *Hammann,* was also sunk. Total American losses were 92 officers and 215 men. Japanese losses: 4 carriers, 2 cruisers, 275 aircraft, 4,800 men.

GUADALCANAL CAMPAIGN

Guadalcanal Marked Our First Actual Offensive Operations in the South Pacific Theater of the War

Our invasion of the Solomon Islands, especially the landing at Lunga Bay on Guadalcanal at about 8:30 on the morning of August 7, 1942, marked our first important offensive operations in the Pacific. Our Marines pushed toward Henderson Field, chief objective, and took it with little ground opposition as the defenders had fled into the jungle. The enemy attacked from the air and on the night of August 8–9 a strong force of Japanese cruisers and destroyers entered Savo Sound and surprised our warships. Our heavy cruisers *Quincy*, *Vincennes*, and *Astoria* and the Australian heavy cruiser *Canberra* were wrecked; the American heavy cruiser *Chicago* and the destroyers *Ralph Talbot* and *Patterson* were damaged. The loss was serious as it enabled the enemy to land supplies and reinforcements on Guadalcanal. Such efforts brought about six great surface and air battles during a five-month period. Besides Savo Island, the chief sea engagements were the Battle of the Eastern Solomons in August, 1942; the Battle of Cape Esperance in October, 1942; the Battle of Santa Cruz in October, 1942, in which the carrier *Hornet* was lost; the Battle of Guadalcanal in November, 1942, in which seven destroyers and the light cruiser *Juneau* (carrying the five Sullivan brothers) were sunk; and the Battle of Tassafaronga, November 30–December 1, 1942.

In October Army units began to reinforce Marines, and on December 9, 1942, the Marines were completely withdrawn, leaving Army forces to garrison the island. By Feb. 10, 1943, the remaining Japanese had been mopped up and the six-month campaign ended.

Japanese Shinto temple, seized by the Marines at Henderson Field, Guadalcanal, served as headquarters for Marine and Navy fliers. Surviving numerous enemy bombings, it was finally torn down after having been badly damaged.

Guadalcanal offensive began as Marines waded ashore at Lunga Beach on the morning of Aug. 7, 1942. The landing was made so speedily that they were able to seize the newly constructed Japanese airfield and catch eighteen enemy planes on the ground. The Japanese fled into the jungle, leaving their breakfast still cooking and their wash on the line. The beachhead taken by the Marines was part of a broad plain on the northern shore of Guadalcanal.

U.S. Army troops were brought in to relieve the Marines on Guadalcanal beginning October 13, 1942. The remaining Japanese pockets were blasted out with artillery. Here is a 155-mm. cannon busy hurling steel into the Japanese positions. The Japanese had repeatedly but unsuccessfully attempted to relieve their garrison, but by February 8, 1943, our troops, which had been closing in from both sides, joined forces and, except for incidental mopping-up, had cleared the enemy from Guadalcanal.

Henderson Airfield was still unfinished by the Japanese when the Marines landed on Guadalcanal, Aug. 7, 1942. Pentagonal revetments between the white runways were constructed of coconut logs to protect planes from bombs and strafing.

Three Marines, musketeers of the jungle, and brothers too, return weary and bearded from the front lines on their last day of active duty on Guadalcanal. They grin with cause, for they anticipate furloughs home to the United States.

Marine stands on the embattled ridge where 600 Japanese, trying repeatedly to recapture Henderson Airfield, were wiped out. Marines entrenched behind the high ground of the ridge which protected the field, were called upon to fight many bloody engagements at this spot during the early days of our invasion of the island.

Japanese prisoners, sullen and silent, are herded safely behind barbed wire. They have grouped themselves according to rank and service. Except for a few laborers, these men are Imperial Marines. Prisoners of this type were most unusual. The enemy showed preference for a fanatical fight to the death, or self-destruction, rather than surrender, as was the case particularly in Attu, Aleutian Islands. These Japanese expressed great surprise that they were not immediately shot as their officers told them they would be.

U.S. soldiers (*left*), bearded and weary, leave the jungle after a twenty-one day period of fighting against the Japanese. By Feb. 10, 1943, all Japanese on Guadalcanal were reported killed or captured. Total Japanese casualties were estimated at 40,000 men.

Wounded American at Henderson Field, Guadalcanal, is placed aboard one of the cargo planes, operated by Marine Aviation at the South Pacific front lines. At dawn the plane will make a short flight that will deliver the medical evacuee to a nearby hospital base.

U.S.S. Carrier Wasp, turned into a blazing inferno by three Japanese torpedoes, lists to starboard in Guadalcanal waters. She was hit while escorting a convoy through the Solomons on Sept. 15, 1942. Members of her crew can be seen at the bow and stern of the vessel. The fire raged for five hours; then a United States destroyer sank the carrier to keep her out of the hands of the enemy. Ninety per cent of her crew of 1,800 was rescued.

Admiral William F. Halsey, Jr. (*right*), Commander of South Pacific Naval Forces who outgeneraled the Japanese at Guadalcanal, Bougainville, New Britain and New Guinea.

Japanese installations on Tanambogo Island go up in flames from pre-invasion bombing by American carrier-based planes. At noon of Aug. 7, 1942, the Marines landed on the bullet-swept wharf of Gavutu Island at right. Japanese were entrenched in the hill on the center of the island. To get them out, Marines dashed from cave to cave hurling dynamite into openings. Next morning they attacked Tanambogo over a connecting causeway.

Japanese bombers attack the U.S.S. *Hornet* during the Battle of Santa Cruz at which the carrier from which the raid on Tokyo was launched was lost. Bursts of anti-aircraft flak from the carrier, and a destroyer and battleship off to the right, fill the stormy sky. Japanese planes may be detected among the black splotches of smoke, diving on the carrier. A bomb has just dropped astern the *Hornet*. The initial damage to the *Hornet* resulted from a bomb hit and an enemy suicide plane diving into the carrier's stack, spreading blazing oil over the deck and setting her afire.

U.S.S. carrier Hornet lists after Japanese torpedoes and bombs have crippled the ship on the morning of October 26, 1942 (*below*). The cruiser *Northampton* stands by for salvage operations. With fire-control system shattered and ammunition hoists powerless, the *Hornet* was at the mercy of waves of enemy planes. When finally a torpedo reached the boilers, the commander gave the order to abandon ship. An American destroyer sank the *Hornet*, after all efforts to save her had failed.

Two Japanese planes at the battle of Santa Cruz on Oct. 26, 1942, dive to their deaths in fiery explosions (*above*). One plane has already hit the water; the second crashed a few seconds later. This picture was caught at the instant of the plunge of the planes.

U.S.S. South Dakota fends off Japanese torpedo bomber by a hail of anti-aircraft fire. This engagement, part of the Battle of Santa Cruz, did much to demonstrate that, given sufficient anti-aircraft equipment, a battleship can handle itself against aircraft.

U.S.S. President Coolidge, the $8,000,000 former luxury liner, struck a mine off the New Hebrides Islands while serving as a troop transport late in 1942. Here, soldiers and crew are shown clambering down her sides by rope and net. Survivors then swarmed ashore, and only two men were lost out of more than 4,000. The 22,000-ton ship became a total loss. Beached on a reef in an effort to save her, she later slipped off and went to the bottom.

Four Japanese transports were hit by both U.S. surface vessels and aircraft, and beached at Cape Esperance, about seven and one-half miles west of American positions on Guadalcanal, on Nov. 14, 1942. They were part of a huge armada the enemy was bringing from Buin and Rabaul.

Japanese troopship Yamazuki Maru is beached after being knocked out during the Battle of Guadalcanal, Nov. 13–15, 1942. Forced to the beach by American forces, the ship was completely gutted by fires caused by the bombing and shelling.

Cruiser San Francisco came home on Dec. 12, 1942, for repairs, after victorious battle of Nov. 13, 1942. The *San Francisco*, off Savo Island in the Solomons, sank a battleship, cruiser, and destroyer. Rear Adm. Daniel J. Callaghan and Captain Cassin Young, the ship's master, were killed. Lieut. Com. Bruce McCandless, though wounded, took charge and brought the ship through three days of bitter fighting.

CAPTAIN EDDIE RICKENBACKER

Our World War I Ace, Forced Down in the Pacific, Is Rescued After an Ordeal of Twenty-Three Days

Captain Edward Vernon Rickenbacker was our foremost ace in World War I. His record of twenty-six German planes shot down stood in World War II until 1944. He won the Congressional Medal of Honor and was the idol of air-minded American youth.

While on a mission in the South Pacific for the United States Army, Captain Rickenbacker's plane ran out of fuel and was forced down at sea, October 21, 1942. He and his crew were able to launch their three rubber life rafts before the plane sank, but could save little food; their water rations lasted but a few days. Rafts tied together, the eight men floated under the scorching sun of the days and the chilling temperatures of the nights. One of the crew died and was buried at sea. Planes of our Army and Navy covered thousands of square miles, crisscrossing Rickenbacker's supposed route. The drifting men prayed for deliverance day after day and read the New Testament. They trapped and ate a gull that landed on Rickenbacker's head, caught rain water during thunder showers that relieved the terrific heat. On November 9 three men on one raft became separated from the others. On the twenty-second day a Navy plane sighted a life raft 600 miles north of Samoa, in the Phoenix Islands area, and picked up Captain W. T. Cherry, Jr., Rickenbacker's pilot. With his guidance, a flying boat discovered Rickenbacker himself and two companions on a second raft. The final three men were rescued from a small island. All were hospitalized at our base in Samoa and eventually recovered their health.

Lost for seventy-two days in the South Pacific, this Marine pilot was rescued by a Navy patrol plane. Forced down at sea, he took to his life raft and paddled from island to island until he reached a settlement and natives aided him.

Eddie Rickenbacker is helped out of a Navy patrol bomber. Six members of his crew were also rescued after their plane was forced down in the Pacific.

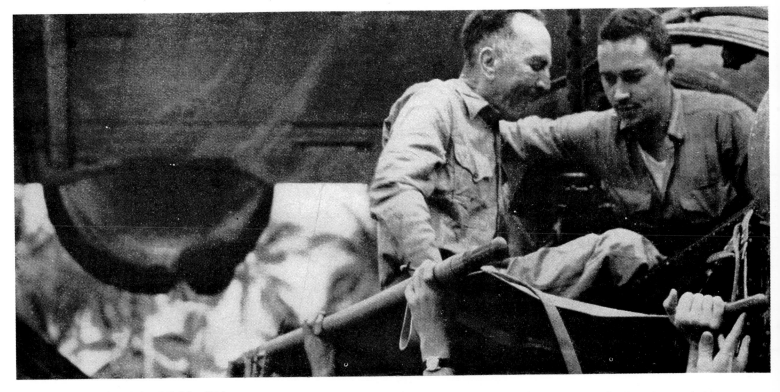

Brig. Gen. Nathan F. Twining, U.S.A., and fourteen of his crew of a Flying Fortress spent five gruelling days and six nights in small rafts in the open Pacific before being rescued on January 27, 1943. The Fortress made a forced landing while on one of its many combat missions in the Solomon Islands area. The picture below, taken from one of the two Navy Catalina patrol planes which made the rescue, shows crew member bringing a tow line out to the raft.

ATLANTIC CONVOY PERIOD

Second Year of the Invasion of Russia— First Mass Air Attacks of Continent

In the European war theater the first six months of 1942 were largely a period of preparation by the United States and Great Britain for offensives to come in the latter part of the year. On the Russian front, in late 1941, the Germans had pushed as far as the outskirts of Moscow, had taken and lost Rostov, and had begun the siege of Sevastopol. In the spring of 1942 they advanced in the Ukraine and the Crimea and on July 1, 1942, succeeded in capturing Sevastopol. The Germans in their spring and summer offensive took Kharkov, Rostov, Orel, Kerch, and other key Russian cities. Hitler had his mind set on capturing the oil fields of the Caucasus, but the Russians stubbornly held on to them. He had his choice of pushing south to cut off Lend-Lease shipments to Russia or of laying siege to Stalingrad. Hitler chose the latter course, and his armies stood at the city's gates on August 25, 1942. Hitler had Goebbels announce daily Stalingrad's imminent fall. But the months went on through fall and winter, and the Russians still held out. The opposing forces fought from yard to yard, from house to house, from room to room. Toward the end of the year the Russians set in action a counteroffensive, taking advantage of the dreaded Russian winter. The Red troops pinned the Nazis in a narrow corridor before Stalingrad and cut their divisions to pieces. Field Marshal von Paulus of the Sixth Army and sixteen other Axis generals, German, Italian, and Rumanian, surrendered in the basement of a ruined Stalingrad department store on January 31, 1943, the remnants of an army of some 330,000 tough German troops, now reduced to less than 100,000 men. Fighting ended on February 2.

From that point the Russians in their winter offensive drove the Germans back from one defense line to another, recapturing the key cities the Germans had taken during the campaigns of the previous two years.

During this period the Americans and British were delivering huge convoys of supplies to the Russians through Iran and by the northern route to Murmansk. Troopships were bringing Army units to Northern Ireland and England. The R.A.F. had begun serious bombing of German war plants and the first thousand-plane raid took place on May 30, 1942, in which Cologne was badly battered. The Commando raid on Dieppe was staged on August 19, 1942, a bold, thrilling venture which tested invasion techniques, but was costly in casualties, particularly to the Canadians, who made up five-sixths of the assault forces.

Tanker along the Atlantic convoy route, torpedoed by an Axis submarine, sends up black columns of smoke as flames reach her vitals. Despite stifling heat the crew brought the flames under control in a few hours. The ship was finally brought to an Atlantic port, repaired, put back into service some months later.

Rescued crew of a U-boat sunk in the Atlantic is led ashore from a British destroyer. The men were blindfolded to prevent their obtaining possible military information. The use of small aircraft carriers, enabling fighter planes to patrol for submarines which tried to break into convoys, resulted in an increasing toll of sunken U-boats in 1943–1944.

U.S. tanker afire in mid-Atlantic is saved by heroic efforts of crew. Nazi torpedoes smashed the oil storage compartments, but the crew finally extinguished the flames.

Nazi submarine sinks stern first after being bombed by American plane. Cowering in the shadow along the sides of the conning tower, several crew members await their fate.

Convoy of twenty-four British merchantmen in the North Sea (*above*) steams through a fog, protected by escorting warships. Lifeboats were outswung, ready for instant use should the convoy be attacked. The struggle in which the merchantmen fought the U-boat is one of the epic stories of World War II. After March 1943, the submarine menace was reduced by use of small aircraft carriers.

Nazi submarine is caught in the act of sinking an 11,000-ton British freighter. This picture was taken by a member of the U-boat crew. Nazi submarines often surfaced after torpedoing a ship in order to obtain information concerning the merchantman's cargo and destination. After the intelligence officer questioned the men, they were often set adrift in open boats and left to their fate.

Britain's "Biter," a merchant ship converted into an aircraft carrier, keeps sea lanes open for United Nations. Ships such as this reduced greatly the toll taken by U-boats of Allied vessels. Her Hurricane fighters are lined up on deck despite rough seas, ready to ward off enemy attacks.

Plane is catapulted (*right*) from armed merchantman. In 1941 Germans were sinking many ships through attack by their long-range bombers. To checkmate the enemy, Prime Minister Churchill suggested that fighter planes should be carried in each convoy. Thus resulted the most successful counter-warfare against U-boats devised by the Allies. After flight, each plane was crash-landed in the water, the pilot picked up by destroyer, and the plane lifted aboard.

"Abandon ship" comes to a United Nations freighter aflame and sinking after it was torpedoed off the eastern coast of Canada. One man leaps into the water, throwing his belongings in ahead of him. Another sailor is swimming to the raft. Crew was frantically trying to get away from ship before boilers exploded.

Three British seamen, emaciated and numbed to the bone, are saved after Nazi submarine sank their ship in mid-Atlantic. Clinging in desperation with freezing fingers to a tossing raft, they still had strength to catch the line thrown to them from a U.S. Coast Guard-manned cutter patrolling the sea lanes.

Eighty-three days on a raft in mid-Atlantic, three merchant seamen—two Dutch and one American—are helped aboard a Navy ship on January 24, 1943. These survivors, after their vessel had been sunk by a German submarine, existed on raw fish, fowl, and rainwater.

Chinese seaman, unconscious from long exposure, is rescued in North Atlantic by British minesweeper. His vessel was sunk by a Nazi submarine, with a loss of ninety lives, 160 miles off Halifax, Nova Scotia, one of the more dangerous zones in the Atlantic.

Military Tribunal in Washington, D.C., tries German saboteurs. Attorney General Biddle, in white, reads testimony during trial. At his right, listening, is J. Edgar Hoover, Director of the F.B.I., which tracked down and arrested the saboteurs on June 27, 1942. The trial, held by a tribunal of seven generals under Maj. Gen. Frank R. McCoy, began July 8 and ended Aug. 1, 1942. It was suspended for four days while the Supreme Court, in its first special session in twenty-two years, weighed the authority of the examining commission. The commission's finding, reached on Aug. 3, was approved by the President and the death sentence carried out Aug. 8, 1942.

Ernest Peter Burger

Heinrich Harm Heinck   Richard Quirin   Edward Kerling   Hermann Otto Neubauer   Herbert Hans Haupt   Werner Thiel

George John Dasch

Nazi saboteurs arrested in America carried a two years' supply of money, explosives, maps, and plans for destruction of war plants and transportation in the East and Middle West. Six were executed, one was sentenced to life, one to thirty years' imprisonment.

Unclaimed bodies of Nazi saboteurs lie buried on United States soil at Blue Plains, D.C. (*right*). Identification numbers painted on crude boards mark the graves of these saboteurs who were landed from enemy submarines on June 13 and 17, 1942.

Belgian prisoners in German concentration camp at Huy, Belgium, circle around inner courtyard during a ten-minute "exercise period" allowed them once a day. Most of those held here were intellectuals and professors of Belgian universities who defied German decrees. Some marched with hands manacled behind their backs. Conditions in Nazi camps were appalling; prisoners were subjected to tortures and brutalities.

Victims of the Gestapo, dejected and bitter, pass endless days in a Nazi concentration camp near Paris (*below*). Many of these men fought Fascism for years —in Germany, Italy, Spain, Czechoslovakia, Poland— escaping from one country after another as Hitler conquered the free peoples of Europe, only to be caught in France. The Gestapo was utterly ruthless, and prisoners such as these gradually disappeared.

Nazi guards bind a young French sailor to execution post in a Paris prison (*above*). Germans avenged murdered Nazis by seeking and shooting a hundred "hostages" for each Nazi slain by zealous French patriots resisting German occupation. After the fall of France in June, 1940, the French underground inside of France kept the spirit of resistance alive during bitter years and prepared to throw their country's weight to the Allied forces when the day of liberation arrived.

Norwegians show contempt for Nazi conquerors by turning their backs on German troops marching through Drobak. The people of Norway, forced to bow to their Nazi overlords, still carried on a continuous and successful underground resistance despite the German occupation. Many young Norwegians hid in mountainous parts of the country and organized against the invaders.

Polish prisoners in line (*above*) wait for their noonday meal in a Nazi concentration camp. More than 2,000,000 Poles were transported from their homeland after Poland fell in September, 1939, and were forced to perform slave labor in Germany, working either in munition and armament factories or in laboratories.

Heinrich Himmler was the dreaded mastermind of Germany's secret police. Fanatically devoted to the Nazi cause, he was repeatedly sent by Hitler to occupied countries to quell anti-Nazi resistance and suppress growing sabotage.

Bessarabian peasant begs Nazi executioners to spare his life. These men were guerrillas or demobilized soldiers, a few of thousands who bitterly resisted German occupation by attacking Nazi troops, or sabotaging Rumanian industry.

Lidice, in Czechoslovakia, will ever be a symbol of Nazi brutality. On May 27, 1942, Czech patriots bombed and shot Reinhard Heydrich, the German Gestapo official known as "the Hangman," who was "protector" of Czechoslovakia. He died in a Prague hospital on June 4. In reprisal for suspected harboring of the killer, all male citizens were executed, the women placed in concentration camps, and the children sent to German institutions. Lidice was razed to the ground.

Malta was under almost continuous bombardment for more than three years. A building left unscarred was a rarity. Allied landings in Sicily in July, 1943, brought an end to Axis air blasting of the island. Malta will be known in history as the spot most bombed by the Axis air forces. It was Mussolini's first target when Italy declared war on Britain on June 10, 1940. The island played a key role in the struggle for mastery of the Mediterranean, for it menaced Axis supply lines to Africa and protected Allied convoys.

Galleries of great antiquity, dug deep into solid rock, protected Malta's people from the bombing. On April 16, 1942, at the height of Axis attacks King George awarded the island the George Cross for "heroism and devotion that will long be famous in history."

The statue of Queen Victoria stood undamaged in the square of Valetta after 2,500 raids. First important reinforcements to relieve defenders of Malta came in May, 1942, when the American carrier *Wasp* and several British carriers brought fighter planes.

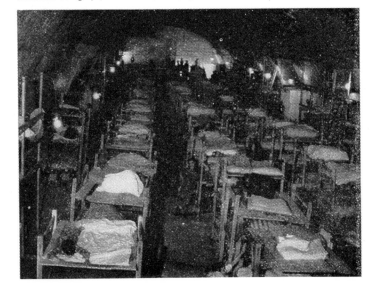

THE COSTLY RAID ON DIEPPE

This Venture, Exhibiting a New Technique of This War, Was a Tragic, Thrilling Experiment in Invasion

The raid on Dieppe began at precisely 4:20 A.M. on Wednesday, August 19, 1942. Before dawn squadron after squadron of planes roared out from the airdromes of southern England and began bombing gun positions sixty-five miles across the Channel at Dieppe. In the gray dawn 6,000 men in landing craft neared the beaches. A great majority were Canadian, but British Special Service forces Americans, and French were among the raiders, all thoroughly ready after months of training. Dieppe was flanked by two batteries, one at Varengeville, five miles west, and another at Berneval, the same distance east. In order that the raid be successful, these batteries had to be silenced. At Varengeville, the Commandos landed by surprise and carried through their flanking movements toward Dieppe. On the east, however, landing forces ran into a strongly escorted German convoy which the Allies had not suspected of being there. Four heavily-armed trawlers turned their guns upon the invaders; but one of the landing craft reached the beach. At 5:10 A.M., preceded by a half hour's shelling by destroyers, men and tanks stormed Dieppe frontally. They attained some of their objectives, but casualties were great, due to the shelling by the guns at Berneval which had not been put out of action.

Overhead was fought incessantly the greatest air battle of the war up to that time. The R.A.F. reported the loss of ninety-eight planes and claimed that 182 enemy planes had been shot down.

The withdrawal of the Commandos began at about 11:00 A.M. Allied losses were practically fifty per cent of the force taking part in the raid. A heavy price had been paid for the advantages gained.

Three Canadian soldiers, two wounded, surrender at Dieppe during raid of Aug. 19, 1942. Canadian losses totaled 3,372 men killed, wounded, and missing. Although costly, the raid tested invasion on a small scale and thus enabled the Allies to perfect techniques required for the giant assaults to follow.

The Commando fleet lies off the chalk cliffs of Dieppe, as landing barges bring back wounded from the beach. Canadians comprised five sixths of the attacking force of about 6,000 men. An estimated 1,000 planes afforded an umbrella for the raiders. The raid marked the first daylight attack in the Commando technique, and the first occasion in which tanks were landed on enemy shores.

Dieppe beach looked like this after the raid on August 19, 1942. Wrecked tanks, a beached transport, and scattered debris indicate the fierceness of the struggle. The objectives of the raid were to test German defenses at a point known to be heavily guarded and to destroy batteries and a radio location center which was detecting Allied convoys in the Channel.

Tank landing barge was seized by Germans after it had been abandoned by British at Dieppe on August 19, 1942. Bodies of Allied dead have been covered with blankets. Barges such as this one were tested under battle conditions for the first time during the Dieppe raid, which uncovered many problems to be faced in planning for the invasion.

Canadian wounded, taken off the beach at Dieppe, are helped aboard a British destroyer. The raiding forces were Canadian, British, American, and French units trained in commando tactics and equipped with weapons needed for sudden attack.

Canadian Commandos in invasion barges advance toward shore of Dieppe under Nazi dive-bombing attack. Raiders were discovered at 3:30 A.M. Aug. 19, 1942, by trawlers who warned Nazi coast defenses. Despite this, some Allied forces reached center of town.

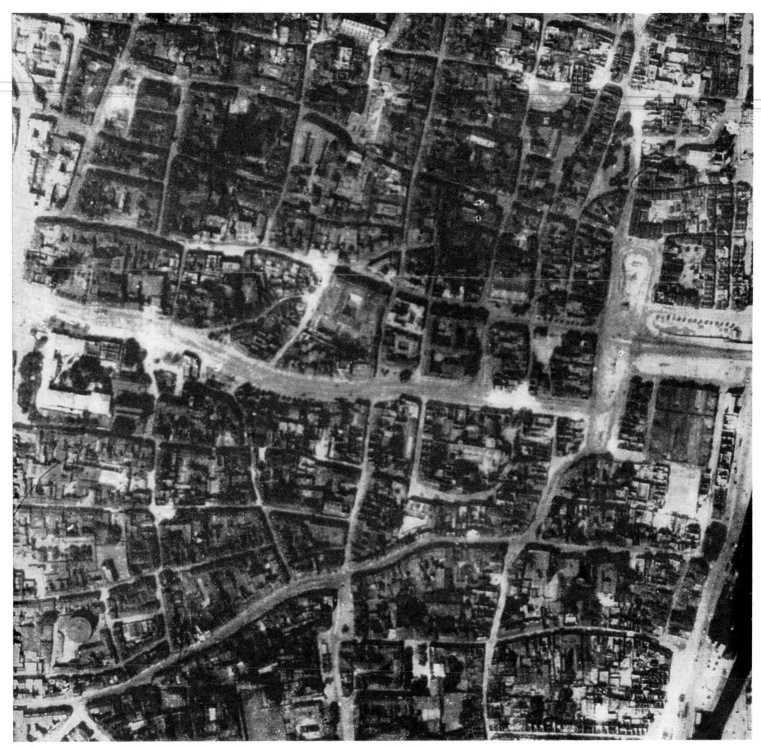

Cologne was the target of the first 1,000-plane raid by the British, on the night of May 30, 1942. Over one million incendiaries were dropped on the city, which suffered terrific damage. The Cologne raid was really the beginning of mass bombing of Nazi Germany by Allied air forces. These had reached a strength sufficient for both day and night attack.

American fliers who participated in the first American raid over Nazi Germany, on Jan. 27, 1943, gather under their Flying Fortress "The Eight Ball." The bombers destroyed twenty-two enemy fighters. Only three American bombers were missing. The Eight Ball was reported lost in 1944.

Admiral von Tirpitz, 35,000-ton German battleship, hides from the British Navy in Altenfjord, Norway. It was severely damaged on Sept. 22, 1943, when British midget submarines raided the lair from which it preyed on Allied convoys.

THE ROCK OF STALINGRAD

The Turning Point of the German Invasion of Russia Came When the Nazis Failed to Conquer Stalingrad

Stalingrad represented the second high tide of the invasion of the Germans into Russia. In November, 1941, on their initial push, some of their troops had reached the suburbs of Moscow, only to be forced to retreat to previously prepared winter positions. In August of the following year, after the Germans swept through southern Russia trying to capture the Caucasian oil fields, which they did not quite reach, they turned northward to Stalingrad, the great modern industrial city on the Volga River. They were flushed with success, as one after another of the key points of the Russian defense lines had fallen into their hands. Hitler and Goebbels went so far as to announce the collapse of Russian resistance in Stalingrad. The city's beautiful buildings and its modern stores and factories became piles of rubble which the Germans and Russians used as cover for machine-gun nests. Finally, in late November and December, the Russians began counteroffensives below and above Stalingrad, and their enveloping movements caught the besieging German forces in a trap. Hitler ordered his army to fight to the last man. Their escape cut off, some 91,000 troops surrendered. In all, the Russians killed or captured 330,000 Nazis. The frustration of the Germans before Stalingrad was the turning point in the Russo-German war.

Four Russians are executed by a Nazi firing squad (*above*). A German practice, when executing Russian prisoners, was to place them so that their bodies fell into pits which the victims themselves had dug. This photograph was found on a dead German soldier.

Nazi sets the woman to trap the man (*right*). Rumanian has promised the wife of a Russian soldier hiding in the house that her husband will be spared if he surrenders. The Nazi with bayoneted rifle, ready to spring if the Russian should appear, indicates promise will not be kept.

Russian infantry drives toward the German rear across the snow-covered flats northwest of Stalingrad (*below*). First wave advances cautiously following Russian tanks, as machine gunners and riflemen lend cover.

Russian soldier returns to his native village after its deliverance from the Germans, incidental to the recapture of Rzhev in August, 1942. Rejoicing to find his wife and two children alive and well, he is pictured marching down the street surrounded by his comrades.

Russian Cossacks attack on the southwestern front, as the Soviets launch their counteroffensive, late in the fall of 1942. These famed cavalrymen by their swiftness of movement over the Russian Steppes effectively harassed the rear of the German armies in their retreat across Russia.

Russian automatic rifleman, taking shelter near Stalingrad, is about to fire on an ambushed Nazi. A shell from the heavy barrage laid down by the Germans in their advance toward the city has just hit another building and throws up immense clouds of smoke and debris.

Russians counterattack from a factory on outskirts of Stalingrad. Germans began the siege on Aug. 25, 1942. The Nazi position at Stalingrad became precarious in November, 1942.

Russian prisoners (*left*) are carted away to be shot by the Germans. After months of brutal treatment in a Nazi concentration camp, victims were too dazed and weak to protest. Shortage of food caused Germans to kill prisoners and Russian civilians so their own men could be supplied.

In a Stalingrad backyard Russian machine gunners blast away at the Nazis (*below*). The lines were often but thirty to forty yards apart. From room to room in the shattered hulks of factories and apartments Germans and Russians fought and killed each other with grenades and tommy guns.

Russian women emerge from an air-raid shelter in the city of Stalingrad after the fighting for the city had ended, February 2, 1943. Stalingrad marked the high tide of German success and frustration in Russia.

Red Army flame thrower directs an effective and destructive fire at a crumbling brick wall behind which Germans were making a final stand during the cleanup operations in Stalingrad.

Nazi machine gunners attack a Soviet village during the German drive across the southern Ukraine toward the Caucasus, in 1942 (*below*). Germans have taken cover in a river bed.

American trucks, guarded by a Russian soldier, are lined up at the Soviet supply base at Tabriz, Iran. Lend-Lease munitions, industrial and agricultural supplies, totaling $1,634,148,000 in value, were shipped to Russia in 1942. Landed and assembled at an Iranian port, they were driven 750 miles to Tabriz for final inspection before being sent to the Soviet front. In 1943 Lend-Lease shipments to Russia were announced as $3,034,986,000.

Nazi Field Marshal von Paulus, right, commander of Hitler's Sixth Army, surrenders to the Russians in the basement of a Stalingrad store on Jan. 31, 1943. Russian generals, left, are Rokossovsky and Voronov. Sixteen other Axis generals also surrendered to the Russians.

German troops surrender at Stalingrad, exhausted and resigned to their fate. Hitler's armies before Stalingrad were first-line troops. The Sixth Army which surrendered there had covered itself with glory in western campaigns, but was no match for the staunch Russians.

Inter-Allied Supply Conference at Iran speeds delivery of Lend-Lease material to Soviet Russia. Here at Red Army headquarters, American, British, and Russian officers met daily to work out problems arising from the flow of vital equipment from the United States, via the Persian Gulf, to the Russian fighting fronts. The system of Lend-Lease, passed by Act of Congress on March 11, 1941, was designed to aid the nations fighting the Axis.

NORTH AFRICAN CAMPAIGN

Rommel Driven 1,500 Miles in Fifteen Weeks Across Libya — Axis Surrenders

In mid-September, 1940, Italians under Marshal Graziani, attacking from Bardia, Libya, drove the British to Sidi Barrani, Egypt. Later the British retired to Matruh. Between December 9, 1940, and early February, 1941, the British under General Wavell pushed the Italians back as far as El Agheila, taking on the way Sidi Barrani, Bardia, Tobruk, and Bengasi. In March, 1941, the Germans under Rommel forced the British back to Sollum, Egypt, where the Nazis were held April 30, 1941. Led by General Auchinleck, the British launched a new offensive and drove the Germans to El Agheila, in the middle of January, 1942. Rommel attacked again in the latter part of January, and by the first of July the British were at El Alamein, within seventy miles of Alexandria and dangerously close to Cairo and the Suez Canal.

The British line at El Alamein was strong, its right flank at the Mediterranean coast, its left at the Qattara Depression. Alexander replaced Auchinleck and Montgomery replaced Ritchie as Commander of the Eighth Army. The British ob-

tained tanks and heavier artillery from America and were reinforced by units of the American Air Force. On October 23, 1942, the British set down the heaviest barrage of the war. Infantry followed up the attack and the Germans gave way, retreating 1,500 miles in fifteen weeks — one of the most remarkable retreats and pursuits in all history. The Nazis lost Tripoli on January 24, 1943, and by January 30, 1943, had taken position behind the Mareth Line.

Americans and British had landed at ports of Northwest Africa on November 8, 1942, and pressed eastward into Tunisia. The Germans then proceeded to occupy all of France. The French scuttled their idle fleet at Toulon on November 27, 1942, to prevent its falling into Nazi hands. General Eisenhower, commanding Allied forces, coordinated encircling movements that pocketed Axis troops near Bizerte and Tunis. The last of these troops surrendered on Cape Bon on May 12, 1943.

Meanwhile, the Casablanca Conference had been held, from January 14 to 24, 1943. President Roosevelt and Prime Minister Churchill with their advisers had formulated plans for the months to come, in which the Allies were to obtain the offensive in the European theater. At the meeting it was decided to accept nothing less than the unconditional surrender of the Axis.

Australian infantry in the battle of Egypt advances over the western Libyan desert, employing special tactics and strategy. General Sir Harold Alexander, in the final North African campaign, forced Marshal Rommel, "the Desert Fox," to retreat across 2,000 miles of the desert.

Fighting Poles man foxholes in Egyptian desert. The Poles interned in Russia following Russo-Polish war were freed in 1941, joined Polish units in Cairo, and made the largest single national contingent fighting for the Allies in the desert, excepting the British.

Field Marshal Erwin Rommel, German commander-in-chief in North Africa, arrives at an airport in Tripoli in August, 1942, after a conference with Hitler (*below*). With him, right, is a soldier of the Afrika Korps. Rommel, a brilliant tactician, took command of Axis African forces in 1941, after British had driven Italians from Sidi Barrani, Egypt, nearly to Bengasi.

Fighting French, in high spirits, reach the British lines (*above*). They were part of the forces that made an epic stand for sixteen days against continuous Axis armor and air power at Bir Hacheim. Practically surrounded, they refused three times to surrender and fought their way out of the pocket on June 10, 1942, when they carried their wounded with them to safety.

Germans land reinforcements for Rommel's army in North Africa. Behind the disembarked soldiers are the transport planes which flew them in from Crete, Greece, or Italy. A large part of Rommel's supplies was destroyed by the British fleet and air force operating in the Mediterranean.

British infantrymen in Libya, hot on the heels of retreating Axis forces, charge through smoke and sand-dust ignoring the disabled tanks. The British Eighth Army had cleared Egypt of Axis troops by Nov. 8, 1942. By Nov. 12 Montgomery's army had crossed the Libyan frontier, and on Nov. 13 his forces reached Tobruk. From that point the retreat was greatly accelerated. Nazi supplies were kept under constant bombing from the air.

General Sir Harold Alexander, left, **and General Sir Bernard Montgomery,** right, won the desert victory for the Allies. The British were holding desperately to the El Alamein line seventy miles from Alexandria, in July, 1942. General Alexander replaced General Auchinleck as commander-in-chief and General Montgomery succeeded General Ritchie as commander of the British Eighth Army. Reinforced and rearmed, the Eighth Army started from El Alamein on Oct. 23, 1942, and drove the Axis troops across the desert.

British night attack near El Alamein, Oct. 23, 1942, opened the campaign to drive the Germans and Italians from Egypt, Libya, and finally from North Africa. Camouflage was designed to conceal type, size, and number of British guns from enemy observation.

Australians charge Axis machine-gun positions on the first day of the El Alamein attack, Oct. 23, 1942. The artillery barrage which preceded the attack was one of the most devastating in modern warfare and began the Nazi retreat of 1,500 miles.

New Zealanders in armored cars round up Axis prisoners taken in Egypt, incidental to mopping-up operations after Rommel's armies broke and retreated westward in October, 1942. The prisoners were sent to Alexandria and many of them eventually to camps in the United States. Italians made up the large majority of the prisoners which were taken during early days of the withdrawal in Libya.

Axis troops hug the earth as Allies with artillery and air bombing blast their shallow trenches (*below*). The Germans in their 1,500-mile retreat in fifteen weeks were unable to dig in to make a stand for long at any point, under Alexander's continuous pressure. They finally reached the Mareth Line Jan. 30, 1943, where they held off the British and American forces until dislodged on March 29, 1943.

British crew trains its machine gun on Axis outpost somewhere in the vast expanses of the Libyan desert (*above*). The soldiers' helmets were canvas-covered to prevent their becoming unbearably hot from the desert sun beating down. Fighting in the desert tried endurance of strongest-hearted and most physically fit, through days of intense heat and nights of fog and creeping chill. Note men carried full packs.

Rommel's armies broke after El Alamein, on Oct. 23, 1942, and retreated westward, often disorganized and desperately trying to slow up the Allies' pursuit. The British-American air force bombed the main roads, wreaking havoc on the German sources of supply and lorries loaded with troops. The few coastal roads in Libya made Rommel's retreat toward the Libyan-Tunisian frontier extremely difficult.

AMERICANS IN NORTH AFRICA

The Americans and their British Allies Take Over the Offensive in the European Theater of the War

Probably the greatest mass landing in all history up to that time was made by American and British troops on the shores of North Africa on November 8, 1942. The troops came ashore at a number of points on the west and northern coasts — at Casablanca, Fidala, Oran, and Algiers. Huge convoys coming from America and England, and carrying troops, supplies, and landing barges, stood off the coast in pitch-black night. When dawn approached, transports and auxiliary ships launched their landing barges, and our men pushed ashore. At Casablanca the unfinished battleship *Jean Bart* opened fire, but was quickly put out of action by our warships. At Fidala three of our transports were sunk by German submarines. At Oran the French, under German officers, fought and casualties there were greater than at any other landing point. At Algiers our troops quelled resistance in a few hours. Within four days from the time the Americans came ashore, practically all resistance from the French had ceased and an armistice was signed between the French and the Americans. This immense operation placed the Americans in control of large territories in northwest Africa and changed the entire course of the war, putting British and American forces on the offensive in the European theater. The Allied forces joined the British Eighth Army in Tunisia shortly after the first of the year and in a campaign ending on May 12, 1943, drove the Axis from Africa.

Aboard a landing barge, American soldiers, thoroughly trained and equipped, await tensely the moment of landing on a North African beach, Nov. 8, 1942.

Convoy of United Nations ships in perfect formation steams across the Atlantic to land men, armament, and supplies at ports of Algeria and French Morocco, in North Africa, on Nov. 8, 1942; 850 vessels were in the armada.

Landing barges brought American, British, and Canadian troops to beachheads on the coast of North Africa on Nov. 8, 1942. These amphibious operations were carried out at daybreak while American and R.A.F. fighter planes gave necessary air protection from Nazi bombing. The invasion plan for North Africa called for three main points of attack: Oran, Algiers, and Casablanca. United States Army troops supported by British naval units were to land at Oran and Algiers. Americans alone attacked at Casablanca.

American invaders (*below*) wade through surf from their landing barge to assigned positions on the North African beachhead at the break of dawn, Nov. 8, 1942. Two British sailors, right, lend a hand to their Allies. Other types of landing craft later brought tanks and motorized infantry to beachheads. General Mark W. Clark and a small party landed before troops to secure maps and information from pro-Ally French officers.

H.M.S. Hartlett (a former American Coast Guard cutter) and H.M.S. *Walney* crashed through the boom at Oran, to let landing barges enter the harbor and deliver troops to the beach where they could reach the enemy (*above*). The *Hartlett* was shelled and wrecked by French shore batteries. The French troops at Oran stoutly resisted our initial landings on Nov. 8, 1942, but by the following day Allied forces had taken three airfields near the city with 2,000 prisoners. By Nov. 10 they had captured the city itself as well as its naval base, Mers-el-Kebir.

American soldiers land from their transports on the quay at Mers-el-Kebir, near Oran, Algeria, carrying equipment and personal belongings (*left*). Oran surrendered on Nov. 10, 1942. Algiers had been taken Nov. 9, while Casablanca fell to the Allies on Nov. 11, 1942. With its surrender all French Morocco and Algeria passed under Allied control. Three American transports were lost during the landing at Casablanca.

Supplies and equipment are piled up on the shore west of Oran. French garrisons in Oran, an objective of the American forces, surrendered after spirited resistance, Nov. 10, 1942. The next day, all of Morocco and Algeria passed under Allied control.

American troops swarm ashore at Surcouf, Morocco, with *Old Glory* flying, on the morning of Nov. 8, 1942. American casualties incurred in landings were comparatively light: United States Army and Navy missing and dead, 860; wounded, 1,050.

Jean Bart was badly damaged when the French warship, berthed at Casablanca, opposed American landings covered by U.S. naval units, Nov. 8, 1942. The strategy of the campaign, which opened a new African front and was coordinated with the British offensive in Libya, was to form a vise that would press Rommel's forces out of Africa.

German Armistice Commission was taken into custody in Casablanca immediately after Americans landed on Nov. 8, 1942, and placed in prisoner-of-war camps. Hitler had sent the commission to French Morocco shortly after the armistice had been signed at Compiègne on June 22, 1940, to further collaboration between the Nazis and the Vichy French colonies. The commission also served as a listening post for Germans in Africa.

American troops wipe out snipers' nests (*below*) during a street skirmish in Algiers, French Morocco. Few such instances occurred, as the French offered comparatively little resistance to the invaders in Algiers, which fell by nightfall of Nov. 8, 1942, the same day Allied troops landed. Within seventy-six hours, the initial armed French resistance was overcome and the Allies held all of French North Africa up to the border of Tunisia.

French and native soldiers and sailors (*above*) captured by the Allies in the four days of fighting in North Africa, are freed after the signing of the armistice between the Allies and French, Nov. 11, 1942. The Allies also released political prisoners of the Gestapo and Vichy Government.

Admiral Jean Darlan stands between Generals Dwight D. Eisenhower and Mark Clark at a ceremony held at Allied headquarters in North Africa. Darlan, as High Commissioner, surrendered French North African colonies to Allies Nov. 11, 1942. He was assassinated Dec. 24, 1942.

103

French destroyer lies in mud of Toulon Harbor after her magazines have been blown up. The Nazi tank arrived too late to help prevent the scuttling of the ship. The French sank three of their battleships, five heavy cruisers, three light cruisers, twenty-five destroyers, and twenty-six submarines. Only 25,000 out of 220,000 tons fell into German hands. Even the 26,000-ton *Dunkerque* and *Strasbourg* went down.

French scuttled their fleet (*left*), Nov. 27, 1942, to prevent its seizure by the Nazis who occupied all of France following the Allied invasion of North Africa. It was the greatest mass sinking since Scapa Flow.

The Dupleix, a 10,000-ton French cruiser (*below*), burns and settles at her dock after having been abandoned by her crew during the scuttling operations at Toulon. This is another example of thorough destruction of the French fleet. The picture was taken from an Italian-made film captured after the Toulon episode.

CASABLANCA CONFERENCE

This Notable Conference Set a Precedent in Cooperation Among Peoples of Free Nations

At Casablanca, between January 15 and 24, 1943, was held the first of a series of history-making conferences which were designed to solidify the war effort of the United Nations against the Axis. President Roosevelt and Prime Minister Churchill were accompanied by the combined Chiefs of Staff of Great Britain and the United States, who were in constant session during the ten days of the conference.

The entire field of the war was surveyed, theater by theater, throughout the world, and all resources were marshaled for a more intense prosecution of the war by land, sea, and air. Complete agreement was reached between the leaders of the two countries and their respective staffs upon plans and enterprises which were to be undertaken during the campaigns against Germany, Italy, and Japan, with the view of drawing the utmost advantage from the favorable turn of events at the close of 1942. A prime object of the conference was to provide means to draw weight off the Russian armies by engaging the enemy as heavily as possible at the best selected points.

Exigencies of war prevented the attendance of Premier Stalin of Russia and Generalissimo Chiang Kai-shek of China, but they were apprised of the proceedings. The conference, in brief, laid the basis for the victory in North Africa, the occupation of Sicily, and the invasion of the Italian mainland. It also framed the edict of "unconditional surrender" for the Axis.

Gen. Charles de Gaulle and Gen. Henri Honoré Giraud clasp hands at the Conference, before President Roosevelt and Prime Minister Churchill.

President Roosevelt and Prime Minister Churchill, seated on the lawn of the Sultan's villa surrounded by their staffs, read their joint communiqué.

ALLIED VICTORY IN TUNISIA

The Nazis, Driven into a Pocket in Northern Tunisia, Surrender May 12, 1943, Losing 335,000 Troops

Though Rommel had been chased across the Libyan desert by the British Eighth Army, the Fuehrer was apparently confident that he could still beat the British and the unseasoned American troops. Reinforcements and supplies were flown into Tunis and Bizerte, beginning immediately after the Americans landed at bases in North Africa. The Nazis were well situated in the ports of Tunis and Bizerte and in the mountainous country of northern Tunisia, and Rommel reorganized his forces behind the Mareth Line. The Allies were handicapped by long supply lines, green troops, and lack of airfields. Beginning at the end of January, 1943, the Allies took the offensive and their campaign was on in earnest by early February. On Feb. 20 the Nazis broke through the inexperienced American troops in the Kasserine Pass and almost split the Allied forces. On March 28 Montgomery's Eighth Army smashed the Mareth Line with a flanking stroke around the south end, while American forces under General Patton moved southeast toward Gabes. On April 7, 1943, the two armies joined forces on the Gapa-Gabes road and drove the Nazis northward. Mateur was taken on May 3, 1943, and Bizerte was cut off. Tunis fell on May 7 to the British. Axis resistance in North Africa ended in Cape Bon on May 12, 1943. General von Arnim, Commander of the German forces succeeding Rommel, was captured by the Allies. For the first time in World War II Allied forces had won a decisive victory over the Nazis.

American privates on outpost duty keep a sharp lookout from foxholes on the Tunisian battle front. The Anglo-American drive in Tunisia began soon after the American invasion on Nov. 8, 1942. It was temporarily checked in the middle of February, 1943, but on February 24 American forces reoccupied Kasserine Pass from which they had been driven by Axis troops. By the middle of March, Rommel's positions on the Mareth Line began to crumble.

This panorama shows what a Tunisian battlefield looked like. American troops in the Tunisian hills advance in open formation on enemy positions which are being bombarded by American artillery to cover their movement. Bursts from American guns can be seen along Axis-occupied hilltops in the distance. The severest reverse for the unseasoned American forces in Tunisia occurred at Kasserine Pass, in the middle of February, when they were pushed back by the Nazis.

Anti-aircraft barrage over Algiers makes a brilliant display during night raid by German planes, March 26, 1943. Flak and tracer bullets which American gunners fired against the raiders formed a weird pattern in the blackness of an African night. This spectacular picture shows sheer terror of the pyrotechnics of an air raid.

German troops, somewhere in the northeast corner of Tunisia, early in 1943, watch anxiously for an Allied air attack. The Germans converted the outlying hills around Tunis and Bizerte into fortresses bristling with field pieces, mortars, and machine guns.

Brig. Gen. Theodore Roosevelt, Maj. Gen. Terry Allen, and Lieut. Gen. George Patton, Jr. (left to right) watch operations from a foxhole during the final days in Tunisia. General Roosevelt, son of former President Theodore Roosevelt, died July 12, 1944, in Normandy.

Indian stretcher bearers, under fire, remove a wounded Gurkha from battlefield during the British Eighth Army's break-through along the Mareth Line. At right, another casualty receives attention. After Rommel had been forced from the Mareth Line on March 29 he was driven northward with the Eighth Army at his back and the British First Army and the Americans coming in from his left flank. Sfax was captured on April 10, Sousse on April 12, and before the end of April the Nazis were cooped up in north-eastern Tunisia where they were facing defeat.

British Eighth Army tanks and trucks (*below*) break through Gabes Gap to the north of Gabes, a Tunisian port about 200 miles south of Tunis, in one of the decisive operations of the Tunisian campaign. The Axis forces abandoned the Mareth Line on March 29, 1943, and on March 30 British forces occupied Gabes itself, ten miles away. This withdrawal by the Germans enabled the British to push on and attain their triumph at Wadi el Akarit, where the hard-pressed Axis troops had attempted to stand but were driven out April 8, 1943, by the British Eighth Army.

Armored .patrols of the U.S. Second Corps and the British Eighth Army (*above*) joined forces along the Gapa-Gabes road on April 7, 1943. British forces driving eastward met the American units thrusting from the west, completing the pincer strategy which pocketed the Nazis in Eastern and Northern Tunisia. In this picture Tommies and doughboys greet each other joyfully. Two British soldiers dance a jig with an American.

Flying Fortress, while bombing Nazi supply lines in North Africa, was rammed by a German fighter plane whose pilot had been killed. The collision nearly cut in half the fuselage of the Fortress. However, the tail gunner remained at his post and although attacked by other Nazi planes succeeded in routing them. The pilot was able to land the ship and crew safely at his own base an hour and a half after the encounter.

American intelligence officer questions Nazi prisoner (*below*) captured in the fighting around El Guettar in January, 1943. German prisoners, by the rules of International Law, were required only to reveal their names and rank, but many volunteered military information useful to the Allies.

Hysterically joyous crowds (*above*) greet Allied forces as they enter Tunis on May 7, 1943. A sea of arms and hands gave the Victory Salute. Allied planes spared the city proper, bombing only the shipping on the Tunis waterfront to prevent the escape of the Axis troops. Hangars, runways, and installations at El Aouina airport northeast of the city, which Nazis had used, were destroyed.

Hitler's best troops surrendered by the thousands during the last days of the North African campaign in Tunisia. Realizing that they could not extricate themselves, these men were relieved to become guests of the Allies. A large portion of the prisoners was sent to American camps.

The prison camp at Mateur was filled with Germans and Italians in the last days of the Tunisian campaign. More than 9,000 prisoners were taken in one day, May 9, 1943. Between October 23, 1942, and May 12, 1943, when resistance ended, Allied forces in North Africa took a total of 335,000 prisoners. Most important prisoner was German commander, Col. Gen. Dietloff von Arnim, who had taken over when Hitler called Marshal Rommel back to Germany.

American bombers attack Axis air transports, flying just over the water in the Sicilian straits, ferrying Nazi reinforcements into Tunisia for Rommel's troops. American bombers shot down twenty-five out of thirty-five Nazi planes encountered, making too costly the German reinforcement effort.

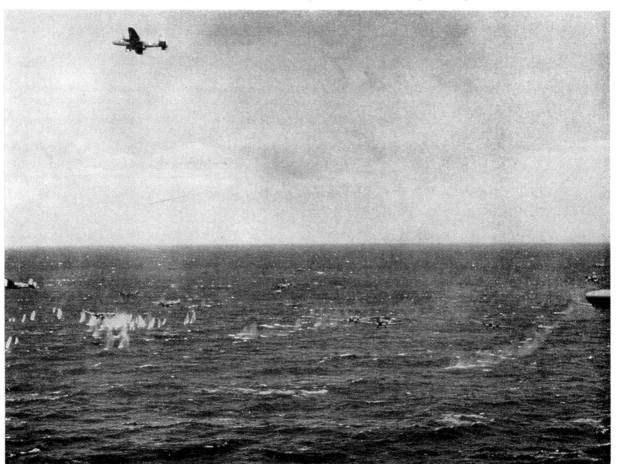

British destroyer rounds up Germans who tried to flee in rubber dinghies to Pantelleria, after the Nazi defeat in Tunisia. Some soldiers were caught by patrols of the Royal Navy as far as twenty miles from land. The great majority of Germans were satisfied to surrender when they realized that they were hopelessly trapped in the Tunisian pocket at Cape Bon. Many attached white flags to their trucks and drove into the Allied lines; others marched into captivity. By May 12 all resistance in Tunisia had ceased. In the final round-up of the trapped Axis forces some 200,000 troops surrendered, including over 50,000 Italians, while the booty included 1,000 guns and 250 tanks. More than seventeen generals were taken, including the Axis commander Dietloff von Arnim and the Italian commander Giovanni Messe.

General Eisenhower reviews detachment of the WAC in North Africa. Organized for noncombatant service and established by law on May 14, 1942, the Women's Army Auxiliary Corps was authorized for service overseas. The corps was trained in all basic phases of Army work, except handling weapons. On July 1, 1943, it was officially named the Women's Army Corps.

Allies bomb island fortress of Pantelleria. Black smoke rolls over the airfield. Two Boston bombers, their bombracks empty, head for Tunisia. At the far end of the airfield are the entrances to underground hangars and workshops. Isolated completely from supporting mainland bases, the island was unable to survive devastation of an air blitz. Pantelleria surrendered June 11, 1943, after seventeen days of bombardment.

Pantelleria, which was bombed almost incessantly by Allied planes and warships for seventeen days, following the surrender of the Axis forces in Tunisia, became an outstanding example of how a military objective may be reduced by air and naval attack without the support of troops. The bombardments continued from May 29 to June 11, 1943, the day a white flag on Semaphore Hill indicated surrender. The fall of Pantelleria and Lampedusa paved the way for the invasion of Sicily.

LATER SOLOMONS ACTION

New Guinea Campaigns of 1942–43—
Bismarck Sea—Rendova, New Georgia

After the Japanese had captured Singapore on February 15, 1942, they had pushed down into the Netherlands East Indies and succeeded in obtaining control of these rich island territories by March 8, 1942. They then moved in the direction of Australia and New Zealand. Late in January, 1942, the Japanese landed troops on New Britain, New Ireland, and the Solomons. Also on March 8, 1942, Japanese troops landed at Lae and Salamaua, on New Guinea, and a day or so later at Finschhafen. By late March the Japanese with specially trained troops began a drive to take Port Moresby. Another group of enemy troops took a shorter road linking Buna, about 140 miles southeast of Salamaua, with Port Moresby. By September, 1942, the Japanese had succeeded in getting over the Owen Stanley Mountains and were thirty miles from Port Moresby, where they were stopped.

On September 25, 1942, the Australians began a major offensive against the Japanese, gradually pressing them back over the Owen Stanley Mountains. The Australians, reinforced by American troops, drove the Japanese into the Buna-Gona area, on the lower northeast coast of New Guinea. On December 10, 1942, the Australians seized Gona and on December 15 the American and Australian forces captured Buna. Sanananda Point, farther along the coast, was taken on January 22, 1943. In July, 1943, MacArthur announced the seizure of the Mubo area. During July and August the Allies bombed Salamaua and Lae, which were the next major objectives of the New Guinea campaign. On September 7, MacArthur tried for the first time a mass parachute attack in the Markham Valley, behind the Japanese ring of defenses surrounding these strategic bases. On September 14 Salamaua was captured and on September 18, 1943, the Japanese were driven from Lae. The Allies went on to take Finschhafen farther up the coast on October 2, 1943.

On June 28 to July 1, 1943, our forces landed on New Georgia and Rendova Islands in the northern Solomons. Their main objective was the Munda Airfield on New Georgia. Other landings were made on Vella Lavella, Choiseul, and the Green Islands. On November 1, 1943, our troops landed on Bougainville Island after an intense bombardment of enemy positions.

Wounded Australian soldier receives first-aid treatment behind jungle underbrush less than 100 yards from Japanese positions at Gona, New Guinea. He was then removed to a dressing station farther behind the lines. Other Australians crouch in the jungle grass, out of line of enemy fire. Gona was captured by Australian forces on December 10, 1942, after the Japanese had put up a savage last-ditch battle for this important base. Five days later, Buna village fell.

Japanese captured at the fall of Gona sit dejectedly under guard of Australian soldiers. Only sixteen prisoners were taken. All others fought to the death or committed suicide when defeat was inevitable. The last pocket of resistance in Gona was cleaned out November 24, 1942.

R.A.A.F. bombing plane (*below*), hit by Japanese anti-aircraft fire, is blown to pieces in mid-air. Tail and wings can be seen floating down amid the wreckage, as fuselage plummets toward the ground. The plane was one of a squadron which was raiding Japanese positions in the Gona region of New Guinea late in 1942. However, Allied planes and pilots engaged in combat in South Pacific areas exerted such superiority over Japanese air forces that after Solomons and Buna-Gona campaigns they had obtained almost complete mastery of skies in that region.

Australian soldier (*above*), lost for nine weeks behind Japanese lines, is borne out of the Mubo area of the jungle in northeast New Guinea by friendly natives. He lived on grass and fruit and, traveling almost entirely by night, was able to make his way to a native village in the interior, where he was hidden from Japanese patrols, fed, and cared for until it was possible for the natives to take him back to safety behind the Allied lines. Many such tales of suffering and courage in the face of almost insuperable odds have come out of the dense jungles in the South Pacific area.

Australian Tommy gun squad sit before the common grave of Japanese killed in hand-to-hand fighting in the Gorari region of New Guinea. More than 100 of the enemy were killed in this engagement. Australian troops cleared the Japanese from the Gorari district on Nov. 13, 1942.

Blinded Australian makes his way along a jungle path, carefully guided by a Papuan native. The soldier was wounded in the battle for Buna, New Guinea. The native gave the man first aid and brought him back to the base of operations, the entire journey taking two days. Although enemy resistance was fierce, the Allies captured Buna, Dec. 15, 1942.

Australian-manned General Stuart tank slugs it out at point-blank range with a Japanese pillbox at Giropa Point in the Buna area of New Guinea, during the fighting late in 1942. The enemy was entrenched behind coconut logs and cement. Australian infantry following the tanks wait on the alert to pick off Japanese as they are routed from their positions.

Mortar crew dispatches a three-inch shell into Japanese positions. In the brush ahead on observer lies on his stomach, watching the effect of the explosion. He telephones back to the mortar sergeant, at the left, who directs angle and rate of fire. When the enemy positions have been sufficiently softened up, the infantry will move ahead.

Japanese dead are shown a little distance up the same beach from slain Americans in bottom picture. The landing barges were Japanese, knocked out by Allied bombing and strafing when the enemy tried to bring in troops to reinforce his desperate toehold in the Buna sector.

American troops crawl through a swamp to attack Japanese at Buna, New Guinea. Japanese snipers were hidden deep in the jungle, in foxholes covered with leaves so that only their machine guns protruded, or in pillboxes too strong to be wrecked by mortar.

Three American boys lie dead on the beach at Buna, New Guinea, after the battle of Buna-Gona was won in mid-December, 1942. Japanese snipers had hidden in the wrecked landing barge near by and had surprised the Americans during their mopping-up operations. The Allies won Buna village on Dec. 15, 1942, but enemy units continued to hold out at nearby Buna Mission.

American soldiers who fought at Sanananda Point, New Guinea, are brought out of the jungle in a jeep, their bodies wracked with fever. They were evacuated to Australia and given the utmost in modern medical care by Americans specially trained to handle diseases peculiar to the jungle.

Australians ford a stream (*below*) as they close in on Japanese positions in the Sanananda Point sector, the last of the three enemy pockets of resistance in eastern Papua, New Guinea. During the New Guinea campaign, the Japanese had been pushed from near Port Moresby across the Owen Stanley mountains and had been cleared out of Gona on Nov. 24, 1942, by Australian troops. The long Papuan campaign came to an end on Jan. 22, 1943. Fighting quieted down, but General MacArthur's headquarters announced the seizure of the Mubo area in July, 1943.

Dead Japanese are sprawled on the beach (*above*) before Buna Mission, New Guinea, in December, 1942. Hiding in the wrecked landing barge, they were picked off as they came out to fight. American soldier shot these Japanese with his pistol, then cleaned out others still in barge.

American gun crew goes into action to blast out a Japanese machine-gun nest during mopping-up operations in the area from Buna to Sanananda Point in New Guinea. Japanese positions were hidden in the almost impassable undergrowth in the left background. Buna was taken after bitter fighting by American and Australian forces on Dec. 15, 1942, and Sanananda Point was captured by the combined forces on Jan. 22, 1943. The Japanese were routed from their entrenched jungle positions in the area by artillery shelling, aerial bombardment, and fierce hand-to-hand combat.

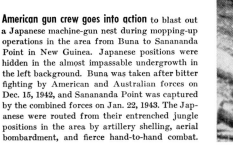

Camouflaged Japanese troop transport is bombed and set afire, south of the Bismarck Archipelago, by our Army planes. Thick black smoke arises from the foredeck. The ship had been covered with foliage so that it could move through the island-studded waters without detection.

Japanese destroyer is stopped dead (*below*) by Allied bombs in the Battle of the Bismarck Sea on March 2–3, 1943. This action, which took place at night, is lighted by flare bombs. Gray splotches on the water are oil slicks. This battle was a major disaster for the Japanese.

Japanese merchantman (*right, above*) in the Bismarck Sea Battle on March 2–3, 1943, suffers a direct hit by an Australian plane. In the mast-height attacks, some vessels seemed literally to blow up in the faces of plane crews, scarring the undersides of their planes with flying debris.

U.S. Army Air Force bomber roars over the decks of this Japanese destroyer as its crew scurries to find shelter. The enemy ships were attacked at mast height, which caught the Japanese by surprise. Such tactics were most effective in the Bismarck Sea Battle on March 2–3, 1943.

RENDOVA—NEW GEORGIA

We Press the Offensive in the Northern Solomons, Invading Vella Lavella, Choiseul, and Green Islands

After the Guadalcanal campaign had ended, our troops were able to take the offensive in the Solomons area, attacking the enemy at places of our own choosing. On June 30, 1943, two units of United States Marines and an Army force, under protection of a barrage of naval guns, made surprise landings on Rendova and New Georgia Islands. Two days later our forces had driven the Japanese off Rendova Island. Munda Airfield on New Georgia Island, which the enemy had used effectively as a base for their planes during the Guadalcanal campaign, became one of our main objectives. It was taken by the Americans on August 6. The Japanese garrison put up bitter resistance, but all of New Georgia Island fell into Allied hands by the last of August, 1943.

Meanwhile, our troops landed on other islands of the New Georgia group — Vella Lavella, Choiseul, and the Green Islands, setting the stage for the invasion of Bougainville. The Japanese desire to reinforce their occupation troops, particularly on Rendova and New Georgia, led to the Battles of Kula Gulf, which occurred on July 6 and 7 and on July 12 and 13. Our task force entered Kula Gulf between Kolombangara and New Georgia Islands at two o'clock in the morning of July 6, to protect American landings. They found there Japanese units, and the two fleets fought at point-blank range. Our cruiser the *Helena* sank two enemy cruisers and two destroyers. Then a torpedo tore off her bow. As she was going down she sank another enemy destroyer. A second battle occurred a week later. In the two naval engagements that were fought in the Kula Gulf the Japanese lost at least thirteen and possibly seventeen of their ships.

American infantryman works his way through the New Georgia underbrush, past a dead Japanese. The Americans met fierce resistance from the Japanese entrenched deep in the jungle. Munda Airfield was taken Aug. 6, 1943.

First wave of Marines storms the beach at Rendova in heavy rain. They take cover as they begin the advance inland. At dawn of June 30, 1943, U. S. transports disgorged men and matériel before the Japanese shore batteries could fire. Escorting destroyers silenced the enemy guns. By mid-afternoon the Rendova garrison was wiped out. Simultaneous landings were made on New Georgia, and Marine artillery on Rendova shelled Munda Airfield across the channel.

U.S. warship hurls a stream of anti-aircraft fire against Japanese bombers during the night battle for Vella Lavella Island, north of New Georgia. Thirty Japanese landing barges and a destroyer, attempting to retake the island, were sunk on Aug. 18, 1943, by a task force under Admiral William F. Halsey, Jr. Three days earlier specially trained "Barracuda" troops landed on Vella Lavella. After the conquest of the central Solomons, Admiral Halsey's forces moved to the northern islands.

American infantrymen wade across a jungle stream to attack Japanese positions in the fighting of November, 1943, on Arundel and Sagekarsa Islands. The action was designed to consolidate our positions in that area of the Solomons. The Japanese were hidden in dense jungle across stream.

Flame thrower sprays a Japanese pillbox on New Georgia, in mopping-up operations after the fall of Munda on Aug. 6, 1943. Tanks, guns, and infantry made little headway due to the heavy undergrowth of the swamps and jungle, so flame throwers were brought up which enabled our forces to gain the last tough mile to Munda in the next two days.

Naval task force bombards Munda Airfield, New Georgia, in the early morning of July 12, 1943. To soften up enemy positions, a hail of shells was poured into shore points guarding the airfield. Spectacular picture reflects the eerie terror of naval battle in the unbroken blackness of a tropical night. White streaks are tracer shells setting range for guns.

American patrol returns after wiping out a Japanese nest deep in the jungle at Munda, New Georgia. In the foreground is a guard covering the men as they emerge from the underbrush during fighting for strategic airfield, which was taken from the Japanese on Aug. 6, 1943. The garrison there was annihilated. The New Georgia campaign ended with the occupation of Bairoko Harbor on August 25. Numerous barges filled with enemy troops attempting to escape across Kula Gulf were sunk by our PT boats and aircraft.

Survivors of an Allied ship torpedoed in the Indian Ocean wait for rescue. Fortunately, after drifting for five days the lifeboat reached a friendly island. Deeds of unique heroism were enacted day after day by those intrepid men who manned the merchant ships which kept supplies moving to the war fronts in every part of the globe. The torpedoing of their ships by lurking U-boats, particularly in the early years of the war, meant death to a large proportion of the crews, with often but a slim chance of rescue to those who managed to get into lifeboats.

Oil-soaked survivors of the U.S.S. Cruiser Helena (*below*) answer roll call on board their rescue ship after the Battle of Kula Gulf. The *Helena,* with other ships of a task force, had steamed into Kula Gulf, between Kolombangara and New Georgia Islands, at 2 A.M. on July 6, 1943, preparatory to an American landing. A Japanese fleet was also there. The *Helena* sank two enemy cruisers and two destroyers before she in turn was sunk, by a torpedo.

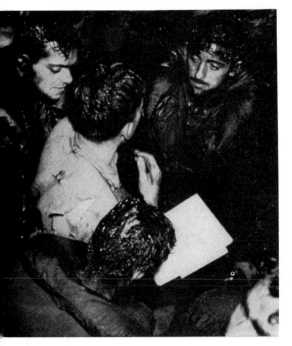

This great picture, entitled "Water" (*above*), won the Pulitzer Prize for "an outstanding example of news photography." An Associated Press photographer took the picture of the Lascar sailor begging for a drink, as the lifeboat drifted toward the northwest shore of Sumatra.

This lifeboat was never seen again (*left*). Survivors of a ship torpedoed in the Indian Ocean sail away seeking land or a rescue ship. What happened to crew and boat will probably never be known. This picture was taken from another lifeboat, seen in the accompanying pictures.

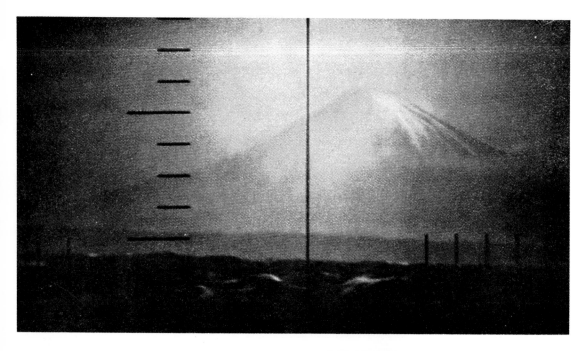

Fujiyama, Japan's sacred mountain (*left*), is photographed through the periscope of an American submarine which has suceeded in approaching close to the Japanese home islands. This remarkable picture, the first time that Fujiyama had ever been so photographed, tells the story of the skill and daring of U.S. submarine crews who slipped their boats through Japanese minefields and coastal defenses to prey upon enemy shipping, at the door of Japanese harbors, sinking a large percentage of cargo ships and tankers so badly needed in supplying their outposts.

Japanese ship (*below*), the same vessel as at center left, is shown up-ended as she goes bow first to the bottom of the Pacific. The entire drama took only a few minutes all told. The *Wahoo* sank eight Japanese vessels during this patrol of enemy waters, but in 1944 she was reported missing. The war of attrition carried on by our submarines in Pacific constituted a bright chapter in the annals of our naval forces.

American submarine, U.S.S. Wahoo, torpedoes a medium-sized Japanese cargo ship (*above*). This picture, taken through the submarine's periscope, shows the enemy vessel just after it had been struck by the torpedo. The ship was taken by surprise in the half darkness. As the torpedo from our submarine reached its vital forward-quarters section, the vessel tilted, with its bow already going under for the final plunge.

Japanese destroyer sinks, after being hit by two torpedoes from an American submarine which took this picture through its periscope. Two white-clad Japanese sailors on the bridge make a futile effort to scramble to safety. The ship, one of the latest and largest types in the Japanese Navy, keeled over and went down in a period of nine minutes. Rising Sun insignia on the turret serves as an identification for aircraft. In the Pacific our submarines created a remarkable record, as an estimated three-quarters of Japan's ship losses were caused by submarines.

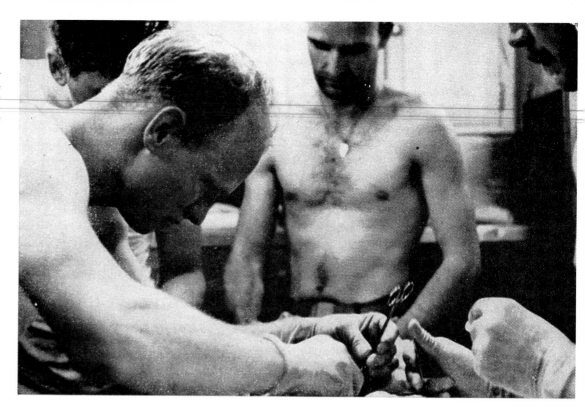

Pharmacist's mate performs an emergency appendectomy on a fellow crew member while one of our submarines is submerged in enemy-controlled waters. The patient recovered completely and after an eight-day convalescence was able to carry out light duties aboard vessel.

Japanese merchantman of 9,000 tons (*below*), thoroughly camouflaged, lies unsuspectingly at anchor in an enemy-controlled harbor in the Pacific. Picture was snapped through the periscope of one of our daring submarines which evaded enemy defenses to slip into the harbor.

Three torpedoes from the American submarine (*above*), carrying death and destruction, have crashed into the Japanese cargo ship shown in the accompanying picture. Heavy smoke rolling up from the stricken vessel has blotted out all except the bow. The submarine crew got away.

Control room of U.S. submarine, like the entire ship, is crowded with men and machinery. American submarine crews are carefully selected and trained. The sinkings by our submarines made it difficult for the Japanese to supply their outposts or to derive profit from their conquests.

THE ALEUTIAN CAMPAIGNS

We Wipe Out the Japanese Garrison on Island of Attu in May 1943, and Occupy Kiska Aug. 15, 1943

On May 11, 1943, American landings were made on the Japanese-occupied island of Attu, bypassing Kiska which lies farther to the east in the Aleutian chain. Attu, thirty-five miles long and twenty miles wide, is rugged and mountainous, therefore making our efforts to drive out the Japanese garrison particularly difficult. The American forces landed from opposite sides of the island, at Holtz Bay and Massacre Bay, their object being to crush the enemy in a pincers movement. The Americans battled the defenders on the beaches and then forced the Japanese into the mountainous areas fringing the tundra, from which they fought fanatically. An unusual feature of the battle was the large number of suicides among the Japanese. At one time during the fighting they infiltrated our lines and ran berserk. Before their ammunition was exhausted they killed themselves, thus failing to carry out the orders of their officers to kill as many Americans as possible. Only twenty Japanese prisoners were taken. All fighting ceased, with the Americans in complete control, on May 30, 1943.

American and Canadian troops landed on Kiska on August 15, to find the Japanese had evacuated the island under cover of the fog, retiring to their bases in the Kurils. Bomb-shattered installations on Kiska indicated that at one time as many as 10,000 Japanese troops were on the island. The Japanese retirement from Kiska ended Japan's military and naval threat in the entire northern Pacific area.

American landing barges push their way through slate seas and fog as our forces begin the attack on Attu, May 11, 1943. Landings were made at Holtz Bay on northern side of the island and at Massacre Bay on southern coast.

Americans and Canadians landed on Kiska on Aug. 15, 1943, bringing ashore full equipment and armament for the troops. Enemy forces evacuated the island before Allied invasion. The fourteen-month defense of Kiska cost Japanese twenty-nine warships and thirty noncombatant ships sunk or damaged.

American crews of 90-mm. gun units try to locate Japanese positions on high ground surrounding the shore area of Attu. In the initial fighting the Japanese put up stubborn resistance on the beaches, but were soon driven into the mountains. From there they continued to pour shells on our troops.

U.S. mortar crew hurls shells into Japanese positions in this land-battle action on Attu Island. Note tense attitude of men as they wait for explosion. Troops in trench in background are ready to attack enemy hill positions as soon as mortar fire has done its work.

Beachmaster directs landing operations as American troops invade rocky Attu Island in the Aleutian chain. Loud speakers were used to transmit landing instructions to barges. For nineteen days United States forces battled heavy blizzards as well as Japanese.

American troops at Massacre Beach, on Attu, fire against Japanese snipers on hillside beyond. On this mist-shrouded tundra, our men battled freezing cold and snow eight to twenty feet deep to dislodge the enemy from high mountain ridges. Final conquest of the strategic but almost uninhabitable island was won in bitter hand-to-hand fighting. Attu's airfield, unfinished by the Japanese, was then quickly completed and used to bomb Kiska.

Wounded American on a stretcher is swung from a landing barge to a mother ship in Massacre Bay, at Attu, in the Aleutian Islands. The American forces invading Attu on May 11, 1943, suffered heavy casualties as they crossed the level tundra near the beachheads and plunged toward the central ridges in the face of Japanese machine-gun fire. The Attu campaign was completed on May 30, 1943, when the Japanese Imperial Headquarters at Tokyo admitted that its garrison had ceased fighting in the Aleutians.

American dead await burial on Attu. At each man's head is a board to which his identification is attached. Total American casualties were 342 killed, 1,135 wounded, and 58 missing. Japanese casualties were 1,845 known dead.

American soldiers on Attu clear out enemy dugout during mopping-up operations. The Japanese had built an elaborate system of caves and tunnels, forming a network throughout the island. Sniper nests consisted of tiny underground houses connected by tunnels.

U.S. pilot shot down over Kiska was buried here by the Japanese. The sign reads: "Sleeping here, a brave air-hero who lost youth and happiness for his mother land, July 25, Nippon Army." This inscription, in contrast to the usual Japanese attitude, was evidently written by an American-educated soldier.

Japanese two-man and three-man submarines of the types that attacked Pearl Harbor were destroyed by the enemy at its base on Kiska, before reoccupation by Allies. Cut off from supply lines, the Japanese were unable to withstand furious air and naval bombardments.

American and Canadian troops occupy Kiska, Aug. 15, 1943. The Japanese had succeeded in evacuating an estimated 10,000 troops under cover of the heavy fogs of the region. The capture of Attu on May 30, 1943, had isolated Japanese forces remaining in the Aleutians.

FRANKLIN DELANO ROOSEVELT

The first of the World War II Presidents, he died while in office, April 12, 1945. Before entry of the United States into the war, December 8, 1941, he advocated assistance to the Allied nations through lend-lease and the Atlantic convoy system.

HARRY S. TRUMAN

Elected Vice-President in 1944, he became the nation's leader upon the death of President Roosevelt. His pledge to press to a successful conclusion the country's war against the Axis powers was fulfilled when the Japanese surrendered to Gen. Douglas MacArthur, September 1, 1945.

UNITED STATES BATTLESHIP *ARIZONA* EXPLODES AT PEARL HARBOR, DECEMBER 7, 1941, AFTER A DIRECT HIT BY A JAPANESE PLANE. THE *ARIZONA* WAS THE ONLY ONE OF OUR BATTLESHIPS THAT BECAME A COMPLETE LOSS.

THE HEART OF LONDON, SHOWING THE DESTRUCTION AFTER THE CITY WAS BOMBED BY THE GERMANS DURING THE AIR BLITZ OF SEPTEMBER, 1940. ST. PAUL'S CATHEDRAL IN THE BACKGROUND WAS ONLY SLIGHTLY DAMAGED.

PRESIDENT FRANKLIN DELANO ROOSEVELT DELIVERS A MOMENTOUS ADDRESS ON POST-WAR GOALS BEFORE THE CONGRESS OF THE UNITED STATES ON JANUARY 7, 1943, ASSEMBLED IN JOINT SESSION IN THE HOUSE OF REPRESENTATIVES.

A CONVOY OF UNITED NATIONS CARGO SHIPS PROCEEDS ON ITS WAY ACROSS THE NORTH ATLANTIC GUARDED
FROM THE U-BOAT MENACE BY A DIRIGIBLE SUPPLEMENTING ESCORT VESSELS AND CARRIER-BASED PLANES.

LANDING BARGES AND SMALL CRAFT COME ASHORE AT KISKA IN THE ALEUTIAN ISLANDS ON AUGUST 15, 1943. ALLIED FORCES FOUND THAT THE JAPANESE HAD ALREADY SURRENDERED THEIR LAST FOOTHOLD ON NORTH-AMERICAN SOIL.

UNITED NATIONS FORCES COMPOSED OF AMERICAN, BRITISH, AND FRENCH TROOPS, WITH THEIR FLAGS FLY-
ING, MARCH VICTORIOUSLY THROUGH TUNIS AFTER THE SURRENDER OF THE AXIS ARMIES ON MAY 12, 1943.

INVASION BOATS ARE DRAWN UP TO SHORE AFTER THE LANDING OF ALLIED FIFTH ARMY IN ITALY ON SEPT. 9, 1943. IN THE DISTANCE RISE THE FOOTHILLS OF THE APENNINES.

An LST unloads jeeps and troops below Salerno during the invasion of Italy. A pontoon dock extends from the LST, facilitating unloading.

American infantry of General Clark's Fifth Allied Army comes ashore on the morning of Sept. 9, 1943, to establish a beachhead below Salerno.

MARINES IN CAMOUFLAGED SUITS AND CARRYING FULL PACKS LEAVE THE BEACHHEAD AT TARAWA ON NOVEMBER 21, 1943, TO STORM THE AIRPORT. ONE SOLDIER HAS ALREADY HURDLED THE BARRICADE IN THE FACE OF JAPANESE FIRE.

GENERAL OF THE ARMY DWIGHT DAVID EISENHOWER

Appointed Supreme Commander Allied Expeditionary Forces, European Theater
of War, December, 1943; Chief of Staff, United States Army, December, 1945.

GENERAL OF THE ARMY DOUGLAS MacARTHUR

Appointed Supreme Commander of the United Nations Forces in the Southwest Pacific,
March, 1942; Supreme Commander Allied Powers for Japanese surrender, August, 1945.

MOUNT CASSINO, THE STORMY PETREL OF THE ITALIAN CAMPAIGN

The town of Cassino and the ancient Benedictine Monastery atop Mount Cassino emerge from clouds of smoke during the bombardment preceding the Allied attempt to capture this sector in the early months of 1944. The town of Cassino lies at the bottom of the deep mountain slope. The Germans were driven out of Cassino, May 18, 1944.

WAVE (WOMEN ACCEPTED FOR VOLUNTARY EMERGENCY SERVICE, USNR)

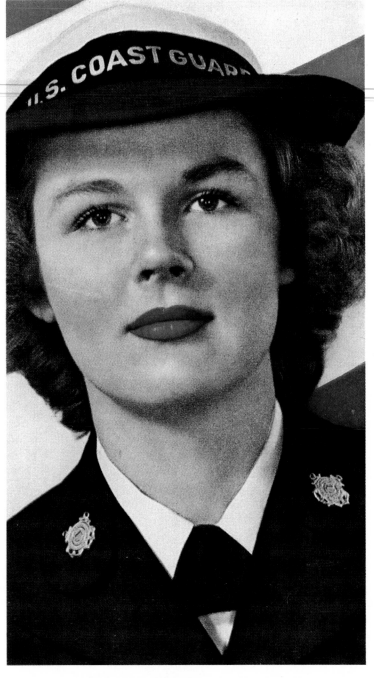

SPAR (WOMEN'S RESERVE OF THE UNITED STATES COAST GUARD)

WAC (WOMEN'S ARMY CORPS)

MARINE (UNITED STATES MARINE CORPS WOMEN'S RESERVE)

WORLD LEADERS CONVENE AT POTSDAM

Berlin Conference in Potsdam, from July 17-Aug. 2, 1945, planned for peace, extermination of Nazism and militarism in Germany, administration of the conquered Reich, and the final destruction of Japan. Seated, left to right, are Prime Minister Attlee, President Truman, and Premier Stalin. In rear are Fleet Admiral Leahy, and Foreign Ministers, Bevin, Byrnes, and Molotov.

Flames from a Kamikaze are extinguished by flight deck crew of the U.S.S. *Intrepid*. Named for the "Divine Wind" that once saved Japan from invasion, the *Kamikaze* or suicide planes struck their hardest blow at Okinawa. The Japanese lost 4,232 planes.

Nagasaki lies in ruins after atomic bomb attack of Aug. 9, 1945. *(below)* More than 30,000 were killed outright at Nagasaki, and thousands died later from after effects. Of 50,000 buildings, 18,000 were demolished.

THE U.S.S. *MISSOURI* AT WAR AND IN PEACE
Giant American battleship fires salvo from her 16-inch guns, *above*. Note projectiles in flight. At right, Gen. Yoshijiro Umezu signs Japanese surrender aboard the *Missouri*. Gen. MacArthur and Lieut. Gen. Sutherland look on.

THE INVASION OF SICILY

With 3,000 Ships and 160,000 Men the Allies Drive the Axis from Sicily

American and British forces launched the invasion of Sicily, on July 10, 1943, with landings at several points on the southern and eastern coastline of the island. The Americans of the Seventh Army, under Lieutenant General George S. Patton, Jr., came ashore at Licata and Gela, while the British Eighth Army, under General Sir Bernard L. Montgomery, landed at Syracuse. More than 3,000 ships of all types carried an invasion force of 160,000 men. It was later revealed that 85,000 tons of our ships were lost during the operation. The Axis forces on Sicily consisted of about 250,000 troops, including four German and twelve Italian divisions. Parachute and glider troops were dropped behind Axis lines. Although the invasion had been preceded by heavy air and naval bombardment, German and Italian forces put up a bitter battle on the beachheads, and for a short time during the day of the landing at Gela our troops were in danger of being pushed back into the sea. Allied warships gave needed support and saved the beachhead.

The general strategy of the campaign called for the American troops to press northwest in the direction of Palermo, with Canadian contingents taking the east-central part of the island, and the British Eighth Army pushing up the eastern coastline. The British Eighth Army met gradually increased resistance until on the plains before Catania its progress was held up for several weeks. In the center of the island the Canadians moved ahead, while in the west the American Seventh Army speedily spread out. On July 16, Agrigento was taken and on the 21st of the month, Enna. American troops reached Palermo, the capital of Sicily, on July 23, and the city surrendered without firing a shot. Thus all of western Sicily was cut off and captured. In two weeks the Americans took 50,000 Italian prisoners. From this point the Seventh Army moved eastward, with every mile contested, along the north coast toward Messina.

The offensive of the Eighth Army was resumed after the capture of Catania on August 5. Troina was taken on August 7, Adrano and Bronte on the 8th, and Randazzo on the 13th of August. By this time the Germans were evacuating their troops across the Strait of Messina. The thirty-eight-day Sicilian campaign ended with the capture of Messina on August 17, 1943.

American parachute troops make last-minute adjustments to their heavy packs and parachutes before they are ordered aboard the Douglas C-47 transports which carried them to Sicily. Each man wore on his right arm, for identification, an American flag. They had been thoroughly trained for many months for the first real test in this war of the effectiveness of our paratroops in invasion operations. These men landed in Sicily in the rear of enemy lines in the dawn of July 10, 1943. They were preceded to Sicily by glider-borne troops which were able to concentrate in great strength during the early hours of invasion.

Battalion commander aboard transport plane in flight announces to the American parachutists that they are bound for Sicily to start the invasion of the island, July 10, 1943. Neither air troops nor land forces knew their destination until they were under way. This secrecy was necessary in order that no information reach enemy ears, allowing him to prepare and thus make our task more difficult.

Six United Nations auxiliary ships (*below*) were hit and lost during the invasion of Sicily. The vessels in the background have just been bombed by Italian and German planes and are belching smoke and flames. These ships of the auxiliary fleet were standing off Gela where the Americans landed. It was later revealed that the Allies used over 3,000 ships of all sizes and description in the invasion of Sicily.

Allied invasion barges (*above*), in an enormous fleet, mass in North African port preparatory to invasion of Sicily. Others already on their way steam out into the Mediterranean under escort of our fighting ships. Allied forces reached Sicily on July 10, 1943, with the Americans coming to shore on the southern coast near Licata and Gela, while the British landed at Syracuse.

Invasion of Sicily to American paratroopers was grim business. These men set off the spark for the invasion when they landed on July 10, 1943, a few hours before British, American, and Canadian infantrymen stormed the beaches in the biggest operation of land, sea, and air forces, to that time, in history. In the confusion, some planes carrying our parachute troops were mistaken for enemy planes and were shot down.

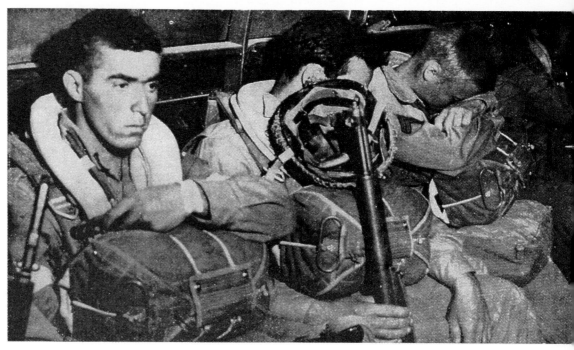

German planes bomb American convoy off Gela, Sicily. In high-level and dive bomber attacks the enemy tried repeatedly to smash the Allied invasion armada, but only 85,000 tons, a small percentage, were sunk.

American supply ship carrying ammunition and gasoline is set afire by a bomb dropped from a Nazi plane during Allied landings at Gela, Sicily. While air forces based in North Africa afforded effective air cover for our troops during the invasion, Nazi planes at times were able to get through to harass our operations. The Allies lost six of a fleet of 3,000 vessels.

British troops land on Sicily at dawn on July 10, 1943. A fleet of 3,000 ships converged on designated points, and troops, guns, tanks, and supplies were rushed ashore under incessant bombardment by enemy artillery.

American invasion barges push close to the shore near Licata, Sicily, on the morning of July 10, 1943. U.S. troops of the Seventh Army, under Lieut. Gen. George S. Patton, Jr., landed at Licata and at Gela.

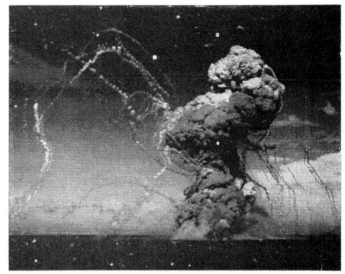

Pyrotechnics light the sky (*above*) as the American cargo ship explodes near Gela, Sicily, on July 10, 1943. Oily black smoke billowed high into the sky, with ribbons of fire shooting in all directions. Before the fire reached the munitions and gasoline, the crew was removed to safety.

The American cargo ship seen in the two above pictures is shown as the explosion from gasoline and munition stores reached its full burst of destructive splendor. A number of hours elapsed between the time the Nazi bomb struck the ship and the final explosion. The crew stubbornly fought the spread of the flames until the fire reached the inflammable cargo.

American Paratroopers who landed behind German lines in Sicily were caught in the bombing of American positions by German 88's and heavy tanks. These men were killed on July 13, 1943, near Vittoria, Sicily, during initial operations which resulted in successful invasion of the island.

American gun crews with the hitherto secret weapon (below), the Bazooka, gather on a Sicilian street corner. The Bazooka achieved a remarkable record in the Tunisian, Sicilian, and Italian campaigns. On Sicily it was considered the deadliest anti-tank weapon, as its shells could penetrate the heaviest armored enemy vehicle.

Italian troops carry high the white flag as they approach the British lines to surrender (above), in Sicily, during the Allied invasion in July, 1943. The picturesque Sicilian countryside at the eastern end of the island, with its heavy verdure, is clearly seen in this dramatic picture.

British infantry mop up straggling snipers left behind to protect the enemy's retreat near Augusta, Sicily. The city was taken by the British Eighth Army, which forced the Nazis to evacuate it after a heavy naval bombardment. It was surrendered to the victorious invading forces on July 12, 1943.

Allied wounded were brought from the fighting zones back to bases where they were given immediate treatment, and then moved to ports such as Syracuse. Here, wounded soldiers on stretchers cover the entire deck of a British landing craft in this Sicilian harbor. They are waiting to be placed aboard a transport which will take them to North Africa where they will receive the utmost in medical care in hospitals.

American forces on July 23, 1943, captured Palermo (*below*) with its excellent harbor, the principal port of Sicily. During our occupation the Axis air forces bombed it, when they were not driven off by our planes. In this picture the Chemical Warfare Branch of the U.S. Army has laid down a smoke-screen to protect the city.

United States soldiers conduct mopping-up operations in a small Sicilian town (*above*). Italians were prone to surrender to the invading Allied forces; the Germans on the contrary planted snipers and booby traps to delay as long as possible the Allied advance. The Nazis were thus able to reorganize their defenses.

Princess Patricia's Canadian Light Infantry, famous western Canada unit, mop up a German transport convoy. They then advanced into Valguarnera, Sicily, and thence to Enna, where they joined the American forces. The Canadian troops, proceeding through the east-central part of the island, encountered stubborn resistance in the mountainous country where the Germans had entrenched themselves.

People of Catania, once freed from the restraint of the Fascist government whose officials had fled before the Allied advance, turned to looting. In this picture crowds wait below while looters throw goods from balconies of houses of local Fascist party members. Pent-up vengeance of Sicilians upon Fascists was thus partly satisfied.

British Eighth Army soldiers pursue German snipers through a square in Catania in the course of mopping-up operations. Catania, the chief port of eastern Sicily, was captured on Aug. 5, 1943. The mountainous country enabled the Germans to put up a stubborn resistance, until they were driven out by shelling and infantry attacks.

German prisoners taken near Valguarnera, in Sicily, are lined up by Canadian soldiers of the Edmonton Regiment. During the first three days of fighting in the island this regiment took 3,000 Italian prisoners. The Canadians after the landing in Sicily July 10, 1943, moved through the island between American and British forces.

U.S. Forces press on through Troina, which was captured on Aug. 6, 1943, by the Seventh Army under General Patton, in the toughest battle our troops had fought to that time. This town was a focal point of the German defense line in Northern Sicily, fifty miles distant from Messina.

British Eighth Army troops (*below*), despite enemy resistance, push through the smoke of bursting bombs to attack a Sicilian railway station. Discarded helmets and gun belonged to Italian infantry. British forces raced inland after Syracuse had been captured, joining American units at Ragusa. But the main contingent of the British Eighth Army struck northward along the coast toward Messina on the northeast tip of Sicily.

Canadian soldiers mop up in Sicilian town of Centuripe (*above*), following its evacuation by the Germans, Aug. 3, 1943. The Nazis made a desperate defense at Centuripe, entrenching themselves in the mountains in and about the town. The Allies were forced to blast the enemy out with artillery followed by infantry attacks.

British Eighth Army gun crews with twenty-five pounders shell Axis forces retreating toward Messina. The Eighth Army, late in the campaign, was progressing north and east toward Messina where they met American and Canadian forces. On Sept. 3, 1943, the British crossed the strait of Messina and effected a landing on the Italian mainland.

American soldier, wounded in the fighting in Sicily, is brought on stretcher to a small village. A private of the Army Medical Corps administers precious blood plasma which has been contributed by Americans back home. Plasma flows through tube into soldier's veins. Sicilian townspeople, sitting in doorway of their bombed home, watch with grave interest. Thousands of lives were saved during the fighting in Sicily by such promptness in administering both plasma and sulfa drugs to wounded soldiers who might otherwise have died from shock while being transferred to casualty stations behind the lines. Large supplies of plasma were kept close to battle line, ready for use on battlefields or for emergency operations at base hospitals. Mortality rate in first World War was seven out of one hundred. In World War II this percentage was reduced to 1.2 per cent.

German teller-mines, abandoned by retreating Nazi armies before they could be put to use, cover a field near Roccopalumba, Sicily. Thousands of these mines were ingeniously buried along roads and in fields over which the Allied armies would pass in pursuit of the enemy. A discus-shaped container about four inches thick and one foot in diameter, the teller-mine was most dangerous of all Nazi anti-tank and anti-personnel devices. It held about eleven pounds of high explosives which could be set off by 300 pounds of pressure. Engineer Corpsmen, with mine-detectors, were sent ahead of the advancing Allied troops to render the traps harmless.

Badly wounded U.S. soldiers (*below*) were speedily evacuated by transport planes from Sicily to the base hospitals established in North Africa. In the foreground, an Army nurse is ministering to one of the casualties from the front, while Medical Corpsmen are keeping close watch over the precious cargo.

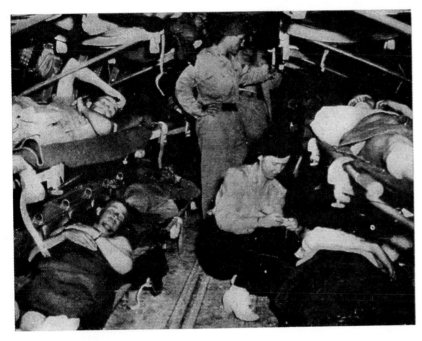

Lieut. Gen. George S. Patton, Jr. (*above*), Commander of the Seventh Army during the invasion of Sicily, bends over to offer his sympathy to one of his wounded men waiting to be evacuated to a base hospital. General Patton was famous for his carrying of a pearl-handled revolver strapped on each hip. Early in April, 1943, he was relieved of his command in Tunisia to train Allied troops for the Sicilian invasion. On the first day of fighting he took command and personally led his forces ashore.

Prison compound, in Gela, Sicily, was built by Italians and originally intended for Allied captives. In this picture it is well filled with Italian and German captives taken in the fighting during the Allied invasion of the island. The guards in the foreground are Army military police. Trenches surrounding the enclosure were dug to ensure protection against possible air raids. Axis casualties in Sicily were approximately 165,000 men killed, wounded, or missing. The total casualties of the Allied fighting forces during the campaign were 31,158 men killed, wounded, and missing.

American and British troops mop up snipers in Messina, left behind to delay the advance of the Allies after the main body of Germans had fled to the Italian mainland. Using barges, ferries, or any other craft afloat, almost three German divisions escaped across the Strait of Messina despite continuous Allied bombing and strafing. The Italian troops were left to shift for themselves and soon surrendered. The taking of Messina on Aug. 17, 1943, ended the thirty-eight-day Sicilian campaign.

Happy Sicilian calls a greeting to Allied troops which entered Messina Aug. 17, 1943. The British and American forces converged on the city from their respective directions. They received a tremendous welcome from the populace who looked upon the Allies as their liberators.

Germans placed anti-aircraft guns on mainland opposite Messina, to protect German evacuation from Sicily. Although many Nazis crossed the narrow straits, 135,000 Axis prisoners were taken, and 260 tanks, 502 guns, and 1,691 aircraft captured or destroyed.

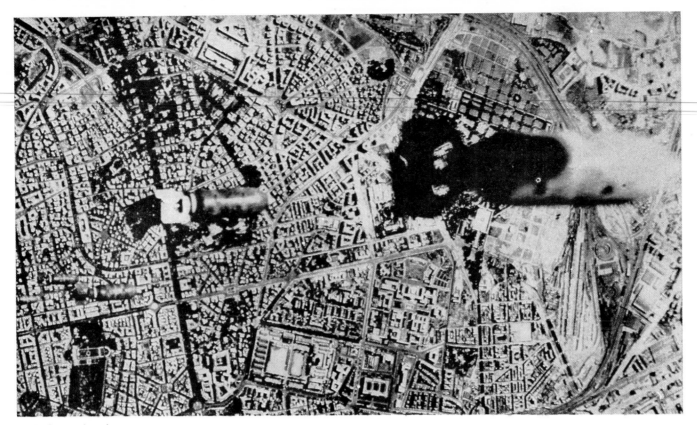

Bombs drop earthward on July 19, 1943, to destroy the Littorio marshaling yards in Rome. Carrying out the mission were 272 American heavy bombers and 249 medium bombers of the U.S. Ninth Air Force. The planes dropped 1,101 tons of high explosives, sparing the religious buildings except the Basilica di San Lorenzo.

American bombers circle over Rome during an attack. The raids were deemed necessary by the Allied High Command to stop, if possible, the Germans from using the Eternal City as a base for military operations, and retard supplies and additional troops reaching the fronts in southern Italy by destroying railway installations in and about Rome. The American pilots had carefully studied detailed maps of Rome in order to avoid striking any of its famous churches or historical monuments.

San Lorenzo railroad yards are smashed by bombers of the U.S. Ninth Air Force, based in North Africa, in the first Allied raid on the Rome area, July 19, 1943. The raid was preceded by the dropping of leaflets warning civilians to evacuate the area and explaining the necessity for the raid, and also assuring the people of Rome that only areas located in the military zones would be bombed. For utmost accuracy in precision bombing, the raid was carried out in daylight, with a loss of only five planes.

Pope Pius XII, on a tour of inspection of air-raid damage, prays outside the ruined Basilica di San Lorenzo, in Rome. Italian and German communiqués claimed 717 persons were killed, 1,599 wounded, and eleven religious buildings hit in first raid on Eternal City. The Pope confirmed only destruction of the Basilica di San Lorenzo.

Basilica di San Lorenzo (*left*), adjacent to one of Rome's important railway terminals, was hit in the first American raid on Rome. The Nazis tried to capitalize on the damage for propaganda purposes. The object of the raid was to destroy railroad yards through which the Nazis were reinforcing and supplying their armies in southern Italy.

Bomb craters cover the airstrip at Crampino Airfield in Rome after American B-26 Marauders blasted air and railway installations in the Italian capital on July 19, 1943. The raid climaxed a gigantic softening-up process preceding Allied invasion of Italy.

THE OUSTING OF MUSSOLINI

Il Duce Is Arrested on July 25, 1943, by the King
After Being Voted Down by Fascist Grand Council

After twenty-two years as dictator of Italy, Mussolini's star set on July 25, 1943. On July 19 Mussolini had had a conference in northern Italy with his Axis partner who, seeing the writing on the wall, had proposed that the greater part of Italy be given up to the Allies. Mussolini brought these tidings back to his King and the Fascist Grand Council. After a heated discussion, on the night of July 24, Mussolini was voted down by a reported majority of nineteen to five. Among those voting against Il Duce were Count Grandi and Count Ciano, Il Duce's son-in-law. The announcement that King Victor Emmanuel had "accepted the resignations" of Mussolini and his Cabinet was made over the Rome radio on July 25, at 11 P.M. Rome time. It was also announced that the King had asked Marshal Badoglio to form a military government to replace the Fascist regime. Mussolini, arrested on orders of the King, was transferred from one place to another and finally to the Grand Sasso d'Italia, in the Abruzzi. The Nazis, in order to prevent Mussolini's falling into the hands of the Allies, sent parachute troops and men of the Elite Guard and Secret Security Service to Abruzzi to rescue him from the custody of the Badoglio government. He was flown back into German-held territory. The Nazis then released pictures showing Hitler welcoming an aged and emaciated Duce. The sudden end to Mussolini's career must have been a rude shock to Hitler who then made Mussolini head of a puppet "Italian Fascist Republic."

Adolf Hitler greets the deposed Duce after his arrival by plane on German territory. Thus after twenty-two years Mussolini's star set, suddenly and ingloriously—a tame anticlimax to his career, as not a shot had been fired in his ousting. But his going could not prevent disaster for Italy, for the Germans opposed Allied forces invading the mainland from Messina on Sept. 3, 1943, and at Salerno six days later, and Italy became a battleground. After Italy's surrender the Nazis made Mussolini head of a shadow regime.

A Roman holiday (*right*) marks Il Duce's downfall and the official end of Fascism on July 25, 1943. Pictures of King Victor Emmanuel and Marshal Badoglio, Italy's new Premier, decorate the truck, but notably absent, for the first time in twenty-two years, are pictures of the erstwhile dictator Mussolini, who had been imprisoned on orders of the Italian King.

Mussolini is rescued from Italian custody in Abruzzi by Nazi paratroopers, after his arrest by Marshal Badoglio. At a Grand Council meeting of the Fascist Party on July 24, 1943, Il Duce presented Hitler's proposals for abandoning most of Italy. Nineteen of twenty-four members, including Count Ciano, refused to support him, demanding his resignation.

Cheering Italians (*below*) celebrate Mussolini's downfall with mass demonstrations. The placards read "Long Live the Army." Marshal Badoglio proclaimed martial law to curb looting of homes of Fascist officials by throngs released from Fascist rule.

At the Quebec Conference, held between Aug. 11 and Aug. 24, 1943, President Roosevelt and Prime Minister Churchill with their full staffs mapped out and clarified political and military policies in the light of the many gratifying events which had taken place during the preceding months. Necessary discussions were held to provide for the forward actions of the fleets, armies and air forces of Great Britain and the United States. As their forces were engaged in continuous action against the enemy in several quarters of the globe, it was indispensable that unity of aim and method be maintained at the summit of the war direction. The joint statement by Roosevelt and Churchill added that military discussions turned largely upon the war against Japan and aid to China. Full reports of the discussions affecting the war against Germany and Italy were furnished to the Soviet Government. Seated with President Roosevelt and Prime Minister Churchill, is Prime Minister Mackenzie King of Canada.

Over this table during Conference at Quebec, Canada, war leaders of the United Nations (*right*) exchanged ideas which were designed to contribute to the pattern of eventual victory for United Nations armies. The combined staff of war chiefs laid out a blue print for future operations. At extreme left and nearest the camera may be seen Lord Louis Mountbatten, later Chief of the Southeast Asia Command in Burma, and on the opposite side of the table are Generals Marshall and Arnold and Admirals King and Leahy. In a speech at the Conference President Roosevelt said: "During the past few days in Quebec the combined staffs have been sitting around a table, which is a good custom, talking things over, discussing ways and means in the manner of friends, in the manner of partners, I may even say in the manner of members of the same family." The Conference approved unanimous recommendations of combined chiefs of staffs.

Four American Liberators, skimming the tree-tops, pass into the target area against a background of flame and smoke from oil fields set afire by previous waves of raiders over Ploesti, Rumania. Bombers flew at zero level over two seas and at least two countries in the greatest low-level attack ever known. Many planes flew so near the ground that explosions from their own bombs nearly wrecked them.

American planes completely destroyed the distillation and cracking plants at the Columbia Aquila refinery at Ploesti, Rumania. Smoke still rises from one of the many burnt-out oil storage tanks. Damage is also visible on railway sidings and among storage buildings. The Americans practiced for months before the raid, constructing a replica of the Ploesti fields and refineries on which to perfect this bombing technique. Although the results were satisfactory, the raid proved costly to the Allies. Casualties were numbered at 400.

Through gaps in the rising clouds of flame and black oily smoke, American Liberators swoop down on the Astra Romana refinery at Ploesti, Rumania, already burning from direct hits. Consolidated B-24's swarmed over the target area in squadrons of thirty-six planes, dropping their lethal loads of 300 tons of incendiaries and high-explosive bombs on this valuable oil source to Hitler. Seventy-five per cent of all production in the Ploesti area was crippled for sixty to ninety days after the attack. The actual raid, during which our fighters shot down fifty-one enemy planes, lasted only one minute although months of secret planning preceded it.

Astra Romana refineries, at Ploesti, were transformed into a sea of flame and smoke as American Liberators unloaded their bombs on these oil fields which furnished Hitler with thirty to fifty per cent of the oil required for his war machine. Fires still raged five days after the raid which took place on August 1, 1943. Eighty per cent of the installations were disabled and the raid, carefully planned over a long period of time, was a brilliant success, which prompted General Lewis H. Brereton, head of the Middle East Command, to say that this devastating attack on the Rumanian oil fields and refineries at Ploesti had "materially affected the war."

An American intelligence officer, at a Libyan base, questions pilots and crews who raided Rumanian oil fields in Ploesti. One hundred and seventy-five Liberator bombers participated in the daylight raid which involved a 2,400-mile round trip. Twenty per cent of the planes were lost.

THE SPENCER AND CAMPBELL

Our Coast Guard Cutters Write Heroic Chapters in the Battle of the Atlantic Against the U-Boat Menace

One of the outstanding epics in the Allied war against the German submarine was the sinking by the Coast Guard-manned cutter *Spencer* of a U-boat that was trying to break into a large convoy crossing the North Atlantic. This cutter of 2,300 tons, 327 feet in length and "paper skinned," outmaneuvered, outfought, and sank the German submarine, and then rescued from the icy water forty Nazi seamen who were screaming for help. The U-boat, lying in wait, was detected by the cutter which gave the warning. The submarine tried to escape by running under the convoy, but depth charges finally forced the U-boat to the surface. The *Spencer* and a companion cutter opened fire. The U-boat's deck became a mass of wreckage and resistance ceased. A Nazi seaman was seen clinging to a stanchion near a deck gun. Another shot from the *Spencer* landed and the seaman disappeared. Soon after the submarine sank. The *Spencer* sent out boats to pick up hysterical survivors.

In a second tale of heroism, the *Campbell* during a period of twelve hours engaged six U-boats. In the last of the six battles the cutter steered a direct collision course for the Nazi submarine and blazed away at the U-boat at point-blank range. When the submarine had been disposed of, the *Campbell* had a twelve-foot gash below her waterline and her engines and electrical system were dead.

Depth charge explodes off the stern of the cutter *Spencer*, serving to bring the U-boat to the surface. This operation took several hours. The submarine was detected at 3 A.M. and it did not appear above the water until 11 A.M. It was sunk after it attempted to break into the center of the large convoy.

Sailors aboard the U.S. Coast Guard-manned cutter Spencer watch a K-gun, which is employed to hurl depth charges, go into action following detection of an enemy submarine. This was the opening operation in a battle to bring the submarine to the surface. In the air, at right, is the depth bomb, just projected.

Nazi U-boat lies helpless (*right*) after being brought to the surface by depth bombs from the U.S. Coast Guard-manned cutter *Spencer*. The conning tower of the submarine has just received a direct hit and is smoking from the damage. A Nazi sailor with his back to the *Spencer* clings desperately to a stanchion of the conning tower. He soon disappeared under the fire from the *Spencer's* guns. As the U-boat's engines have been put out of commission by the depth charges and shelling, it wallows in the trough of the waves which break over it. A few minutes later the crew abandoned their sinking ship and were in the black waters, wearing their bright orange life jackets.

Nazi U-boat settles in the water (*left*) as the Coast Guard cutter bears down upon it. One Nazi can be seen cowering against the conning tower, hopeful of rescue. Another crew member is barely visible in the water, at the right. He, as well as other crew members who were able to get free from their ship, was picked up by boats sent out by the *Spencer*. The *Spencer* had by this time ceased firing as it was evident the U-boat was finished. In the battle a number of the crew of the *Spencer* were wounded by shells from the submarine. After U-boat survivors were brought aboard, the *Spencer* rejoined the convoy which had proceeded under protection of other cutters and destroyers.

Survivors are rescued by Coast Guardsmen from the cutter *Spencer* before the submarine makes its final dive. In addition to the damage done by depth bombs, the cutter shelled the U-boat. In this picture the stern can be seen completely submerged, while the prow rears upward. The submarine sank almost exactly an hour after she surfaced under the hail of depth bombs.

Nazi officer pleads for rescue, after his U-boat was sunk in the North Atlantic in February, 1943, by the Coast Guard-manned cutter *Campbell*. The submarine had tried to intercept a merchant convoy. After March of 1943 the U-boat menace was steadily reduced through the introduction by the Allies of small carriers.

ITALY INVADED BY ALLIES

Italy Unconditionally Surrenders to the Allies—The Fifth Army Lands at Salerno

On September 3, 1943, Italy unconditionally surrendered to the Allies. The terms of the armistice were signed by representatives of General Eisenhower and Marshal Badoglio. Mussolini's resignation had been accepted on July 25 and he had been arrested. The announcement of Italy's unconditional surrender was withheld at the request of the Allies until September 8. On September 3, Montgomery's Eighth Army had crossed the Straits of Messina into Reggio Calabria, four years to the day after Great Britain and France had declared war on Germany. The announcement of the armistice on September 8 came a few hours before the Fifth Army under General Mark Clark landed near Salerno, south of Naples.

Montgomery's Eighth Army, consisting of British and Canadian troops, moved north and east along both coasts at a rapid pace. The Fifth Army, consisting of two divisions of British and one division of American troops, found the Germans waiting for them in well-entrenched positions. Thus for several days the battle was in doubt. However, by the 16th of September the tide had turned against the Germans and on the following day the Fifth and Eighth Armies made contact south of Salerno. These armies pushed northward up the Italian Peninsula, and by September 20 it was evident that the Nazis were preparing to evacuate Naples. Before leaving, however, they looted and gutted Italy's second largest city. They demolished docks and warehouses and filled the harbor with sunken ships. On September 20 Foggia with its airfield fell to the Eighth Army, and on October 1, General Clark's forces entered Naples.

General Clark sent the bulk of his Fifth Army in pursuit of the Nazis toward the Volturno River which was crossed, after a bitter defense by the Germans, on October 12. The ancient city of Capua was taken on October 8 and Caserta with its royal palace fell on October 9. But after this the campaign slowed down with the arrival of the rainy season, the stiffening of Nazi resistance, and the difficulties imposed upon the invading armies by the mountainous terrain. The Allied advances became pitifully small. The Fifth Army reached the heights overlooking Cassino in late December, 1943, and fought for the town, against stubborn Nazi resistance, until its fall, May 18, 1944.

Italy surrenders unconditionally to the Allies. The Italian armistice was signed, on Sept. 3, 1943, by representatives of General Eisenhower and Marshal Badoglio (in civilian clothes). The terms of the armistice were approved by the governments of the United Kingdom, the United States, and the Union of Soviet Socialist Republics. Notice of the unconditional surrender was not released to the public until five days later, Sept. 8, the moment judged most favorable to the Allies. The next morning the American Fifth Army invaded the Italian mainland, landing at Salerno, sixty miles to the southeast of Naples.

German paratrooper stands alone in the streets of Rome, watched by crowds of hostile Italians. When the armistice was announced, Nazis under Field Marshal Kesselring seized Rome, Sept. 10, after a bloody battle with seven Italian divisions. They took over "protection" of Vatican City, in spite of protests, making the Pope virtual prisoner. Northern Italy was also occupied after severe fighting. Italian prisoners were sent into forced labor in Germany. Italian troops in other parts of Europe also laid down their arms, or, as in the case of Yugoslavia, joined guerrilla and Partisan units to fight the Germans.

Ships of the Italian fleet steam into Malta harbor to surrender to the Allies under the armistice, in September, 1943. Several ships were sunk by German bombers as they fled, but more than 100 escaped, including six battleships, eight cruisers, twenty-seven destroyers, nineteen submarines; also fifty lesser craft and 70,000 tons of merchant shipping.

Flying Fortresses over the Brenner Pass, gateway between Italy and Germany, go on to North African bases after bombing the Messerschmitt factory at Regensburg on Aug. 17, 1943. They carried on "shuttle bombing" by which planes alternated between English and North African bases, lessening the flying distance to points in Germany and Austria. These bombings were discontinued because of the difficulty in servicing the planes in North Africa.

B-17 Flying Fortress, hit by flak while bombing Nazi positions near Naples, twists over on its back and plunges earthward. One of its wings has been blown off and the controls have been shattered. The crew managed to right the ship and before it crashed five of its members were seen to escape by parachute.

Canadian troops pour into Italy preceded by a terrific artillery barrage from Messina, two miles across the straits from Italy. The key rail terminals of Reggio Calabria and San Giovanni were quickly taken, and the Allied troops then fanned out across southern Italy. To save their positions, the Nazis hurried reinforcements into the peninsula. German forces occupied Rome on September 10, 1943.

Invasion of Italy began as units of British Eighth Army with their equipment streamed ashore at Reggio Calabria at dawn on Sept. 3, 1943. Four years to the day after the outbreak of World War II, the Allies had seized their first foothold in Europe.

U S. Coast Guard and Navy beach battalion men, during landing operations, hug the shaking beach at Paesternum, just south of Salerno, as a Nazi plane drops bombs about them. In the background, debris from a bomb hit can be seen in the air. The beachhead was established by one American and two British divisions, which found the Germans well-entrenched on high ground.

German soldier, in the hills bordering the beachhead at Salerno, fires upon a crew beside their burning tank. First landings were made at 3.30 A.M., on Sept. 9, 1943, under withering enemy fire. German Tiger Tanks pushed back the first invaders, but, under the protective barrage of warships off shore, the Allies established a beachhead.

Allies land at Salerno, Sept. 9, 1943, amid shelling by Nazis from surrounding hills. Shrapnel-wise Military Police crouches at the sound of an enemy shell burst, while other troops pay little attention, being intent upon getting their supplies ashore. The Luftwaffe also stubbornly opposed the Allied landing, from near-by bases, and air battles developed overhead as Allied planes flew 2,000 sorties a day at the height of the struggle. Allied naval units moved close to the shore to blast out the Germans at point-blank range. For several days General Clark's Fifth Army was required to fight a seesaw struggle with the Germans.

Amphibious tanks of the armored corps, each mounting a 105-mm. gun, make their way up the beach at Salerno on the morning of Sept. 9, 1943, as the Fifth Army under Lieutenant General Mark Wayne Clark lands on the Italian mainland. The officer at the right directs operations over a public-address system.

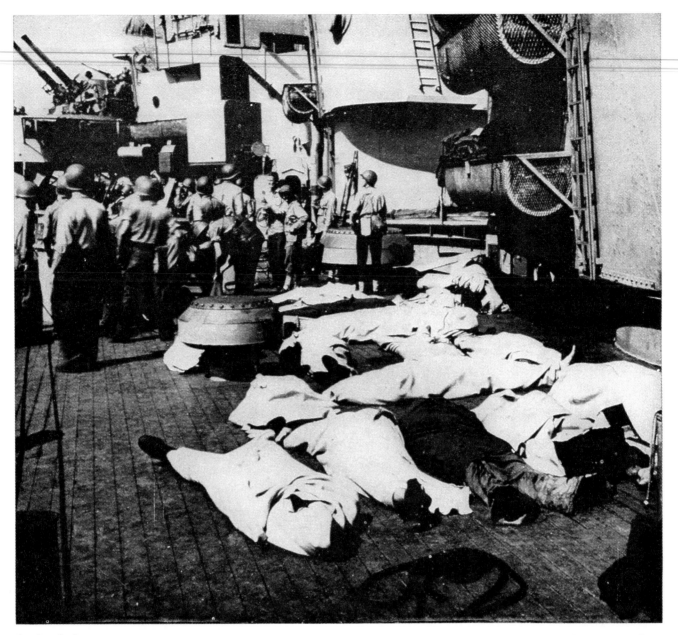

American dead lie on the deck of the *Savannah*. The 10,000-ton cruiser was damaged when a bomb from an Axis plane smashed into one of her gun turrets, during the landings at Salerno in September, 1943. The fire from the exploding bomb was brought under control within twenty minutes. Those wounded by the explosion were treated by the ship's medical officers and transferred to other vessels which conveyed them to safety out of the battle zone. Despite the damage, the cruiser continued against the enemy with other units of the combined navies helping to cover the Allied forces. The *Savannah* was commissioned March 10, 1938.

Survivors of the sinking of the U.S. destroyer Rowan, smeared with blood and oil stains, await medical attention in the sick bay of the rescuing ship. The *Rowan* was sunk on Sept. 11, 1943, as the destroyer was supporting the landings of the United Nations forces at Salerno.

Allied soldiers, in the formless anonymity of war dead, lie in an Italian field behind Salerno. Comrades from the Fifth Army prepare their graves. American casualties in the first four weeks of the Italian campaign were 8,307 men, including 511 dead and 2,368 missing.

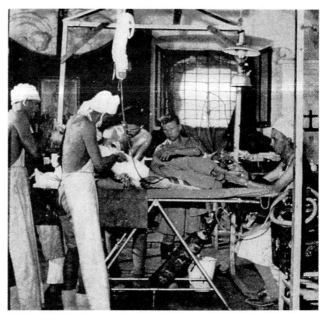

Wounded German prisoner, in great agony, is assisted to a dressing station during the Allied landings at Salerno, supported by two British soldiers. No distinction was made between friend and foe in treatment of the wounded.

British medical team applies a plaster cast to the leg of an Allied soldier, while life-saving plasma drains into his veins. This unit worked night and day in a church, attending the wounded who had been brought back from Chiunzi Pass.

American Infantry, under protective cover of machine-gun fire, advances cautiously through an olive grove as Allied troops, after breaking through the Salerno mountains, continue their northward drive over difficult terrain toward Naples. Heavy fighting developed in the mountain barrier between Salerno and the plains of Naples in late September, 1943. Although vast quantities of land mines and booby traps together with stubborn rear-guard actions by the retreating enemy forces slowed down their advance, the Allies were able to drive the Nazis from Naples which was occupied by the Fifth Army on October 1, 1943. Mt. Vesuvius, seen in background, afterward burst into active eruption.

U.S. Paratroopers, reinforcing Ranger battalions, rest in their cliffside foxholes at Chiunzi Pass, key to the plains of Naples. The enemy, strongly entrenched in caves and rocky heights, had to be blasted out of the mountains between Salerno and Naples with heavy artillery and high explosive bombing, then mopped up in hand-to-hand fighting. The terrain in this part of the coastal region was too rough and difficult for flanking and infiltration movements. The Allies broke through from Salerno at the end of September, 1943.

Frenzied crowd welcomes the Allied Fifth Army on Oct. 1, 1943, as it enters Naples. Before they retreated from the city the Nazis indulged in an orgy of terror, with executions, looting, and wholesale demolition. Foodstocks, civilian vehicles, public utilities, buildings of Naples University, hotels, and police headquarters were wholly or partially destroyed. Officers of the Allied Military Government were confronted with the gigantic task of repairing the destruction, preventing epidemics, and feeding the starving populace. Many mines had been left behind by the Nazis, but the climax of horror came a week later when a time-bomb exploded in the new post-office. The morale of the public sank still lower.

Naples harbor presented this scene of destruction when the Germans, driven out of the city by the Allied army on Oct. 1, 1943, retreated northward. Repeated bombing of the harbor area by Allied air forces had sunk many of the ships, but the greatest part of the shipping and docks was destroyed by the Germans before they left Naples.

Italian church near Naples is transformed into a hospital during fighting incidental to the clearing out of Nazis from the area around the city. Any undamaged building had to be used for emergency care of the wounded.

Lieut. Gen. Mark Clark, commander of the Allied Fifth Army, tours the city of Naples. General Clark missed death by the timely discovery and removal of a 1,500-pound explosive charge left by the Nazis in his hotel headquarters.

American army nurse wades ashore in Naples harbor, while a human chain passes supplies to dry land. Nurses were desperately needed during the early days of Allied occupation.

Fifth Army troops rest in a Naples street after the battle for the city. Though weary and grimy, they cheer an American comrade who walks down the street with a local Italian belle.

Nazis, before they left Naples, destroyed the city's water system. The inhabitants, in serious straits, were thus forced to obtain water wherever possible. The picture shows a long queue waiting before the outlet of the city's main sewer. American troops, which occupied the important port on Oct. 1, 1943, found a starving population living amid total devastation.

Naples was a ruined city when the Nazis finally abandoned it before the Allied occupation. They destroyed anything that they thought could be useful to the Allies. The harbor was cluttered with dynamited ships. Transporation systems, including tracks and rails, rolling stock, gas, electric and water utilities, as well as sanitary systems, were completely wrecked. The Germans also pillaged churches and shrines, and burned cultural landmarks of no possible military value; 200,000 books of the Royal Society were soaked in gasoline and set afire.

NAPLES POST-OFFICE DISASTER

The Nazis Plant a Time-Bomb in New Post-Office Which Kills One Hundred Civilians and Soldiers

The Nazis evacuated Naples on October 1, 1943. Before they left they did a thorough demolition job in all areas remotely susceptible of military use. Public buildings, warehouses, hotels, police stations, the buildings of Naples University, and docks were blown up, while the harbor was rendered unnavigable for some time to come by ships cunningly sunk in the channels. The Germans placed a time-bomb containing several tons of high explosives in the new Naples post-office. They had chosen this building for their purpose as it stood in the busiest section of the city, and thus the bomb would be likely to kill the largest number of people. A week later the bomb exploded, showering Italian civilians, including many women and children, with its deadly missiles and debris. The whole pavement about the post-office was flung into the air. Unfortunately the explosion occurred at a time of greatest activity during the day, when hundreds of Neapolitans were visiting the post-office trying to communicate with their relatives in other parts of Italy occupied by the Allies. Some soldiers were also included among the dead.

The Naples post-office was the only public building that had been left intact by the Germans. The reason for this became evident when the explosion occurred. One appalling aspect of the disaster was the great proportion of children killed. British and American Red Cross services worked at high pressure for hours, assisted by soldiers of the Fifth Army, as they cared for the wounded and transported them to hospitals and first-aid stations.

Hysterical, screaming man (*above*) staggers away from the Naples post-office disaster after the explosion of the Nazi time-bomb. Fumes and debris fill the air. Blood streams from the man's hands and face, while a dazed boy stares.

Naples post-office disaster was probably the most atrocious act of cruelty by the retreating Germans. Allied soldiers quickly came to the aid of the stunned and dying victims. A German delayed-action bomb, planted by the Germans a week earlier, exploded on Oct. 7, 1943, killing more than 100 people, civilians and soldiers. Several hundred more people were killed and injured in similar explosions.

Naples post-office blast victim writhes in pain on stretcher (*below*), as other casualties are put in ambulance. At the right another victim is taken from the debris.

Italian woman in Naples gratefully kisses the hand of a smiling but embarrassed American armored corps officer, as throngs of joyful civilians press forward to welcome men of the Allied Fifth Army who liberated their city.

American soldiers and an army nurse (*left*) pose in the throne room of one of the Italian royal palaces in Naples shortly after the occupation of the city. The historical gold throne had been removed for safekeeping.

Lieut. Gen. Mark Clark, commander of the Allied Fifth Army, and members of his staff, seated in the sanctuary, attend Mass in the Cathedral of St. Januarius, Naples, on Oct. 10, 1943, after entering the city on Oct. 1, 1943, twenty-two days after the landings below Salerno.

French Goumiers, Arab mountain troops of the French army, stream into Ajaccio, capital of Corsica, in September, 1943. Corsican patriots had been carrying on a guerrilla war against the German and Italian occupation forces. They were reinforced by French regulars and commandos and also by an American Ranger unit. By October 5, 1943, the 20,000 Germans on Corsica were driven into the northeast corner of the island and either surrendered or fled to the mainland. A force of 85,000 Italian troops gave half-hearted help.

Bombs hurtle down on the Monserrato Airfield, near Cagliari, the capital of Sardinia, during a raid by the Allied air forces in September, 1943. By September 20 two Italian divisions which were loyal to Badoglio defeated the German occupation army.

Germans, routed by French troops, American Rangers, and native patriots, evacuated Corsica on Oct. 4, 1943. This heavily loaded ferry is taking German trucks to the Italian mainland. Corsica was taken from France by Mussolini on June 10, 1940.

Nazi ME 323, one of the heaviest armed of German planes, goes down in flames off Cape Corse, Corsica, outfought by a Martin B-26 Marauder. Germans suffered an air disaster when nineteen Junkers-52 transports evacuating troops from Corsica were destroyed in September, 1943, by American fighters. Though there were some 85,000 Italian troops, they played little part in the campaign which began on Sept. 20, 1943, when French Commandos from North Africa, with an American unit, landed and put down German resistance.

British troops of the Fifth Army, under heavy fire, drive across a wrecked railroad bridge over the Volturno River toward Cancello, in mid-October, 1943. As a rule the Nazis destroyed bridges as they retreated, forcing the Allies to cross rivers in assault boats. British Commandos, landing north of the Volturno, drove inland, causing the Germans to flee northward.

Nazis demolished these Volturno bridges to delay the advance of Allied troops in Italy. North bank of the river was stubbornly defended by the enemy for many days. On Oct. 8, 1943, the Nazis launched a fierce counterattack to hold Lieut. Gen. Mark Clark's Fifth Army on the opposite shore. Photograph was made from a reconnaissance plane.

American engineers build a pontoon bridge across the Volturno River after shock troops in rubber boats have secured a bridgehead on the other bank. Crossing was made Oct. 12, 1943, when Allied troops staged a frontal assault. At the Volturno River the Germans held the Allies for a number of days, while they strengthened their next barrier known as the Gustav Line. These defenses and heavy rains for months practically halted the Allied advance.

Germans captured by the U.S. 168th Infantry at Caiazzo, after our forces crossed the Volturno River on Oct. 12, 1943, are marched off to a rear-line prison camp. The Germans had been left behind to burn the town. In the group of prisoners are several German medical corpsmen. The Nazis in Italy, as elsewhere, destroyed, as they retreated, useful material. Demolition squads, specially trained, made ghost towns of beautiful Italian villages.

Mussolini's armored railroad car, captured in Naples area, provided anti-aircraft protection for Fifth Army forces moving to the front. Car was a present from Hitler, who on the fallen dictator's birthday, July 29, 1943, also sent him a set of Nietzsche's works.

Canadian artillery hammers at German positions near Atella. The Fifth Army in early October, 1943, forced the German troops to fall back to the Volturno River, a natural defense line which enabled them to hold up the Allied advance for many days.

Japanese-American infantry move up to the front in Italy to fight for their adopted country. This battalion was organized in Hawaii, which supplied a comparatively large number of recruits to both our Army and Navy. These men, born in the islands and taught in American schools, were indoctrinated with American ideas. They fought with units of Allied armies, and reports of their performance under fire were particularly favorable.

FROM NAPLES TO CASSINO

Rain, Mud, and the Terrain Slows Advance of the Allied Armies North Through the Italian Peninsula

On October 1 the Germans left Naples. General Mark Clark threw the bulk of his army behind the retreating Nazis, pursuing them toward the Volturno River, the south bank of which the Allies reached on October 7. On October 8 they occupied the ancient city of Capua. On October 18 the Americans and British pushed sufficient men and tanks across the Volturno to take Cancello. Meanwhile the Eighth Army, fighting its way through passes in the Apennine Mountains, occupied Bresso and Oratino. By the end of October mud, rain, and the mountainous terrain affected the speed of the Allied advance. On December 8 the Fifth Army won control of the dominating heights overlooking German positions in the Liri Valley, so-called gateway to Rome. On the hundredth day of the Fifth Army's invasion of Italy, December 18, 1943, the Americans won a bloody, tough battle in taking San Pietro. On December 28 the British Eighth Army captured Ortona, after a bitter fight for this Adriatic coastal town. Late in December the Fifth Army reached the heights before Cassino. San Vittore and Cervaro, outposts of German Cassino defenses, were captured in turn on January 8 and January 12, 1944. Then the Fifth Army came within sight of the ancient Benedictine monastery atop Mount Cassino, which the Nazis had made into an artillery strongpoint. For more than four months the Anglo-American forces waged a bitter struggle for the ruins of Cassino with the strongly entrenched Germans.

Grave of an unknown American soldier, somewhere in Italy, is marked only by a rough board. His identification was destroyed when he was killed. If it is humanly possible, the identity of the soldier will eventually be established.

American soldier of the Engineer Corps (*left*) of the Fifth Army cleans out a German mine field in the Apennine Mountains. One of our men killed by a mine lies at the left. The Apennines, a rugged range running the length of Italy, constituted a formidable obstacle to Allied progress up the peninsula to Rome. The Nazis effectively slowed the forward progress of the Allied armies through Italy by sowing land mines and booby traps which had to be cleared out and rendered harmless before troops could pass in the difficult country.

Nazis captured on the Italian front by New Zealand troops are inspected by Gen. Sir Bernard L. Montgomery, at left, commander of the Eighth Army in Italy until Feb. 7, 1944, and Gen. Sir Alan Brooke, Chief of the British Imperial General Staff. From their bedraggled appearance these prisoners did not live up to Hitler's braggadocio that the Germans are supermen. Apparently these men were not first-line Nazi troops. General Montgomery was called to England as Commander-in-Chief of British Armies under General Dwight D. Eisenhower.

Flying fortresses drop sticks of 500-pound bombs on an oil refinery at Leghorn, Italy. The oil tanks may be seen in the center of the picture, but the targets were the cracking and refining plants surrounding the tanks. Allied bombers during this period also hammered Axis supply lines and installations in southern France and Germany.

British troops of General Clark's Fifth Army follow close on the heels of the retreating Germans. The soldiers scale a wall during mopping-up operations after the main body of the enemy has been forced from the village, which was badly battered by the Allied shelling.

South African flier, shot down into the Adriatic Sea by Nazi flak, is carried by Canadians after he was brought ashore by civilian refugees. South African air and ground forces under the command of the Eighth Army wrote a brilliant record in the war.

Italian village north of Venafro is battered by American artillery. Shells can be seen bursting on the target as this picture was taken, with one shell, lower right, at the exact instant of detonation. The village, which anchored the German defense line, had been transformed into a fortress. Battle raged about the area for more than a month during November and December of 1943. One of the last objectives of the Allied forces before Cassino, it had to be reduced, then occupied by infantry at bayonet point.

Allied Military Government officials question an Italian who has been accused of hoarding wheat. Allied authorities dealt with all such cases with firmness and justice. The Allied Military Government was set up under General Alexander of the British Army.

American forces, entering San Pietro, are greeted by a lone Italian woman who has just emerged from her cave-like cellar where she had taken shelter during the battle for the village. San Pietro was taken by the Americans on Dec. 18, 1943. They won it only after the bloodiest, bitterest, and toughest struggle of the Italian campaign up to that time. The town was pounded to destruction.

Bari, key port in southern Italy, on the Adriatic Sea, was blasted by Nazi planes in a raid on Dec. 2, 1943. Seventeen Allied ships, including five United States cargo vessels, were sunk, with more than 1,000 casualties. This surprise attack hurt the Allies, for it caused destruction of much-needed supplies for Montgomery's Eighth Army.

San Vittore, a beautiful Italian town, was unmercifully subjected to intensive Allied bombing. It had been turned into a fortress guarding Cassino and the inland road to Rome. Fifth Army soldiers study the effects of the intensive blasting which has reduced the town to a mass of wreckage.

Fighting French soldiers trudge through Pozzili (*below*), in southern Italy, on their way to the front. In December, 1943, for the first time since the armistice at Compiègne in June, 1940, French soldiers fighting with the Allies came to grips with the Nazis on continental soil. In the Allied push toward Rome, beginning on May 11, 1944, the French distinguished themselves by their spirit and courage.

Italian troops (*above*), fighting with Allied Forces to free their land, move up to the front. These former soldiers of Mussolini, having foresworn Fascism, were brave and resourceful. They were particularly useful since they fought on familiar terrain. Behind German lines thousands of Italian deserters joined escaped Allied prisoners in guerrilla warfare against the Nazis.

Allied stretcher-bearers struggle down a rocky slope in Italy carrying a wounded soldier to a hospital station. Many of the great heroes produced during World War II were found among Medical Corpsmen, who suffered a high rate of casualties.

177

Canadian infantrymen cautiously move from house to house during mopping-up operations in a rubble-covered street in Ortona, Adriatic port taken by Montgomery's Eighth Army on Dec. 28, 1943. The Canadians waged nine days of some of the most bitter hand-to-hand fighting in the whole campaign to wrest this town from the Germans, who had placed their tanks in cellars as pillboxes, as they had done at Stalingrad. After Ortona was taken at the end of 1943 the front held by the Eighth Army remained stable until the terrain dried up, permitting the Spring offensive of the Fifth Army and Eighth Army toward Rome.

British soldier of General Montgomery's Eighth Army (*below*), stationed in a small village of the vineyard country during the Allied campaign in southern Italy, uses some of his time off duty to help two attractive Italian girls tread grapes in a vat for making wine. This important industry in Italy suffered from the war and had to be carried on by the women while the men were away fighting.

American soldiers, an advance unit of the Allied Fifth Army (*above*), move cautiously through difficult country. In skirmish lines they take cover behind rocks and in depressions, keeping as low to the ground as possible while feeling out German positions just beyond the ridge. Beginning in November of 1943 and continuing until the spring of 1944, rain, mud, and heavy snow slowed down the advance of the Allied armies, fighting over the Apennine mountains, the spinal backbone of Italy. Tanks and heavy artillery could not be put to effective use. The mountainous character of the terrain, favoring the German defending troops, is particularly well shown in this picture.

Canadian tanks and infantrymen advance through ruined and desolate Ortona, late in December, 1943. Ortona, lying on a high cliff overlooking the Adriatic, had to be cleared a house at a time of Nazi paratroopers fighting as infantry. Heavy snow and sleet, enemy flame throwers, and booby traps seriously hampered operations. This was a stubbornly fought battle by Montgomery's Eighth Army.

SOUTH PACIFIC ADVANCE

MacArthur Pushes Along New Guinea Coast, Northward to the Philippines

Salamaua was captured on September 11, 1943, by American and Australian troops driving up the northwest coast of New Guinea. Lae fell on September 16, and Finschhafen, opposite New Britain, on October 2, 1943. On October 12 and 13, 1943, our air forces attacked Rabaul on New Britain Island, a key position for the Japanese, controlling the general area to the south. We sank 119 Japanese vessels and destroyed 177 enemy planes. During November further attacks were made with such damaging results that the Japanese abandoned Rabaul as a naval base. On January 1, 1944, General MacArthur's forces made a surprise landing at Saidor, 110 miles north of Finschhafen, trapping the intervening Japanese forces.

Meanwhile, on October 26 and 27, 1943, Mono and Stirling in the Treasury Islands were occupied, and on October 28 a landing was made on Choiseul Island. On November 1 our forces landed on Bougainville Island. On December 26, 1943, the Marines landed at Cape Gloucester, on New Britain Island, 275 miles from Rabaul, and at Arawe, an air strip on New Britain's southwest coast. The capture of Cape Gloucester and its airfield was accomplished in less than five days.

In 1944 the American forces continued their progress northward up the New Guinea coast. On March 5 they stormed ashore thirty miles above Saidor, again bypassing the Japanese. Australian troops advancing through the Ramu Valley captured Bogadjim, an outpost of Madang, and Madang itself was taken on April 22, 1944. On the same day General MacArthur sent troops ashore on a 150-mile front between Aitape and Hollandia. Hollandia, the administrative center of Netherlands New Guinea, was also captured on April 22, and three airports lying inland were taken by May 1, 1944. On May 17 our infantry landed at Sarmi, 125 miles up the coast from Hollandia. From here our forces crossed on barges to the Wakde Islands, and on May 19 seized the airfield on Insumuar. On May 27, 1944, infantry and tanks were landed on Biak Island in the Schouten group, and by June 22, 1944, we had captured the islands' three large airfields. Our troops took the Sansapor region of New Guinea July 30, 1944, and then bypassed Halmahera to occupy Morotai Island, September 15–18. On October 19, 1944, General MacArthur kept his pledge to the Philippines, landing on Leyte Island with strong American forces.

Australian soldiers pour through the open gates of a U.S. LST (Landing Ship, Tanks) during Allied landing operations east of Lae, New Guinea, on Sept. 6, 1943. The Americans and Australians under Lieut. General Blamey pressed home the attack, to neutralize the Japanese in this section of New Guinea.

General Douglas MacArthur directs American paratroopers from a Flying Fortress on Sept. 6, 1943, in operations which routed the Japanese from the Lae-Salamaua sector of New Guinea. Simultaneously, heavy bombers destroyed the fortified position on Heath's Plantation, northern bastion of Lae, and attack bombers raked Japanese artillery positions in the valley. Salamaua was taken Sept. 12 and Lae four days later, by the largest force of amphibious and airborne troops in the Pacific up to that time.

Paratrooper leaps from plane over the Markham Valley in New Guinea. This surprise operation on Sept. 6, 1943, planned by General MacArthur, was the first paratroop assault carried out in force in the South Pacific. It was preceded by an Allied landing east of Lae.

American paratroopers drop down behind a smoke screen in the Markham Valley to encircle Japanese defenders of the Lae-Salamaua sector. An umbrella of fighter planes protected the landings. These paratroopers consisted of artillery units dropped from air transports. They captured the western approaches of the valley with the aid of Australian troops who marched fifty-five miles over mountains from the interior.

Douglas A-20 attack bomber flies low to strafe Japanese planes on the ground at the airfield of Lae, New Guinea. The Japanese were unable to resist the Allies in the air. They gave up any pretense of obstructing the advance by air-bombing and abandoned their bases in eastern New Guinea, removing all their planes to Hollandia, about 550 miles west of Salamaua. We were thus able to bomb Japanese positions almost at will throughout the Lae-Salamaua campaign, which ended in mid-September, 1943.

Lae waterfront, New Guinea, presented this air view after it was taken by American and Australian troops. Large craters, hangars destroyed, and barges sunk show the punishment this Japanese base took before it was seized on Sept. 16, 1943.

Body of an American soldier awaits burial in a graveyard for American dead on an island in the Pacific. He was killed in the desperate jungle battle for Lae, New Guinea. In background smoke issues from bombed and beached Allied ship.

Victorious American and Australian troops file into battered Lae, Sept. 18, 1943, shortly after the New Guinea base was captured. Allied soldiers on the coast and American paratroopers inland trapped the Japanese in a ring thrown around Lae and Salamaua. When the Allies reached the bases, the Japanese fled northward toward the mountains. There they were ambushed by Australian bush-fighters who, anticipating such a maneuver, were waiting for them behind blockades built by the Australians.

Australian troops are led by friendly natives, packing arms and supplies, through the rocky Ramu River en route to the Upper Ramu Valley of New Guinea. In the course of the journey to forward posts where the Australians made contact with the Japanese, the river was forded thirty times. There were practically no roads through the jungles by which supplies could be sent regularly, and these troops fighting in the outpost areas of New Guinea depended chiefly on the air force for food, ammunition, and supplies which were flown in and dropped by parachute. Tropical vegetation was so dense that trails disappeared in a few days.

Native stretcher-bearers carry a soldier down Shaggy Ridge to a dressing station. In the background are Faria River and Ramu Valley, through which the Australians pursued the Japanese forces after taking Shaggy Ridge, December 29, 1943.

Australian troops in New Guinea advance cautiously through the jungle in an attack at Sattelberg Pass in November, 1943, after tanks forced a narrow passageway. The use of tanks surprised the Japanese and enabled the Australians to capture the plateau.

Japanese anti-aircraft gunners crouch inside their emplacements, as Allied parachute bombs fall upon their installations. This close-up photograph was taken during attack on Japanese airfield in New Guinea in November, 1943, in which more than fifty enemy planes were destroyed by our aircraft. The Allies held air superiority over the Japanese during this campaign from their air base at Finschhafen, which they had captured from the Japanese, Oct. 2, 1943.

American medium tank, pushing its way into the jungle, clears a path for the infantry after our forces landed at Humboldt Bay, Dutch New Guinea. Sharpshooters ride its stern. American troops landed in three sectors of Dutch New Guinea on April 22, 1944, cutting off an estimated 60,000 Japanese soldiers defending the region.

Hollandia Village (*below*), Japanese stronghold and administrative center of Dutch New Guinea, is smashed by United States Fifth Air Force bombers. Bombs drop in Challenger Cove.

General Douglas MacArthur (*above*), disdaining the presence of Japanese snipers, strides down the beach at Humboldt Bay, Dutch New Guinea, accompanied by the Army sector commander. He landed with the second wave of our forces to reach the beach.

American amphibious alligator tanks roll into Sentani airdrome, Japanese air base near Hollandia, Dutch New Guinea, which was captured on April 27, 1944. Swarms of these Alligators, together with other amphibious tanks and landing vehicles, helped capture the important airfield by circling through Lake Sentani in a surprise over-water operation. The soldier in the foreground, crouching beneath the wreckage of a Japanese plane, is on the lookout for Japanese snipers.

American soldiers of General MacArthur's Sixth Army unload supplies and equipment at Morotai, one of the Molucca Islands only 300 miles south of the Philippines. Our troops landed on Morotai Sept. 15, 1944, and in three days seized the island with its strategic airfield.

Japanese naval gun (below) was silenced by American bombers to stop its shelling our forces which landed on Biak Island, May 27, 1944. Capture by June 22 of the airfields on Biak, largest island of the Schouten group, brought the Philippines within a bombing distance of 900 miles. MacArthur's forces then seized the Sansapor region of New Guinea, July 30, 1944, and our conquest of the island was considered virtually complete.

A-20 Havoc of the U.S. Fifth Air Force (above) flies away after blasting oil-storage tanks at Boela, on Ceram Island, in the Netherlands East Indies. Operating from their bases on New Guinea, the planes of General MacArthur's command took a heavy toll of Japanese oil facilities in the Southwest Pacific, hitting as far as Java and Borneo.

American infantrymen, racing through the boiling surf, land on a beach of the Wakde Islands, May 18, 1944. Our forces crossed in barges from Sarmi, on the coast of Dutch New Guinea, which they captured the previous day in a 125-mile amphibious advance from Hollandia. The main objective in the Wakde group, the air strip on Insumuar, the largest island, was seized May 19, 1944.

LANDINGS ON BOUGAINVILLE

The Marines on November 1, 1943, Invade the Last
Important Base Left to Japan in the Solomon Islands

A landing force of Marines under the command of Lieutenant General Alexander A. Vandegrift landed at Empress Augusta Bay, about midway up the west coast of the island of Bougainville, on November 1, 1943. The invasion was preceded by a bombardment of enemy positions by a naval task force. Army troops reinforced the Marines on November 8, and after our beachheads were consolidated, took the offensive against Japanese troops on the island. During the period of these landings our operations were opposed by enemy naval and air forces, but our losses were small, although the Japanese suffered considerable damage to both ships and planes. The ultimate objective of our invasion of Bougainville was to capture the Japanese-held air bases at Kahili, Karu, Buin, and Ballale, on Bougainville, and Buka and Faisi just north of the island. On November 8, after the beachhead had been established, General Vandegrift was ordered back to Marine Headquarters in Washington, and the Bougainville command was turned over to General Roy S. Geiger, USMC. General Vandegrift later became Commandant of the United States Marine Corps, succeeding Lieutenant General Thomas Holcomb. By mid-December our forces had widened their beachhead to allow for an air strip from which planes were operating, but progress was slow due to almost impenetrable jungle.

American Marine, wounded in the initial attack at Empress Augusta Bay, Bougainville Island, early in November, 1943, is hoisted from a barge to a Coast Guard-manned transport lying off shore.

United States warships of a task force pour high explosives and steel into Japanese positions on Bougainville guarding the strategic Buka Airfield. The bombardment prepared for the first landing on the island of our Marines on Nov. 1, 1943. In naval operations leading to the invasion of Bougainville the Japanese suffered considerable damage and retired. We lost no ships and sustained little damage in establishing a beachhead. However, dislodging the Japanese from the large island was a long and difficult task.

Marines wade through waist-deep water to reach the beach at Bougainville in their initial landing on Nov. 1, 1943. Bougainville is 150 miles long and lies within five degrees of the equator. Our men fought through tropical rain, mud, and jungle.

Marines leap from landing barges and push inland at Empress Augusta Bay, Bougainville, on Nov. 1, 1943. Bitter fighting developed and on November 8 U.S. Army troops reinforced Marines. Empress Augusta Bay lies 250 miles from Rabaul.

Jungle-suited Marines on Bougainville Island carry a wounded comrade to a landing barge. Securing a beachhead at Empress Augusta Bay, Marines fought until reinforced by Army troops.

Marine paratrooper was buried on the spot where he was killed on "Hellzapoppin Ridge," Bougainville, November, 1943. The grave was outlined with machine-gun bullets. A cross was placed at the head, with the inverted rifle and flag stuck in the ground behind it.

Marine machine-gun crew operates from flooded foxhole guarding a road-block on Bougainville during November, 1943. This gun took a heavy toll of Japanese lives while repelling attacks in this sector.

Marines guard their wounded on Bougainville. To protect them from a possible Japanese counterattack during a raid behind enemy lines on Nov. 29, 1943, squads of riflemen accompanied the casualties as they were carried back to the beach for medical treatment.

Surgeons operate in this improvised hospital during the fighting in November, 1943, on Bougainville Island. In the foreground a Marine raider lies on a litter waiting to have a piece of shrapnel removed from his head, while the doctors attend other cases inside the tent. Medical units, together with their hospital equipment, moved up with the troops as the battle lines advanced. Japanese snipers on Bougainville took particular pains to harass these improvised hospitals.

American soldier lies dead on the beach of Mono Island, in the Treasury group of the central Solomon Islands. Another lies in the water. Their comrades are seeking the enemy who shot them down. American and New Zealand forces landed on Mono Island in daylight, Oct. 26-27, 1943, preceded by a bombardment from U.S. destroyers.

Trained dogs aid Marines (*right*) on Bougainville Island to ferret out hidden Japanese. These animals greatly reduced loss of life on scouting parties. They carried messages through jungle growth impassable for man and were also valuable for sentry and rescue work, locating wounded men and bringing them assistance. Dogs of the K-9 Corps served on all Pacific fronts. Among many breeds used, Dobermans proved to be particularly successful.

Marines plod through jungle mud (*right, below*) on Bougainville Island to the front lines, in January, 1944. Bougainville, with its malaria, offered probably the most difficult conditions our forces encountered in the Solomons. The campaign was co-ordinated with the clearing of Huon Peninsula in New Guinea and landings on New Britain.

Marine paratroopers (*left, below*) land deep behind Japanese lines on Bougainville Island, Nov. 29, 1943. At the left, a Marine bends over a comrade wounded in the raid. This photograph was taken under fire during a battle in which the Marines held their jungle position for more than sixteen hours against an overwhelming enemy force.

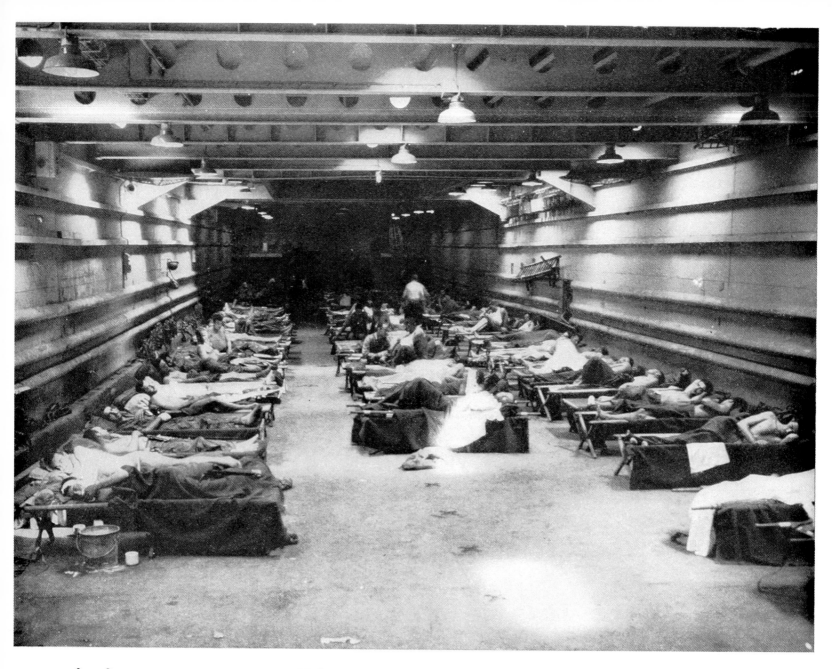

Green Dragon, a ship constructed for many purposes, is used here to transport wounded Marines (*above*) to base hospitals in the South Pacific area for medical and surgical care. On the outward journeys these specially designed LST's (Landing Ship, Tanks), called "Green Dragons" because of color and size, carried supplies to our forces in the South Pacific, transporting tanks, jeeps, and motorized equipment as well as food, ammunition, and materiel. These ships were a development of World War II, designed to meet the requirements peculiar to the global conflict.

Wounded American soldiers lie on stretchers on barges alongside the ship that will carry them from the combat area to base hospitals somewhere in the South Pacific. These men were participants in such campaigns as Guadalcanal, Tulagi, Munda, Rendova, and Vella Lavella. The efficiency with which the evacuation of our wounded soldiers was accomplished in all theaters of World War II has made a bright chapter in United States Army annals. Our wounded and otherwise disabled men all received the most modern treatment known to medical and surgical science.

B-25 Mitchell Bomber swoops low over the flaming harbor of Rabaul, New Britain, during the devastating air attack of Nov. 5, 1943. Clouds of smoke rise from burning shore installations. About 150 Allied planes at masthead height dropped 1,000-pound bombs on enemy merchantmen and warships.

Rabaul Harbor (*below*) presented this sight after the attack by Allied planes, Nov. 5, 1943, on the Japanese stronghold. Ships burning and sinking litter the harbor, while smoke and flames rise from battered shore installations and warehouses which were bombed during the seventy-five minute engagement. Three enemy destroyers, eight merchant ships, and four coastal vessels were sunk, and sixty-seven Japanese planes shot down in this Allied blow.

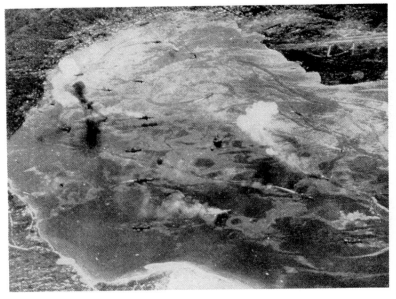

Japanese ships (*above*) scurry to get out of land-locked Rabaul Harbor during the attacks by American bombers on Nov. 5, 1943. Planes from the aircraft carrier *Saratoga* raided the enemy naval base on New Britain Island and several of the twenty-five ships there were hit and set afire as they tried to reach the open sea. Rabaul was under constant bombardment by our planes in order to neutralize or destroy that strong Japanese base.

Japanese freighter, smashed by Allied bombers during raid on Rabaul, New Britain, settles fast at the stern. Rabaul was the main Japanese base in the area. From October through December, 1943, Allied air forces inflicted such destruction at Rabaul on ships, planes, and installations that the Japanese abandoned it as a major base.

American bombers score a direct hit on a Japanese destroyer off Cape Gloucester, New Britain Island. The following day B-25 bombers found the destroyer, still afloat but completely out of commission, and finished the job.

Americans race to the beach (*left*) at Arawe, New Britain, on Dec. 15, 1943, in LCV's (Landing Craft, Vehicles). The men anxiously scan the sky, watching for Japanese planes. A few minutes later enemy aircraft attacked our landing barges and troops on shore, but were driven off by anti-aircraft fire.

American landing craft approach under fire the beach at Arawe, New Britain, Dec. 15, 1943. Japanese planes have just hit one of these landing barges crowded with our soldiers. Clouds of thick smoke almost hide the boats.

Invasion craft is crammed to capacity (*right*) with our Marines and supplies, consisting of gasoline, barbed wire, trucks, jeeps, and other materials needed in beating the Japanese at their own game of jungle fighting. The ship, an LST (Landing Ship, Tanks), manned by Coast Guard and Navy crews, nears the Japanese-held beach, Cape Gloucester, New Britain, during invasion on Dec. 26, 1943.

Landing craft, manned by U.S. Coast Guard and Navy crews, empty their human freight of Marines ashore at Cape Gloucester, New Britain, Dec. 26, 1943, to capture the strategic airfield. This operation at the western tip of the island was designed to force the Japanese northward toward Rabaul, their key base in the Southwest Pacific, and eventually clear New Britain.

Marines wade through three-foot surf at Cape Gloucester, New Britain Island, Dec. 26, 1943. They carried their rifles high to keep the mechanisms dry. On reaching the beach, the Marines pushed inland toward the large airfield which was their immediate objective. The Japanese put up a stubborn resistance.

American Coast Guardsmen and Marines push a jeep just brought ashore from an LST (Landing Ship, Tanks) onto dry ground at Cape Gloucester, New Britain. These ships, developed especially for our large-scale invasion operations, were 328-foot giants capable of carrying vast quantities of trucks, tanks, and guns, and even 100-foot landing craft on their decks. Picture shows size of ships and how close they came to shore for unloading through huge bow doors.

Navy Seabees and Marines put in place a crude bridge across a jungle stream at Cape Gloucester, New Britain Island, in December, 1943, while constructing a road to the strategic airfield near by. The Navy Construction Battalion units, known as "Seabees," cleared the jungle and constructed roads.

Our Marines waded through swollen streams as they made their way toward Cape Gloucester airfield, on Dec. 26, 1943. They kept their rifles and ammunition dry for instant use.

Marines battle at Cape Gloucester, New Britain, in slashing tropical downpour. This 75-mm. howitzer, imbedded to its hubs in the thick mud, batters incessantly at Japanese positions dug into the undergrowth surrounding the airfield. The picture was snapped just as the gun captain raised his arm for the signal to fire this effective weapon.

Grim-faced Marines render first aid to a fallen comrade during battle for Cape Gloucester, New Britain, in December, 1943. This man, after having his wounds bandaged, was taken to a hospital base in the rear where he received thorough treatment before being transferred to a hospital ship. American losses were extremely light.

Marines, tired, dirty, unshaven, but cheerful, prepare to go back to a relief base after twenty-three days and nights of fighting in which they took Hill 660 on Cape Gloucester, Jan. 17, 1944. Fresh troops replaced them in the positions which they temporarily left in order to rest from the hard weeks of uninterrupted fighting.

Major General W. H. Rupertus, Commander of the landing force, applies New Britain's seaside mud to his aching feet, after inspecting the Cape Gloucester area December, 1943.

Momote Airfield, on Los Negros Island in the Admiralty group, was captured by American troops on Feb. 29, 1944. This picture was taken from a United States reconnaissance bomber and shows the Japanese airfield as a narrow strip protected by revetments on either side. The white patches are smoke from bomb blasts. The First Cavalry Division, unmounted, took the Momote Airfield with its 5,000-foot runway and sustained casualties totaling less than one per cent of its forces.

First United States Cavalry Division (*below*) cuts a path to Momote Airfield in a heavy rainfall on Los Negros Island in the Admiralty group. A Signal-Corps man telephones his report to beach headquarters, as soldiers in background prepare to blast by mortar fire Japanese positions hidden in the heavy undergrowth of the jungle. Over 50,000 Japanese troops in New Britain and 22,000 troops on Bougainville Island were cut off from vital supply lines by our capture of Los Negros and Manus Islands on Feb. 29, 1944.

United States Marines (*above*) at Cape Gloucester, New Britain Island, knee-deep in water, pull up stakes and move their tent to higher ground. This picture, taken in February, 1944, graphically illustrates the conditions which our men faced in their campaign to rout the Japanese defenders from the island, 5° below the Equator.

United States Coast Guardsmen help unload wounded American soldiers from an LST (Landing Ship, Tanks) on the beach at Cape Gloucester, New Britain Island. On the shore is seen mechanized equipment which has been unloaded from the bow doors of the ship, including ambulances, trucks, and supplies. The officers' ward room on the landing ship was converted into a hospital for the immediate care of the Marines who were wounded during the operations in which our forces captured the important Japanese airfield six miles inland.

American and Chinese troops cross the Tanai River in Northern Burma as they advance into Hukawng Valley, March, 1944. In a little over two weeks the Japanese were driven out of the valley. The Allies pushed on, attempting to open the Ledo road.

"Merrill's Marauders," (*below*) the first American infantry to fight on the continent of Asia, wade across a stream in Northern Burma in pursuit of Japanese forces. In February, 1944, they drove against main enemy concentrations at Maingkwan.

American infantryman of "Merrill's Marauders" (*above*) unpacks ammunition from a parachute dropped by an American transport plane near a clearing in Northern Burma. Food and equipment were supplied by parachute—only means of access.

Lieut. Gen. Joseph Stilwell, with hands on hips, and Brig. Gen. Frank Merrill, second from left, discuss the capture of Myitkyina Airfield. This airfield, the most important in Northern Burma, was seized on May 17, 1944, by Chinese and American infantry.

NAZI ARMIES IN RETREAT

Soviets Drive Germans From Russia— Rome Falls—Allies Force Gothic Line

After Hitler was turned back at Moscow in November, 1941, he met his second and greater frustration at Stalingrad, where his troops on January 31, 1943, surrendered to the Russians. From Stalingrad to the fall of Odessa and Sevastopol, the German armies were never again able to stage a counteroffensive that made any appreciable headway. On the contrary, the great Russian offensives were unstoppable. During the winter campaign of 1943–1944, the Red Army won the battles for the Dnieper and the Ukraine west of the Dnieper, crushed the German lines at Leningrad and the Crimea, and overwhelmed the German defenses on the southern Bug, the Dniester, Prut, and Siret rivers. Almost the entire Ukraine, Moldavia, Crimea, Leningrad, and Kalinin regions and White Russia were thus cleared of the Nazis. Fifty million Russian people were liberated.

In Italy, after the Allies had stood before Cassino from late December until May, the Fifth and Eighth Armies on May 11, 1944, began their drive on Rome. On May 13 they wrestled Castelforte, a bastion on the Gustav Line, from the Germans.

They then pushed on to the Hitler Line where they took Terracina on May 24 and Cisterna on May 25. Troops of the Fifth Army made the junction with forces holding the Anzio beachhead on May 25. Velletri, controlling the German escape route along the Via Casilina to Rome, was taken on June 1, as well as the strongpoint of Valmontone. Then Nazi resistance seemed to melt away, and Allied armies entered Rome on June 4, 1944. King Victor Emmanuel delegated his royal powers to his son Prince Umberto who became Lieutenant General of the Realm. Marshal Badoglio was supplanted by Ivanoe Bonomi as Premier, who formed a cabinet embracing all factions of political opinion. Marshal Kesselring's forces, badly cut to pieces, fled northward from Rome with the Allies in close pursuit. Halfway to Florence reinforcements stiffened enemy resistance, and the Allied advance was stubbornly contested. The Fifth Army took Leghorn on July 19, 1944, while Ancona on the Adriatic fell to the Eighth Army the next day. With the capture of Florence on August 22 and Pisa on September 2, the assault on the Gothic Line was under way. British forces broke through by taking Rimini on September 21. The Americans pierced the line at Futa Pass, September 24, and at Raticosa October 2. Although by mid-October the Allies were only eight miles from Bologna, the winter months then all but halted their advance.

Cassino stood a lifeless ruin when Allied troops entered the town on May 18, 1944, after four months of siege. The Germans, dug deep in its cellars and stone buildings, held out stubbornly despite incessant shelling and bombing. This was the first photograph which was taken after the fall of Cassino.

Castleforte, the German bastion on the Gustav Line, was reduced to rubble after a terrific bombardment by Allied forces. French troops with the Fifth Army, supported by American tanks and artillery, drove the Nazi armed forces from the town early in the push toward Rome.

French infantrymen (*below*) attached to the Allied Fifth Army march along a road toward Esperia, Italy, on their way to the front ahead of a long line of Fifth Army vehicles. On May 17, 1944, the French troops succeeded in capturing Esperia, an outpost on the Hitler Line.

The ancient Benedictine monastery (*above*) presented this appearance after it was taken by Polish contingents of the Allied Fifth Army on May 18, 1944. The Abbey had been made into a veritable fortress by the Germans who used it as an observation post and as an eminence from which to shell the Allied positions. When it was taken the Allies found it had little more than one wall left standing.

Anzio Harbor, fifty miles below Rome, where the Allies landed in a surprise move on Jan. 22, 1944, is bombed by Nazi planes, which attempted to hit Allied ships in the harbor. No damage was done in the raid to any of our cargo vessels or troop transports. Supplies for six Allied divisions poured ashore despite bombings from Nazi planes which were able to penetrate our air cover protecting the landings.

San Ambrogia stands as little more than a shattered and bomb-gutted cluster of windowless buildings on a hilltop after the town was taken on May 15, 1944, by the troops of the Fifth Army who pursued the Germans toward Rome.

Historic moment (*below*) occurred on May 25, 1944, when the main Fifth Army troops made a junction with our forces defending the Anzio beachhead in the Pontine marshes area. British Tommies and American soldiers exchange joyous greetings. The Fifth Army had driven northward while troops on the beachhead had launched their own offensive toward Cisterna a few days before.

Germans in Cisterna (*above*) approach Allied lines with fear-stricken faces and their arms held high in surrender. Cisterna, a bastion in the Hitler Line, saw one of the decisive battles of the drive on Rome. After the fall of Cisterna on May 25, 1944, the Nazis defenses crumbled.

Terracina, an ancient town in a picturesque Italian valley, shows the scars of battle after its capture on May 24, 1944, by the Fifth Army troops commanded by Lieut. Gen. Mark Clark. Terracina, particularly notable for its beautiful buildings, although the damage was severe enough did not suffer as much as other Italian towns which lay in the path of the drive by Allied armies toward Rome.

Captured Germans with their hands on their heads (*right*) march back to the Allied rear. The constant shelling of enemy positions and attacks by our tanks and infantry disorganized German resistance. These men were captured near Cori and Velletri on June 1, 1944.

German one-man submarine (*left*) is stranded near Anzio, Italy. On the left is the torpedo which is shackled to the driving compartment holding one man. When the submarine was in operation, the driving compartment was above with the torpedo below the surface of water.

Parachutes drop supplies to our men in advanced positions in mountainous country just before Rome. Some of our forces pushed forward rapidly during the last days of the drive on the Italian capital and found themselves behind the German lines where mule trains with food and ammunition could not reach them. Parachutes were thus released from planes of United States Army Air Force.

199

Allied tanks in the streets of Rome are greeted with roars of welcome by citizens of the Italian capital. Roman throngs rose at daybreak on June 4, 1944, to hail the triumphant entrance of American troops and armored divisions into the Eternal City.

Lieut. Gen. Mark W. Clark (*left*), Allied Fifth Army commander, tours Rome. In the back is St. Peter's. Seated behind him are Maj. Gen. Alfred M. Gruenther, Chief of Staff to Gen. Clark, and Maj. Gen. Geoffrey Keyes, Com. Gen., Second Corps.

Scottish bagpipers of the Allied Fifth Army, wearing their traditional kilts, entertain the citizens of Rome, massed before the huge Victor Emmanuel Monument in the Piazza Venezia. Their program consisted of compositions inspired by names of battlefields which saw the heaviest fighting in the Italian campaign.

American infantrymen hurry past the ancient ruins of the Roman Coliseum on the Via Labicana in pursuit of the German armies retreating northward from the Eternal City. By the middle of July, two thirds of Italy had fallen into Allied hands and the Germans had been driven back to "Gothic Line" positions.

Leghorn Harbor (*below*) lies in desolate ruins from Allied bombings and German demolitions. General Mark Clark's 5th Army outflanked the Nazi defenders and captured the city, Italy's third largest port, on July 19, 1944, while British forces took Ancona on the Adriatic. Our troops then pressed to the Gothic Line.

Crowd of 60,000 Romans (*above*) gather in the square of St. Peter's after the "Eternal City" was liberated from the Germans by the Allied Fifth and Eighth Armies. People waited to receive prayer of thanksgiving from Pope Pius. On June 21, 1944, in the Hall of Benediction, the Pontiff granted audience to more than 5,000 soldiers and officers of the Allied forces.

American men and machines pass through a gateway formed by the "Twin Churches" of Rome. At the left stands Santa Maria in Monte Santo and at right, Santa Maria de' Miracoli. In the first hours of Allied occupation, Italian mobs stormed the Fascist headquarters on Piazza Venezia, and opened the gates of Regina Coeli prison, but only minor clashes occurred between Fascist and anti-Fascist factions.

Piers of the Santa Trinita Bridge in Florence are blasted by 8th Army engineers to make way for a *Bailey* span for Allied traffic over the Arno River. The Nazis had destroyed the structure before retreating from the city, liberated Aug. 22, 1944. Meanwhile 5th Army troops pierced the Gothic Line and by October 19 were within eight miles of Bologna.

Sherman tanks and enemy dead line war-torn road of an important junction captured by the American 10th Mountain Division of the 5th Army in Italy. By the end of 1944 the Italian campaign had virtually reached a standstill. In February, 1945, the new mountain troops again started action against German defenses, taking Mount Belvedere, February 21.

Infantrymen of the 85th Division march up to relieve another company on the Italian front. Smoke pots raise a protective screen over the valley, hiding troops and vehicle movements. In a limited assault on March 6, 1945, 5th Army troops captured the town of Bisopra and secured domination of the roads leading from Pistoia and Florence to Bologna.

NAZIS DRIVEN FROM RUSSIA

The Failure of the Nazis at Stalingrad Marked the Decisive Turning Point of Hitler's War Against Russia

After the Germans had surrendered at Stalingrad January 31, 1943, the Russians took up the offensive and by February 8, 1943, they had captured Kursk. Rostov fell on February 14 and then Boroshilovgrad. In late spring the Germans attempted a summer offensive but were checked at all points. On August 5 the Russians captured the city of Orel, dislodging the Germans from the anchor of their entire front. On August 23 they re-entered Kharkov. On September 25, 1943, they captured Smolensk and their armies stood on the left bank of the Dnieper River. By the end of October Soviet troops had crossed the Dnieper barrier and on November 6 they triumphantly entered Kiev. In the north the Russians drove well inside of the old Polish border in the early days of January, 1944. On the southern front the Red troops captured, on February 22, 1944, the great iron-ore center of Krivoi Rog. In a bend of the Dnieper River (Korsun pocket) they liquidated 75,000 Nazi troops. In the south they crossed the Bug River, the Dniester, and finally the Prut River, last obstacle before Rumania. They took Nikolaev on March 28, Odessa on April 10, and Sevastopol on May 10, 1944, thus entirely clearing the Crimean Peninsula.

Soviet guerrillas rout the Nazis in a surprise attack. One German is falling at the instant of being shot, two lie wounded, and another flees for his life.

Units of the Fifth Novorossisk Tank Brigade go into action northwest of Novorossisk. After heavy fighting, the Caucasian city was taken by the Russians Sept. 16, 1943.

German farm workers are evacuated with their live stock from Ukrainian farms before the Russian autumn offensive of 1943. They plod the long road back to the Fatherland.

A major disaster befell the Nazis at Shanderovka, in the bend of the Dnieper River, February 5 to February 17, 1944, when the Soviet armies trapped Nazi troops in the so-called Korsun pocket and wiped out ten divisions amounting to 75,000 men, destroyed 329 enemy planes and 600 tanks. Surviving Nazi troops attempted to break through the encirclement under cover of a Russian blizzard but were pursued by mounted Cossacks who cut them down with swords. The only Germans to escape the trap were 3,000 officers taken out by plane.

Red troops march through liberated Smólensk, in which ruined buildings and smoke rising from the burning city remind them of the vengefulness of the beaten foe. This Russian city, for two years a German stronghold, was recaptured by the Russians on Sept. 25, 1943.

Member of a Russian collective farm village (*below*) was persuaded by the Germans to turn traitor when the Nazi troops occupied his town early in the war. When the village was later recaptured his Russian townsmen who had suffered at his hands took revenge upon him by exposing him before the Soviet authorities.

Young Russian girl is questioned (*above*) by German troopers at Novorossisk, in the Caucasus. Other prisoners stand with their hands up, waiting for their turns to be searched and interrogated. The girl was able to prove her innocence.

Russian traitor to his homeland is given short justice before being brought before a firing squad of Soviet guerrillas. The traitor had first been taunted and whipped. Few incidents of this kind were reported although inhabitants of the places in the path of the invaders were subjected to constant threat and pressure to betray their countrymen and give aid to the enemy.

Russian submachine gun crew fighting on the White Russian front during the offensive in the winter of 1943 rush to attack German concealed positions. The Russians wore white uniforms which proved most effective camouflage among the heavy snows of Russian winter.

Red Army soldiers, gathered in a circle (*below*), raise submachine guns in a ceremony signifying their determination to avenge their comrades who were killed by the Nazis. A deep-seated bitterness was engendered by the atrocities committed by the Nazis on Russian civilians.

Soviet infantrymen (*above*) wipe out a Nazi machine-gun nest during the fighting on the Karelian front in the summer of 1943. A Russian soldier lying prone on the ground for protection hurls a hand grenade into the enemy dugout, smoking from a previous hit. In this region the Finns, reinforced by German divisions occupying the country, attempted to slow the advance of the Red Army into Northern Finland.

Spanish Blue Division "Warriors" fighting on the Leningrad front in January, 1944, surrender to the Russians. This division, bolstered by convicted criminals and murderers, was recruited from all quarters of Europe and was sent to the Russian front by Dictator Franco as a gesture of gratitude for Hitler's aid to the Fascist revolutionary armies during the Spanish Civil War, which ended on March 28, 1939.

Kiev, the ancient capital of the Ukraine and a leading industrial center is left in flames by the Germans who gave up the city to the Red Armies on Nov. 6, 1943.

German officers and their men surrender to the Russians in Sevastopol on May 10, 1944. These Nazis were unable to withstand further merciless bombardment.

Russian soldiers crouch in a ruined doorway during the mopping up of Nazi snipers who were hiding in buildings on the outskirts of Sevastopol in late April, 1944. German positions were reduced to rubble.

United States fliers are welcomed by Russian and American ground crews at a newly established airfield on Russian soil. The startling announcement was made in June, 1944, that Americans under arrangement with the Russian authorities had built airfields at points in the Soviet Union to enable Allied planes of the newly created Eastern Command to shuttle between these fields and Italian and English bases, thus bringing Eastern Germany and Balkan objectives within range.

American airmen are shown in a German prison camp near Berlin. Man on the left bailed out of a bomber and was the only one of his crew to survive.

American soldiers captured in the North African Campaign line up before a mess hall at Stalag IIIB, a prison camp southeast of Berlin. Some of the boys were wearing British uniforms, probably because their own were worn out or damaged in battle. The United States Government furnished our prisoners of war with new American uniforms and miscellaneous articles.

American prisoners in Germany gather before barracks in a camp for captured airmen. One boy who was shot down in November, 1942, sent this photograph in a letter to his mother.

American civilian prisoners in Germany ease their confinement with an impromptu concert at their internment camp. They were diplomats, war correspondents, and other officials.

These American fliers were captured when German anti-aircraft guns riddled their planes and forced them to bail out during the intensive bombing of Germany in the early months of 1944. Nazi newspapers referred to them as "terror fliers." Allied observers estimated over 500,000 soldiers and civilians were required to man the thousands of anti-aircraft defense posts which extended from the coast to Berlin.

The Teheran Conference was held in the capital of Iran from Nov. 28 to Dec. 1, 1943. Premier Stalin, President Roosevelt, and Prime Minister Churchill, shown on the steps of the Russian Embassy, reached a "complete agreement as to the scope and timing of operations which were to be undertaken from the east, west, and south." Plans for the invasion of Fortress Europe were a specific topic, and a full agenda was agreed upon. They pledged mutual cooperation after the war and invited all nations to join them.

Moscow Conference (*above*), held in October, 1943, agreed on the treatment of vanquished foes, made plans for setting up stable democratic governments in enemy lands, and laid the groundwork for a general world peace organization.

The Cairo Conference (*above, right*), held Nov. 22-26, 1943, planned prosecution of the war in the Far East. It was attended by President Roosevelt, Prime Minister Churchill, and Generalissimo and Madame Chiang Kai-shek.

President Inonu of Turkey poses with President Roosevelt and Prime Minister Churchill at the second Cairo Conference, Dec. 4-6, 1943. Later, President Inonu announced that existing Anglo-Turkish treaties were strengthened.

BALKAN GUERRILLA WARFARE

Rival Factions of Chetniks and Partisans Vie for Recognition from the Allies and Bitterly Fight the Invaders

Yugoslav patriots waged the most successful guerrilla resistance in Europe against German forces. This warfare was carried on by rival leaders, Draja Mikhailovitch, Army General of the Yugoslav Government-in-Exile, and Josip Broz, called Tito. The adherents of Mikhailovitch were known as Chetniks and those of Tito as Partisans. When Italy collapsed, some of the Italian troops who had been doing garrison duty in Yugoslavia joined the Partisans and large quantities of equipment and munitions fell into their hands. By the end of 1943 the Partisan Army comprised 300,000 men and women, fighting along a 350-mile front. Although the controversy between the two leaders was rooted in political rivalries, it became clear during 1944 that the Partisan movement was the larger and more important, and was fighting the Germans more successfully. Tito, a Communist organizer, obtained the backing first of Russia, then of Britain and the United States. On July 7, 1944, King Peter formed a new cabinet comprising two each of Serbs, Croats, and Slovenes, with Tito leader of the armed forces.

Fighting Chetniks, with captured German guns, were members of the guerrilla army of General Draja Mikhailovitch, who opposed the Nazis in Yugoslavia. Chetniks and Partisans ended by fighting each other in a bitter civil war.

General Draja Mikhailovitch, leader of Yugoslavian Chetniks and Army General of King Peter's regime.

Tito (Marshal Josip Broz) (*right*), leader of the Yugoslav Partisan forces, is pictured with his Chief of Staff, Major General Arsa Yovanovitch. In 1943-44, Tito's army of 300,000, harassed the Nazis trying to control Yugoslavia.

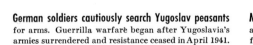

German soldiers cautiously search Yugoslav peasants for arms. Guerrilla warfare began after Yugoslavia's armies surrendered and resistance ceased in April 1941.

Marshal Tito's headquarters was well hidden in the mountains of Yugoslavia. It was reached by a steep and hazardous path cut in the mountainside. From there Marshal Tito conducted the successful campaign of his Partisan forces against the Nazis. In May, 1944, the Nazis located the cabin, bombed it, and nearly captured him.

PACIFIC STEPPING-STONES

Gilberts and Marshalls Speed American Advance — Struggle in China Continues

After a sustained attack by American carrier planes had battered Japanese defenses, on November 20-23, United States forces poured ashore on the Gilbert Atolls, Tarawa, Makin, and Abemama. Our losses on Makin and Abemama were moderate, but on Tarawa the Marines paid a stiff price in human life. Landing barges ran aground on the coral reefs 500 yards from the beaches, and heavy casualties were incurred when the Marines were forced to wade ashore in the face of withering machine-gun fire. The Second Marines wrote a story with blood on the Betio beachhead. On November 21 the airfield on Tarawa was taken, and two days later the fighting ceased. Within four days the Gilberts had been conquered.

Little more than two months later our forces pressed on to the Marshalls, lying directly north. Before the invasion, carrier planes joined by land-based aircraft blasted Japanese garrisons. The impact of the bombardment was terrific, and in less than a week, February 2-5, 1944, Roi, Namur, and Kwajalein Atolls were secured. On February 17-18 our Naval forces attacked the powerful Japanese base at Truk, while landings were made on Eniwetok Atoll and Engebi Island was captured.

By February 20 control of the Marshall Islands lay with the United States. The conquest of each Pacific atoll marked a new stepping-stone for our forces on the long road to Tokyo.

Prospects in China were not so bright. The Japanese moved into the rich "Rice Bowl" area in early November, 1943, and their offensive reached its climax at Changteh in Hunan province. They took the city on December 3, but were forced to relinquish it on December 9 after a bitter struggle. By the end of the year, the Japanese had been pushed out of the "Rice Bowl." However, they had accomplished their purpose of destroying large quantities of rice, leaving China on the verge of starvation. Free China could not exist without crops.

During the early months of 1944, in a new offensive, the Japanese gained control of the Peiping-Hankow railroad. In May they launched another campaign to win the Canton-Hankow line, taking Changsha, the capital of Hunan Province on June 18, 1944. By June 30, the United States Fourteenth Air Force was compelled to abandon its base at Henyang. The air base at Lingling fell on September 7, and on September 17, before evacuating it, the Americans demolished their principal base at Kweilin in Kwangsi Province. Despite these reverses, a new supply route was in prospect at the year's end, as American engineers in Burma forged a road from India to China's Yunnan Province, in the wake of advancing American and Chinese forces.

Japanese pillbox on Tarawa, blasted into utter ruin, is mute but eloquent witness to the bitter fighting on the island in the Gilbert group during the invasion by the United States Marines on November 20-23, 1943. The bodies of dead Japanese, half buried in the sand and scarcely distinguishable, are strewn about the pillbox. This picture is also significant as the winner of one of the two Pulitzer Prizes of the year which are awarded for exceptional photography.

American dead lie on Tarawa beach where they fell after wading ashore on Nov. 21, 1943, in the face of savage Japanese fire. The dead soldiers still wear their full packs. Few that crossed the exposed coral reefs in the initial assault survived the deadly enemy barrage.

Tarawa lagoon saw the heaviest fighting during the U.S. Marine and Army troop landings on the Gilbert atolls, Tarawa, Makin, and Abemama, Nov. 20-23, 1943. In the water are floating bodies and wrecked amphibious tractors. One tractor still hangs on the sea wall.

Marines wounded during the Tarawa battle are placed on rubber boats and towed out to larger vessels. These ships sped them to base hospitals to receive expert medical care. To capture Tarawa, an island only one mile square, Marine casualties totaled 1,026 killed and 2,557 wounded out of the 4,000 men engaged, the toughest battle to that time in Marine Corps history.

Wounded soldier on the Tarawa beach receives blood transfusion to restore his ebbing strength. The blood plasma flows from a flask tied to the butt of a rifle.

The 165th Infantry, old New York "Fighting 69th Regiment," wades toward Butaritari Beach at Makin Atoll, Gilbert Islands, on November 20, 1943, under heavy flanking fire from Japanese machine guns.

Flaming Japanese torpedo plane disintegrates as it plunges into the sea, a victim of anti-aircraft fire from a U.S. carrier during a raid on the Marshall Islands, Dec. 4, 1943. Before invading the Marshalls, Americans paralyzed enemy power.

Marines crawl on their stomachs along Engebi Beach, under partial cover afforded by a jeep. On Feb. 18, 1944, the 22d Marine Division and 106th Army regiment landed on Engebi, the main Japanese position in the Eniwetok Atoll, under Admiral Richmond Turner, who also directed landings at Kwajalein.

Marines dig in along the sandy beach of Namur Island, as they unpack equipment and supplies. American forces landed on Kwajalein Atoll in the Marshall Islands on Feb. 2, 1944, after naval and air forces bombed and shelled the strongly fortified Japanese positions on the island. One Marine, wounded during the landing operations, is carried on a stretcher to a waiting landing barge. Although regarded as stronger than Tarawa, Kwajalein was conquered in less time and with fewer casualties. In the entire campaign we lost 368 men killed or missing and 1,148 wounded.

This Japanese soldier chose death rather than capture, when Marine forces overran Roi and Namur in the Kwajalein Atoll. He removed his right shoe, stuck his big toe in the trigger guard, and fired the bullet into his chest. American forces took twenty of Kwajalein Atoll's principal islands in six days, beginning February 2, 1944. The Marshalls were the first of the Japanese mandated islands to be invaded.

Palau Island in the Carolines, Japanese outpost guarding the Philippines and Japan, was bombed on March 30, 1944, by a U.S. carrier task force. Our planes destroyed four hangars, the phosphate plant, twenty warehouses, and part of the docks. At least three of nine Japanese ships were damaged.

Dublon Island, in the Truk Lagoon, is bombed by U.S. Navy planes during a carrier task force raid on April 29, 1944. A geyser of smoke towers as bombs burst against docks and other shore installations. It was the thirty-fifth time in less than ninety days that American bombers attacked Truk. In the harbor are Japanese ships, many of which were sunk or damaged.

Changsha, in China's rich "Rice Bowl" area, was the center of the bitterest fighting in the Hunan Province. This view shows Nan Tsen Road with pill boxes placed at strategic points. Changsha was taken by Japanese in 1944.

Major American air base at Kweilin (*below*), in Kwangsi Province, China, was demolished by our men, Sept. 17, 1944, as the Japanese drove from Henyang. A half-ton bomb is ready to be rolled into a hole in airfield runway.

Changteh, in northern Hunan Province, was captured from the Japanese on Dec. 9, in the winter campaign of 1943, after some of the bloodiest fighting of the entire Sino-Japanese war. The Japanese losses were extremely heavy. Bodies of their dead were buried in common graves.

Funeral procession (*right*) of a high-ranking Chinese Army officer passes through the ruins of Changteh, China. The officer was killed in fighting in China's Hunan Province. Changteh again saw bitter fighting during May, 1944, when the Japanese tried to isolate Southwest China.

D-DAY COMES, JUNE 6, 1944

Greatest Military Operation in History Launched by Allied Ships and Planes

Before the dawn broke through the pitch black of the night of June 6, 1944, American and British troops poured upon the beaches of Normandy as the beginning of the greatest military operation of all time. This was "D-Day," the consummation of long years of waiting, planning, and preparation— years of anguish and suffering that seemed almost endless before the moment of readiness had arrived. It may be remembered that the vanguard of this great invasion army had reached Northern Ireland in January, 1942, less than two months after America had entered the war. From then our troops in constantly increasing thousands had trained for this enterprise that in magnitude had no precedent in history. For more than two years the American and British Allies had waited before committing themselves to the time and the place of the invasion. But this fleet of 4,000 ships moving across the Channel under a protecting umbrella of 11,000 planes gave notice to Hitler that the Allies had reached an apex of military might. America and its British Ally were now ready to wage global war on their own terms. After thirty months of preparation America possessed the most powerful Navy in all history, the finest equipped and trained Army, and an Air Force whose potentialities were to startle the world in months to come. With D-Day had arrived at last the climactic period of the war.

The Allied invasion fleet made its way across a choppy Channel amidst fog and rain, to the low sandy coast of Normandy, 110 miles from English embarkation ports, to a point forming a somewhat semicircular indentation in the French shore line before it juts out farther west into the Cherbourg Peninsula. Our men laboriously waded ashore in the face of enemy machine-gun fire, hugging the beach until sufficient forces could be assembled to charge the Nazi positions lying inland. Several hours before the first landings parachute and glider troops had dropped down behind enemy lines and sowed confusion among the defenders. Much of the initial success of the invasion was due to these airborne units. Our landing forces were also aided by the big guns of a protecting fleet of Allied warships, which shattered Hitler's Atlantic Wall at that point. The Nazi Luftwaffe was almost completely absent, few enemy planes penetrating the superb Allied air cover. Within forty-eight hours American and British forces had been able to secure a beach strip at least fifty miles in length and from two to ten miles in depth.

A part of invasion fleet of 4,000 ships crosses the English Channel on D-Day, protected by barrage balloons from enemy dive-bombing attacks. The Channel was rough, and many of our men were seasick. Fog and rain also complicated the task of our air forces in furnishing cover for our ships.

American troops on an LCI (Landing Craft, Infantry) are on their way to their rendezvous on the beaches of Normandy early in the morning of June 6, 1944. Some men were smiling, some serious, but as this was the day they were waiting for, all were ready for the great adventure and critical landing.

American armored tank rolls from the bow of an LST (Landing Ship, Tanks) onto the beaches of France. The tank's crew have taken their stations in gun turrets and tower. Our men required support of tanks while advancing inland.

First contingent of United States Army nurses to land in France walk across the invasion beachhead. Underfoot is a traction mat to permit passage of vehicles over the soft sand. These nurses, joined by hundreds of others within twenty-four hours, began immediately caring for the wounded.

Battleship Nevada, bombed to the bottom of Pearl Harbor by the Japanese on December 7, 1941, was later salvaged. Flame and smoke pour from the muzzles of her 14-inch guns as the stout old battleship fires on Nazi shore positions.

Invasion troops, who have just waded ashore from landing boats in the background, take cover behind enemy beach obstacles. These men were firing upon Nazi positions located just back of the beach. The first day was the critical period for our landing forces, when our men were required to battle the Nazis from exposed positions on the open shore. Here our troops suffered the greatest percentage of their casualties.

AIR INVASION OF GERMANY

Combined Air Fleets Softened up Germany for the Land Invasion, Driving the Luftwaffe to Cover

Great fleets of British and American planes did their work in softening up Hitler's Fortress Europe for the land invasion. Cologne, on May 30, 1942, saw the first thousand-plane raid by the Royal Air Force. In October, 1942, the American Air Force joined the British in their air invasion of Germany. In January, 1943, heavy bombers carried out the first all-American air raid on Germany. From then to the very hour of the invasion of France the Allies sent increasing fleets of planes to destroy at the source Hitler's ability to make war, making sure that the invasion, when it came, would not ·fail to be successful. Night after night squadrons of British planes blasted the vital plants upon which Hitler depended to keep his war machine going. By day our own Air Force took up the bombing. On D-Day the Allied air forces escorted the invasion fleet to the beaches of Normandy under an almost impenetrable umbrella of bombers and fighter planes. Then, in cooperation with the invasion armies, they harassed troop concentrations, destroyed bridges and strategic highways. Our Fortresses granted Hitler no respite in blasting war plants still in operation, stepping up the effectiveness of this bombing by shuttling between England, Italy, and bases in Soviet Russia. Our air squadrons fought Goering's Luftwaffe, clipping its wings so that it rarely rose to join combat; and thus our bomber forces dominated the air over Europe. From January 1, 1944, to July 1, in dropping 266,227 tons of bombs on Europe, 3,425 United States planes were shot down while enemy losses were 7,655 planes.

Marauders of Ninth Air Force provided cover for ground forces in Normandy. Two bombers have blasted a road and rail junction behind German lines.

Allied planes fly over the invasion coast of France, dropping heavy loads of explosives on Nazi installations and troops, cooperating with our landing forces. Smoke pours from one bomber, which has been hit by flak from anti-aircraft positions near the coast. Note the closely packed design of falling bombs.

Berlin housewives, their homes destroyed by Allied bombing, obtain food from metal containers provided by the Nazis. In the background is the famous Brandenburg Gate.

Members of an airborne unit were killed in a crash landing of their glider on French soil. The eight men were carried from the wrecked glider and their faces covered with parachute shrouds.

American troops (*right*) wounded in the initial landings in Normandy were brought to the beach, given first aid, and then prepared for transportation to England. Many of the wounded were placed in ambulance planes and flown to base hospitals.

American wounded (*right, below*), evacuated from the beaches of Normandy, are taken off a transport by Medical Corpsmen of a Negro unit at a base hospital in England. An American Military Guard and two receiving attendants carefully watch.

German prisoners (*below*) lined up aboard an Allied transport reach England. Almost every racial type of Europe was represented in this batch of captives—a few of immense haul of prisoners taken in first days of fighting. Third from left, leaning out of line, was a Japanese who had been serving in the Nazi ranks. Many prisoners had been rounded up from occupied countries and were forced to serve in the German army.

General Sir Bernard L. Montgomery (*above*), Commander-in-Chief of the Allied ground troops in France, and Lieut. Gen. Omar N. Bradley, Commander of the American ground forces, meet in their first conference on French soil to discuss strategy of the campaign in the Cherbourg Peninsula, one of the most historic and momentous conferences of the war.

Pier roadway of prefabricated harbor (*right*) on the Normandy coast is route for ambulances carrying the wounded from shore to ship. The steel highway was constructed of a series of small bridges supported on floats which rose and fell with the tides. Built in Britain, these great harbors were towed across the Channel to assist in the liberation of France.

Twisted wreckage of a beachhead bridge on the coast of Normandy juts out into the channel. This American installation was irreparably damaged, shortly áfter it was assembled, by the heavy storm of June 19, 1944. Consequently, only one of the two prefabricated harbors brought from Britain could be used to land men and supplies necessary for operations.

RUSSIA STRIKES FROM EAST

Red Armies Open Their Synchronizing Offensive in June, 1944, Aimed at the Heart of Germany

Three years almost to the day after Hitler's vaunted legions invaded Russia, the Soviet armies on June 23, 1944, launched their summer offensive to synchronize with the Allied invasion in Normandy and the push up the Italian Peninsula. On June 11, 1944, as a preliminary to this main offensive, several Red Divisions breached the Mannerheim Line on the Karelian Isthmus, took Vipurii, and drove the small Finnish army toward Helsinki. So swift was the progress of the Red armies in the offensive begun on June 23 that Vitebsk, the key fortress in the Fatherland Line, was captured within four days. On July 2, when Polotsk fell, the Russians crossed into Old Poland and pushed into the Baltic States of Lithuania, Estonia, and Latvia. Minsk, the last major stronghold held by the Germans in White Russia, fell on July 3. Vilna, the capital of Lithuania, was taken on July 11, and Pinsk, the vital Nazi base in the heart of the Pripet Marshes, was captured on July 14. The Germans had been driven back 265 miles in the first twenty-two days of the summer offensive. In September, powerful Soviet armies started a gigantic drive along the entire Eastern Front. By the end of October, the northern armies had driven through surrendered Finland into Norway and across the Baltic States into East Prussia. In the south, striking out from conquered Rumania, Soviet armies invaded northern Yugoslavia and swept through the Carpathian mountain passes of Transylvania. Soviet forces in southern Poland crossed the panhandle of Czechoslovakia, all armies focusing on the Hungarian Plain leading to Budapest, "side door" into Germany.

Soviet artillery passes down a road under shell fire lined with wreckage—part of the Mannerheim Line on which Finland depended for her defense. Fighting ceased Sept. 4, 1944, when the Finns were forced to capitulate.

Soviet infantrymen (*below*) wade across a stream in pursuit of Nazi forces on the White Russian front behind Vitebsk. The power unleashed by the Russian armies in their summer offensive which began June 23, 1944, was overwhelming, the Germans being unable to slow down the onslaught at any point. During the first week of the drive five major Nazi strongholds fell.

Soviet soldiers fire on retreating Nazi troops, from behind German fortifications near Vitebsk. Vitebsk was the first of the major Nazi strongholds in White Russia to fall to the advancing Red armies.

Vitebsk citizens joyously welcome soldiers of the Red Army, which liberated their city, June 27, 1944, three years after it had been captured.

Red Army makes a triumphant entry into Mogilev, captured from the Germans on June 28, 1944. Russian infantrymen and tank crews wave to the citizens as armored divisions roll along. Mogilev was one of the main fortified points on the "Fatherland Line."

Soviet armored divisions roll past the government building in Minsk, which escaped damage at the hands of Nazi demolition squads. So rapid was the Russian drive into Minsk that the German armies abandoned huge stores of tanks, guns, and heavy equipment.

Bucharest cheers Soviet tanks as they enter Rumanian capital, Aug. 31, 1944. King Michael proclaimed Rumania's surrender on Aug. 23, ordering the nation to aid the Russians. In fury at their lost satellite, the Nazis then air-bombarded Bucharest.

Red Army troops drive to Czechoslovakian frontier. On Oct. 18, 1944, in an attack from Poland, tanks and infantry swept thirty miles into Czechoslovakia on a 170-mile front.

Storm Troopers hunt out Warsaw patriots who on Aug. 1, 1944, rose against their Nazi conquerors. Although Allied bombers flew low over Warsaw to drop weapons by parachute to relieve the patriots, after a bitter and isolated defense, the Poles were forced to surrender.

Russian infantry races to the German frontier from west of Kaunas, Lithuania. By the middle of October, 1944, Soviet armies were awaiting the signal to drive into Germany.

American infantrymen in Fort du Roule, which guards the port of Cherbourg, seek the tunnel entrance to the coastal batteries which continue to fire on our men despite the fact that the fort has fallen to the Americans. In the distance, through the smoke of the bombardment, is the city itself. On June 25, three days after the Nazi commander refused an ultimatum to surrender, fourteen mighty Allied warships pounded Cherbourg from the sea. Our troops then broke into the city and took it June 27, with over 25,000 prisoners.

German commanders surrender Cherbourg to the Allies on June 27, 1944. Lieut. Gen. Carl Wilhelm von Schlieben, facing the camera, Commander of the Cherbourg garrison, and Rear Admiral Walter Hennecke, Sea Defense Commander, discuss terms with Maj. Gen. J. Lawton Collins. The Allies gained an effective port for transporting men and supplies.

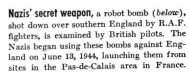

Allied casualties in a steady stream are carried into an LST for transportation to England, while in the background marches a line of German prisoners, also on their way to the British Isles, to detention camps.

Nazis' secret weapon, a robot bomb (*below*), shot down over southern England by R.A.F. fighters, is examined by British pilots. The Nazis began using these bombs against England on June 13, 1944, launching them from sites in the Pas-de-Calais area in France.

Wharves and buildings on the waterfront of Cherbourg (*above*) were found to be a shambles after the surrender of the Germans on June 27, 1944. Immediately American engineers began clearing the harbor and repairing the docks.

American tanks (*right*) smash forward west of St. Lô, July 25, opening the way for the advance southward. Special secret devices enabled them to cut through hedgerows and rout the Nazis.

Stars and Stripes are raised over citadel of St. Malo. "Mad" Colonel Andreas von Aulock, who knew he was doomed but refused to surrender, was finally forced to relinquish the fort to American troops on August 17, after a concentrated eleven-day bombardment.

LST's in Italian port are loaded with battle equipment for the Allied invasion of Southern France. These ships are a small part of the armada assembled in Italy, North Africa, Corsica, and Sardinia to transport troops and matériel for the landings on Aug. 15, 1944.

Citizen army battles to liberate Paris. While Allied armies were encircling Paris, resistance forces within the capital rose up against the Nazis. For six days French patriots 50,000 strong fought to free their city. On the seventh day, Aug. 25, 1944, Allied tanks and troops of the French Second Armored Division entered Paris to aid in the liberation.

Terrified crowds (*left*) dive for cover in the Place de la Concorde as German snipers fire upon them. The Parisians had gathered on August 26 to cheer American and French troops who helped them liberate their city. Although the Nazis had surrendered Paris the previous day, Fifth Columnists had planted snipers on the roofs of buildings.

General Charles de Gaulle and General Jacques Leclerc, at left, review troops of the French Second Armored Division, which, commanded by General Leclerc, was sent to aid the Parisians in their fight for liberation. The Nazis surrendered Paris on Aug. 25.

Grim-faced American troops march in battle array through the historic Arc de Triomphe and along the broad Champs Elysées during the liberation-day parade in Paris on August 26, 1944. Cheered by grateful Parisians, the Americans were on the way back to the front.

Joyful people of Brussels welcome British tanks and troops which liberated the Belgian capital, Sept. 3, 1944. The next day Antwerp was freed, its great port, third largest in Europe, captured intact by swift British armored units.

American bombers pounding at Nazi escape routes destroyed this bridge over the Seine. Fleeing encirclement at Falaise, Aug. 19, 1944, German armies met disaster in a larger trap at the river barrier. Unable to retreat farther, they were cut to pieces by our air and ground forces.

Allied armored column speeds through smoke from burning German equipment as our armies trap Nazi forces in the Falaise area of Normandy. Almost 250,000 Germans were pressed in the gigantic vise. Here and at the Seine River, the German Seventh Army and units of their Fifteenth Army were almost completely annihilated by the Allies.

German prisoners, part of more than 10,000 captured by Canadians at Boulogne, Sept. 21, 1944, march across a bridge to prisoner-of-war enclosure. The Nazis held stubbornly to Channel ports to block the supply of Allied armies.

German demolitions shattered Joan of Arc Bridge in Brest. Ruins of French port show Nazi destructive efficiency, also effect of Allied bombings. American troops besieged the city for seven weeks before the enemy garrison of nearly 40,000 surrendered Sept. 20, 1944.

R.A.F. Halifaxes tow Horsa gliders over the Rhine as the First Allied Airborne Army invades Holland on Sept. 17, 1944. The famed British First Airborne Division went into action around Arnhem, while Lieut. Gen. Sir Miles C. Dempsey's Second Army, in conjunction with the airborne landings, launched an attack across the Dutch border to join these troops.

Allied armor speeds northward across the Nijmegen Bridge toward Arnhem in an attempt to relieve British airborne forces trapped in that area. The Germans clung tenaciously to this strategic span over the lower Rhine, but American airborne troops and British tankmen finally captured it intact on September 21. They then moved toward the Lek River.

British sky troops in the Arnhem perimeter take cover behind a hedge as they tensely await the enemy assault. The Germans were barely 100 yards away when this picture was taken. The Allies began to withdraw their troops on the night of September 26.

"Red Devils" are rescued after their heroic stand at Arnhem. Out of 8,000 paratroopers, only 2,000 survived the historic attempt on Sept. 17, 1944, to establish a bridgehead over the Lek River and gain thereby a northern gateway into Germany.

Smashed German pillbox on the Siegfried Line was blasted by TNT. U.S. Army Engineers demolished these enemy defenses to prevent infiltration into our lines.

Bulldozer tank carries American troops through dragon-teeth barriers of the Siegfried Line near Roetgen, the first German town to be taken by Americans, Sept. 13, 1944.

U.S. First Army soldiers in the Aachen area of Holland crouch, under heavy German fire, for an attack on the Siegfried Line. After rejecting an Allied ultimatum, Nazis in Aachen were severely bombarded. Americans entered the garrison city on October 12, 1944, and remnants of its defenders surrendered unconditionally on October 20.

RETURN TO THE PHILIPPINES

Our Forces Pierce Japanese Defense Ring and Land with MacArthur in Philippines

On the morning of June 15, 1944, our Marines landed on Saipan in the Marianas. This invasion marked the first blow at Japan's inner cordon of defenses. The Japanese were well equipped with tanks, mortars, and artillery which they effectively used against our troops. Before the island fell, July 8, our casualties were the highest of any Pacific campaign. The Japanese fleet sent carrier-based planes on June 18 to bomb our ships lying off Saipan, but the result was a record loss of aircraft by the enemy with little damage to our fleet.

On June 16, 1944, the great new B-29 Superfortresses of the Twentieth Air Force bombed the Japanese steel center at Yawata. Through the next few months the giant bombers continued their raids, hitting Japan, Manchuria, and the stronghold of Formosa. In November B-29's began operating from Saipan.

On July 20 American troops returned to Guam in an assault that wrested the island from the Japanese by August 10. Marines seized Tinian between July 23 and August 1. Pushing on toward the Philippines our forces next attacked the Palau Islands, going ashore on Peleliu September 15 and on Angaur the next day. On September 21 Navy planes from Task Force 58 blasted the Manila Bay area of the Philippines. On October 10 Admiral Halsey's Third Fleet launched crippling sea-air blows at Formosa and other Japanese islands. On October 19, 1944, General MacArthur's forces landed on Leyte Island in the central Philippines.

Goaded by the Leyte landing, Japan finally sent her fleet into action. Three enemy units moved toward the Philippines, one steaming down from Formosa and passing east of Luzon, the second breaking into Mindoro Strait and driving east to the Sibuyan Sea, the third pushing through the Mindanao Sea. On October 23, Admiral Halsey detached a carrier force to halt the Sibuyan Sea naval unit, while Admiral Kinkaid sent a force against the group heading for the Mindanao Sea. On October 24 the bulk of Admiral Halsey's fleet met the largest of the enemy armadas in a great battle northeast of Luzon. This Battle for Leyte Gulf on October 23-26, 1944, proved to be the greatest naval action of the war. The United States Pacific Fleet won a decisive victory, completely crippling Japanese naval strength and assuring our conquest of the Philippines.

American naval task force bombards Tinian Island just southeast of Saipan. As a prelude to the landings on Saipan on June 15, 1944, shore installations were silenced. The huge sixteen-inch guns of a United States battleship, with muzzles belching flame and smoke, hurl tons of hot steel on distant enemy positions, setting up concussions that shake the great ship.

Our troops storm ashore on the island of Saipan. The men crawl forward cautiously, using every possible protective cover. The first wave met little opposition, but following landings were forced to wage a desperate struggle in order to keep from being pushed back into the sea.

Marines dig in on the beaches of Saipan Island. The Marines have dug their foxholes in the sand on the ridge and calmly await the enemy counterattack. This picture was taken a few hours after the first wave of our troops landed on June 15, 1944.

Airfields in China used by the B-29 Superfortresses were built by an estimated 500,000 coolies almost entirely by hand. These bases, which were used in support of the Saipan invasion, brought the Japanese homeland within effective bombing range of these huge new bombers.

The beachhead on Saipan Island in the Marianas was secured and then supplies were rushed ashore from landing barges, army alligators, and other craft. Coast Guard, Navy, Marines, and Army combined in the operations. Smoke hovers over the shore from the barrage by our warships. Four days after the initial landings the Japanese fleet sent swarms of carrier planes to attack our forces, but failed to stop the invasion.

Japanese carrier makes a frantic fight for life in the Philippine Sea on June 19, 1944. One bomb has just landed near the ship's bow and another at her stern. In the foreground an enemy destroyer gyrates crazily to escape bombs. American planes scored a decisive victory over enemy forces.

Vice-Admiral Marc A. Mitscher, Commander of Navy Task Force 58. Mitscher's planes in the Philippine Sea battle sank a carrier, a destroyer, and two tankers, while damaging other units.

Blood transfusion is given a badly wounded soldier in a slowly moving jeep returning from front lines on Saipan. In this emergency transfusion could not wait until first-aid station was reached. Jeeps were always kept at hand.

Blood plasma is given to a wounded Marine by a unit of Medical Corpsmen during the Saipan invasion. In the background a number of other stretcher cases are being prepared for similar treatment. After first aid was administered, the wounded were removed in landing barges to ships standing offshore.

Never in any war in history have the wounded received such meticulous care as in World War II. This soldier wounded during battle for Saipan Island was brought to Hawaii, flown over the largest air evacuation route in the world.

American Marines on Saipan lie in wait, covering the entrance to an enemy cave cut into the hillside. In mopping-up operations hand grenades and flame-throwers dislodged the Japanese.

Amphibious ducks churn up clouds of dust on a fine coral road on Saipan as they haul troops to the front lines. Our forces wiped out the garrison by July 8, 1944.

American Marines take cover as they hit the beach near Asan, Guam on July 20, 1944. Admiral Nimitz's fleet and carrier planes pounded the island for seventeen days in preparation for the assault. American rule over Guam was proclaimed on July 28, but organized resistance did not cease until August 9. During the campaign 17,000 Japanese were killed.

United States Marines advance behind a tank on Guam. Hugging the tank, a Marine Photographer is taking pictures. Between camera shots, his gun accounted for four Japanese soldiers. Orote airfield and naval base were captured on July 28, 1944.

Water buffaloes loaded with Marines from near-by Saipan churn through the sea toward Tinian Island, July 23, 1944. Marine divisions undertook the invasion after a week's rest from the Saipan campaign. Our troops overcame all resistance in a nine-day battle.

Marines take refuge behind an amphibious truck as Japanese gunfire tries to beat back American forces invading strategic Peleliu Island in the Palau group on Sept. 14, 1944. The following day, after a co-ordinated ground and air bombardment, the Marines seized the highly prized Peleliu airdrome. Two amphibious tractors burn in the background.

Wary American Leathernecks advance slowly towards Japanese positions on "Bloody Nose Ridge" on Peleliu. Rocky terrain provided excellent hiding places for enemy snipers, who had to be cleaned out of caves. When organized resistance ceased, American casualties on the Palau Islands totaled 1,022 dead, 6,111 wounded, and 250 missing.

Leyte Island in the central Philippines belches smoke from huge fires as first wave of American forces pours ashore on Oct. 19, 1944. Army Rangers prepared for the attack by landing on Saluan, Homonhon, and Dinagat Islands in Leyte Gulf on October 16, while U.S. air and naval units constantly bombarded enemy defenses on Leyte. General MacArthur, continuing the strategy of by-passing strong Japanese bases, struck between the islands of Luzon and Mindanao, splitting Nippon forces and isolating those to the south.

General MacArthur, fulfilling his promise to return to the Philippines, wades ashore with Lieut. General Sutherland. Meeting little resistance on the Leyte beachhead, American troops surged northward to secure Tacloban and its strategic airfield by October 21.

Dismounted First Cavalry crosses water tank trap built by Japanese to hinder the American advance on Leyte. On Nov. 2 the enemy yielded Carigara to joint artillery and cavalry forces. Across San Juanico Strait, the island of Samar was virtually freed by Oct. 30.

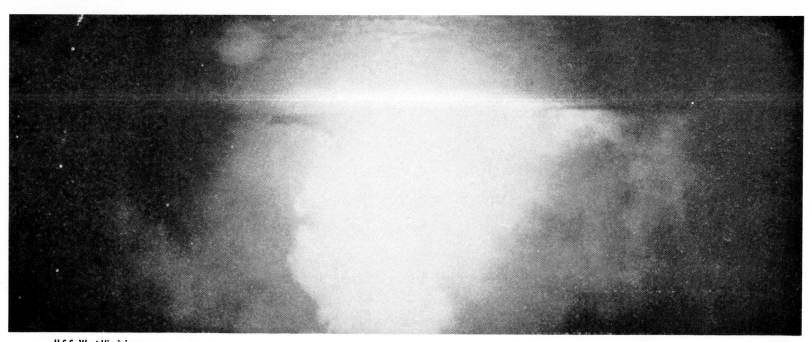

U.S.S. West Virginia blasts enemy ships in night engagement in Surigao Strait, Oct. 25, 1944, during the Battle for Leyte Gulf. Japan sent three naval forces to challenge our Philippine invasion armada. In simultaneous actions in Surigao Strait, off Samar, and off Cape Engaño, units of the U.S. Third and Seventh Fleets dealt a smashing blow to Japanese naval power.

PT boat rescues Japanese survivors of action in Surigao Strait. On October 24–25 the enemy's southern force, advancing in two columns, attempted to pass through Surigao Strait into Leyte Gulf but met first our PT boats and destroyers, and then our big ships drawn up across the channel in a position which enabled them to "cross the T." In the American line were five battleships salvaged from Pearl Harbor. Their 14- and 16-inch guns blasted each enemy vessel as it came into range and turned to flee. Out of 25 ships the Japanese lost more than 19.

Japanese battleship-carrier flees from attacks by U.S. aircraft during sea battle, Oct. 23–26, 1944. Of 60 enemy ships which tried to smash our Philippine invasion, 34 were damaged and 24 were sunk.

Smoke pours from stricken Japanese carrier blasted by planes of the U.S. Third Fleet in the Battle for Leyte Gulf. This ship was sunk off Cape Engaño, October 24.

Burning U.S.S. Princeton is aided by Pacific Fleet cruiser. The 10,000-ton carrier was part of the northernmost of our task force groups guarding Leyte Gulf, which was attacked by swarms of land-based Japanese planes off Luzon on October 24, before the third enemy fleet was sighted. Bombed and set afire, the *Princeton* had to be sunk by American torpedoes when her main magazine exploded. Third Fleet units that night sped northward to meet the new Japanese threat and next day defeated this force, the strongest of the enemy's three-pronged attack.

Escort carrier of the Seventh Fleet narrowly escapes Japanese salvo in action off Luzon on October 25. Fighter planes stand poised for action.

Casualties of the Battle for Leyte Gulf receive medical treatment in the converted wardroom of an American escort carrier. In the emergency sick bay, tables were transformed into beds for the sick and wounded.

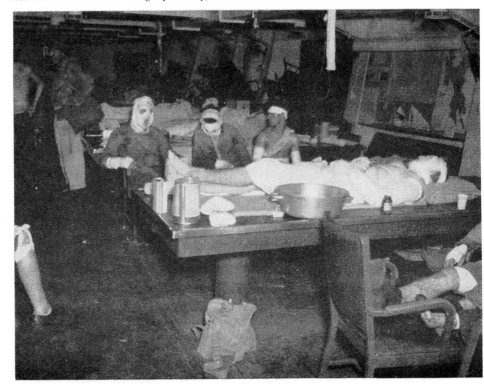

COLLAPSE OF NAZI GERMANY

The Offensive and Counteroffensive—
Conquest of Berlin—Surrender at Rheims

The fall of 1944 saw the beginning of the end in Europe. Canadian forces reached Netherlands territory at the Schelde Estuary on September 22, and began the bitter fight to open the port of Antwerp as a supply base for the Allies. By November 7, with British assistance, the Schelde region had been cleared of the Nazis.

On November 16 General Eisenhower launched a six-army offensive along a front from Holland to the Swiss frontier. On December 16 Hitler opened a powerful counteroffensive. In ten days, while fog and sleet grounded Allied planes, the *Wehrmacht* cut 50 miles into the "Belgian Bulge." By January 29, 1945, the American offensive had stopped the Axis drive and pinched the German armies into the "Belgian Bulge." By mid-January, 1945, the Americans were again inside Germany, advancing toward the Rhine.

The first big Rhine city to fall was Cologne on March 6. Then, on March 7, our troops captured the west-bank town of Remagen

and found the Ludendorff railway bridge still intact. Men and equipment poured across the span; other crossings were made over pontoon bridges. Key German cities fell in rapid succession—Coblenz on March 17, Frankfort on March 29, Hanover on April 10, Leipzig on April 19, and Munich on April 30.

Meanwhile, on the eastern front, Russian armies circled Warsaw and overwhelmed the German garrison on January 17. A five-army drive smashed on to take Tarnow, Cracow, and Lodz on January 19. By February 1 the Red Army was streaming into German Pomerania, Brandenburg, and Silesia. Posen was taken on March 1, Danzig on March 30, and Koenigsberg on April 9. Below the Carpathians, Red armies also forged their way through Hungary, Austria, Rumania, and Bulgaria. Budapest was seized on February 13, and Vienna on April 13. Marshal Zhukoff's armies burst into Berlin on April 22 and battered the city into submission by May 2.

In Italy, Bologna fell on April 22, and the Allies crossed the Po River on April 23. Verona and Parma were taken on April 26. All German forces in Italy surrendered on May 2. On May 7, German leaders signed the formal surrender of Germany at Rheims, France.

Allied vehicles wait to cross canal in flooded section of South Beveland Island in the drive toward Walcheren, Holland. By Oct. 31, 1944, with the help of British units which landed on the southeast shore, the Canadian First Army had completely defeated the Nazis remaining in Beveland. The next day Army Commandos landed on the southern shore of Walcheren in a drive to knock out German batteries at the Schelde estuary. They took Flushing, Holland's third largest port on November 5.

Dutch civilians huddle in dugout as British soldiers aim at German positions during battle for Boxtel in the Netherlands campaign. Crossing the Dommel Canal near Boxtel, the British Second Army captured 'sHertogenbosch and Tilburg on October 27 after stiff enemy resistance and then moved on to the mouth of the Maas River.

American infantrymen, their rifles poised for action, stalk the enemy through Huertgen Forest near Vossenack, Germany. After three months of bitter seesaw fighting the U.S. First Army drove the foe from the shattered forest, captured the town of Huertgen Nov. 30, and surged onto Cologne Plain.

British tanks bear down on Nazi positions on the road to Geilenkirchen, Germany. American Ninth Army troops, joining the Allied assault Nov. 16, helped the British Second Army capture the city by Nov. 19, 1944. Heap of empty shell cases shows the extent of artillery barrage.

Third Army Infantrymen, on the alert for enemy snipers, patrol a section of Metz. Nazi control of the principal Metz fortifications had retarded the Allied advance into Germany. After capturing the fortress city on November 20, Lieut. General Patton's troops rapidly drove on to the rich Saar Basin.

First Army infantrymen crouch in snow-filled ditch during German artillery barrage. By mid-December, 1944, General Hodges' forces were inside Germany on the Roer River, hammering toward Dueren and threatening Cologne. Then, on December 16, the Nazis launched a desperate counteroffensive at the First Army's southern flank.

German soldiers advance past wrecked American jeep. Hitler's élite divisions, piercing our lines in a surprise attack, counted on heavy fog to neutralize Allied air superiority. But many planes took off despite the weather, to give needed support to our ground forces.

Gasoline tins, empty of fuel, are left for advancing Nazis. To prevent its capture by the enemy forces, American troops destroyed all gasoline that could not be moved away to safety. Huge quantities of supplies had been stored close to the front during the Allied offensive.

American troops pause on way to reinforce front-line units struggling to hold the German offensive. Despite heroic resistance by our men, Nazi armored spearheads in ten days overran Luxembourg and drove fifty miles into Belgium. Then, regrouped Allied armies stopped the enemy attack short of Dinant and Namur on the Meuse River.

Supplies are parachuted to besieged garrison at Bastogne, Belgium. Encircled by the Nazis and under constant attack, the 101st U.S. Airborne Division held out from December 19 to 27.

U.S. Army vehicles park in Bastogne Square after siege of the town was lifted. Third Army forces battled four days before breaking through to reach the defenders on Dec. 27, 1944.

Rescuing legions of Gen. George S. Patton's Third Army advance in open formation toward Bastogne after Brig. Gen. Anthony G. McAuliffe, commander of trapped American forces, had rejected a German demand for surrender with the now famous "Nuts!" Tracks in snow indicate deployment of mobile units which used wooded area for cover. Heroic resistance at Spa, Saint Vith, and other vital points in addition to Bastogne, held the flanks of the Nazi salient and kept the enemy from Liege.

Nazi prisoner removes U.S. Army shoes and pants under the eyes of Americans near Geromont, Belgium. Several hundred German spies, specially trained to impersonate our men, were caught behind our lines. After trial, they were executed for wearing American uniforms.

American dead, massacred by the Nazis, lie in the snow somewhere in Belgium. In this and many similar atrocities uncovered by our forces in the "Battle of the Bulge," German troops herded unarmed American prisoners together and brutally shot them down with machine-gun fire.

Wreckage of German equipment, smashed by Ninth Air Force, litters road near Bad Durkheim, Germany. With clearing weather over Belgium, Allied air-power joined land armies in crushing the Nazi attack. Heavy bombers as well as fighters and rocket-firing planes pounded enemy columns without let-up and in one five-day period shot down 600 German planes. The Allies took the offensive on December 26 and by Jan. 13, 1945, had destroyed twenty out of twenty-four Nazi divisions and all but eliminated the "Bulge." Our men reentered Germany on January 29.

Warsaw cheers Polish troops that helped free the city after five years of Nazi rule. Driving 24 miles in one day, Russian and Polish forces took devastated Warsaw on Jan. 17, 1945.

Soviet tommy-gunners observe enemy in fight for Tolkemit. Capture of this German port on Gulf of Danzig, Jan. 26, 1945, sealed off Nazi forces in East Prussia.

Big Three meet at Yalta. At this conference, held in the Crimea from Feb. 4-11, 1945, President Roosevelt, Prime Minister Churchill, and Premier Stalin agreed on plans for the final defeat and military occupation of Germany and on Allied policy toward liberated countries. They also called for a conference on world peace to open at San Francisco on April 25. Yalta was the final meeting of the famous "Big Three." Death came to Roosevelt April 12; Churchill resigned on July 26, upon election of a Labor Government in Britain.

King Ibn Saud confers with the President. From Yalta Roosevelt flew to Egypt and on February 14 received the monarch of Saudi Arabia aboard an American warship anchored near Cairo. Other talks on current problems concerning the United States had been held the previous day with King Farouk of Egypt and Haile Selassie, Emperor of Ethiopia.

Soviet troops advance in Budapest. Encircling the Hungarian capital on Dec. 26, 1944, two Russian armies battled for 51 days before the Nazis surrendered the twin city Feb. 13, 1945.

Longest Bailey Bridge, over Maas River at Gennep, Holland, supplied Canadian First Army as it took Cleve February 12, Goch a week later, and on March 26 stormed across the Rhine.

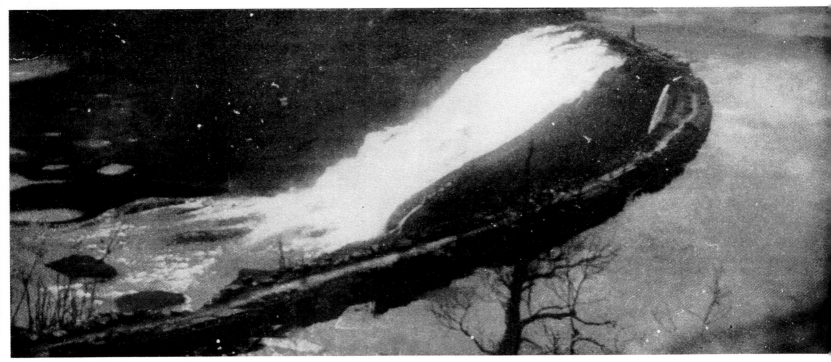

Urft Dam, near Wollseifen, Germany, was taken by U.S. First Army troops on Feb. 4, 1945, in the drive to capture the series of German dams which controlled the waters of the lower Roer River. The American advance toward Cologne had been halted at the river in December because of the danger of attempting to cross while the Germans could at any time flood the Roer Valley. Our forces on February 10 seized the Schwammenauel Dam, largest of seven in the reservoir system, but not before the Nazis had blasted the floodgates, sending torrents down the river.

Wounded American is rescued by stretcher bearer from swollen Roer River during the Allied offensive across the river which opened on Feb. 23, 1945. Foot bridge broke as he was being carried to safety. On the bridge lies a dead American, while another soldier floats down stream on a single pontoon. In background comrades watch as motor craft speeds to lend aid.

Cologne falls to American troops, March 6, 1945. Constant bombing and shelling reduced the Rhineland capital to the mess of rubble shown here. The famous Cathedral was still erect, but retreating Nazis had blown up the Hohenzollern Bridge over the Rhine. Airmen dropped 42,000 tons of explosives, destroying 85 per cent of the city.

American engineers prepare historic Remagen Bridge for Allied traffic across the Rhine. In a quick thrust from Bonn, the Ninth Armored Division of the First Army reached Remagen on March 7, 1945, and captured the Ludendorff railroad bridge still intact. The Germans had planted explosives to blow up the bridge but were prevented from detonating the charges.

Ludendorff Bridge, with damaged girder apparent above stone pier in foreground, is shown before the 1,068-foot span collapsed on March 17, 1945, under strain of Allied traffic and German shelling. For ten days American forces had poured across to strengthen our bridgehead across the Rhine. The Army engineers in a few hours replaced the bridge with a new emergency structure.

General Patton's infantrymen flush German soldier from pillbox in Mainz, Germany, which they entered March 20 as other Third Army units seized Worms and the Seventh Army captured Saarbruecken. Next day the Third reached Ludwigshafen, squeezing tighter the Nazis trapped in the Rhine-Saar-Moselle pocket. On March 22 Patton's forces below Mainz suddenly stormed across the Rhine.

U.S. Army vehicles cross long pontoon bridge over the Rhine. After collapse of the Remagen Bridge, supplies and reinforcements for our bridgehead continued to flow over these structures built by Army engineers. In later crossings by Allied armies, combat engineers worked to erect pontoon bridges even while amphibious craft were carrying assault troops across to secure a new bridgehead.

LCVP's (Landing Craft, Vehicle-Personnel), on Army trucks, go through Belgian town on way to Rhine. These and other craft manned by Navy crews greatly aided our Rhine crossings.

Improvised ferries line Rhine. U.S. 9th Army crossed here on night of March 23–24. To the north Canadian 1st, British 2nd, and 1st Allied Airborne Armies swarmed over toward Wesel.

Third Army jeeps move through wrecked Frankfort-on-Main during the battle for the city, March 26–29. Even while infantry cleared the Nazi stronghold, Patton's armor raced northward for a junction with First Army forces. After the U.S. Seventh Army crossed the river barrier on March 26, seven Allied armies were east of the Rhine, in their final offensive.

Nazi prisoners are marched to rear on the center island of a German *autobahn* near Giessen on March 29, as vehicles of Patton's Sixth Armored Division stream past in the opposite direction, driving toward Berlin. Superhighways such as this crisscrossed Hitler's Germany, connecting key cities, and enabled Allied mobile forces to advance into the Reich with stunning speed.

Men of Seventh Army clear streets of Mannheim, March 29, before pressing into southern Germany, flanked by U.S. Third and French First Armies, on the road to Nuremberg and Munich.

Smoke rises from Danzig as Soviet forces capture the Baltic naval base, March 31. Recognizing Poland's claim, the Russians raised the Polish flag over the former "Free City."

Russian prisoners of war are joyful over release from Nazi prison camp "Stalag 326." The 82nd Reconnaissance Battalion, operating as a mopping-up force for the Ninth Army's Second Armored Division, liberated almost 10,000 emaciated internees. On the verge of starvation, these prisoners broke into warehouses and fought for food.

Ninth Army Infantrymen march through battle-scarred Hanover. Allied bombings and depredations by rebellious foreign workers had made the city a ruined skeleton by the time it fell on April 10. The final offensive had begun. Along the whole western front German cities were being overrun by Allied tanks and infantry.

Red Army soldiers engage in street fighting in ancient fortress of Koenigsberg. Russian forces along the Baltic conquered the long-besieged East Prussian capital, April 9, 1945.

Soviet tommygunners advance through captured aircraft factory grounds in Vienna. The historic capital of Austria fell April 13. Two Russian armies then linked for the push on Prague.

Dying prisoners lie among dead bodies on barrack floors of Nordhausen slave labor camp. The Third Armored Division of the U.S. First Army, entering Nordhausen on April 11, found 3,000 living skeletons and 2,700 unburied bodies. Citizens of Nordhausen were later forced to bury the victims of brutal torture and starvation.

Vast dumps of unburied corpses were found by British Second Army forces when they overran Belsen concentration camp on April 15. Josef Kramer, SS commander of the Nazi death factory, had perpetrated most of Belsen's atrocities during the previous five months. Under Kramer's predecessor prison conditions had been much less harsh for the inmates.

Starved slave laborers were liberated from Buchenwald prison camp on April 10 by U.S. troops of the 80th Division. More than 20,000 living dead were found in squalid living quarters.

Russian prisoner of war, liberated by Third Armored Division of the U.S. First Army, points accusing finger at former guard who brutally beat inmates of the concentration camp.

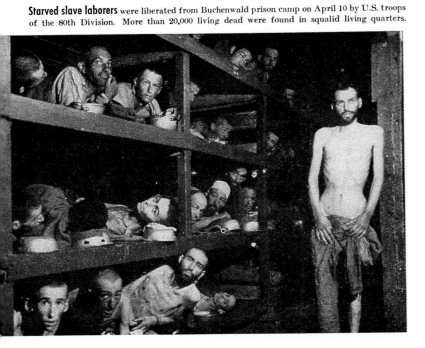

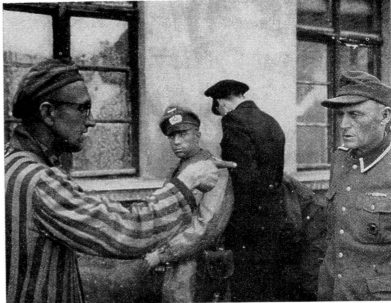

American tank battalion rolls into Brunswick, Germany. The city fell to the Ninth Army on April 13, 1945, and our troops pushed to Hasselburg, twenty miles northwest of Magdeburg.

German jet plane plant was found by U.S. Ninth Army troops 300 meters underground in a salt mine near Engels. The picture shows unfinished Heinkel 162's lined up in the assembly room.

Columns of First Army soldiers march up the sides of the road to Leipzig, Germany's fifth largest city. Troops of the Second and Sixty-ninth Infantry Divisions closed in from all directions and broke through a belt of 1,200 anti-aircraft guns, which were turned on the American forces by Nazi defenders. They took Leipzig on April 19.

V-2 Rocket Bomb was found by British troops near camouflaged German chemical factory in Hahnenberg Forest. From Sept. 8, 1944, to a short time before V-E Day, the Nazis launched 1,050 giant stratospheric rockets against England. The long-range bombs appeared even after launching sites along the Channel were captured.

Tank destroyers advance through rubble-strewn streets of Magdeburg, capital of the Prussian Province of Saxony, after the city was taken on April 19, 1945 by the American Ninth Army.

Nuremberg arena, where Hitler reviewed his *Wehrmacht*, is invaded by men of the 45th Division carrying battle-torn American flags. The shrine city fell to U.S. forces on April 20.

Fifth Army troops in Italy rest in Bologna's Piazza de la Republica. American, Polish, and Italian troops surged into the German bastion on April 21 and made enemy forces retreat to the Po River. The conquest of Bologna was the greatest victory in the Italian campaign since the fall of Rome. The Brazilian units captured Montalto.

Seventh Army tanks roll through war-torn Nuremberg after the citadel was captured on April 20. The terrific artillery bombardment with which U.S. forces had blasted the walled city left no building in the center of town undamaged. The Allies then raced through Bavaria in a sweep to block roads to the Alps.

Soviet self-propelled guns pass through a square in Berlin. Marshal Zhukoff's armies burst into Germany's capital on April 22, and Russian shells and bombs battered the city for ten days before it surrendered on May 2. Defense of Berlin cost the Nazis 343,000 men killed or captured. In foreground is a German tank dug into the ground.

Seventh Army infantrymen ford the Danube on tank destroyer. Nazis destroyed all bridges over the river save that at Dillingen which Americans used in their crossings on April 22. Once across the barrier, our forces sped on toward Munich against crumbling enemy opposition.

First Army soldiers grip hands of Russians at historic Elbe meeting on wrecked bridge at Torgau, Germany. First junction of Soviet and American troops occurred on April 25, 1945, and was quickly followed by others in greater force, cutting the Reich in two from east to west.

Railway marshaling yards at Leipzig, Germany, burn after raid by Ninth Air Force bombers in April, 1945. The effect of the air war in Europe was cumulative. Repeated blows supporting Allied forces, pulverized German utilities and transportation systems, wrecked Nazi war industry, crushed the Luftwaffe, and disrupted enemy organization.

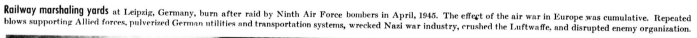

"Big Four" representatives at San Francisco Conference read news dispatch on Germany's surrender. Left to right are Anthony Eden, Edward R. Stettinius, Jr., V. M. Molotov, and T. V. Soong. The San Francisco Conference on International Organization opened April 25. By its close, June 25, a world security Charter had been formulated which was signed by officials of 50 United Nations.

Mussolini lies dead in Milan. Italian partisans executed Il Duce and other Fascists on Lake Dongo, April 28. Three days later the death of Hitler was announced. Reports that he died in the defense of Berlin were followed by rumors of suicide. The passing of the two dictators symbolized the end of the "reign of terror."

Scottish soldier looks down on partly built Nazi submarines in docks at Bremen, seized by the British 2nd Army April 26–28. At least 16 completed ocean-going U-boats were also taken.

American engineers clear path for convoys in Ludwigstrasse, Munich, on May 1. Troops of the U.S. Seventh Army crashed into Munich on April 29 and captured the city by the next day.

Seventh Army Infantrymen take cover in a ditch as they advance into Scharnitz, Austria. On May 1, 1945, American soldiers of the 103rd Division crossed the Austrian frontier and pushed to Sharnitz, ten miles northwest of Innsbruck and on the way to the Brenner Pass. In the meantime, the 44th Division took Stanzach, ten miles to the south of the frontier.

German prisoners of war, taken in Austrian redoubt, march along a road near Auland. Almost 1,000,000 Nazis surrendered in Italy and Austria with cessation of hostilities on May 2.

Hamburg was desolate and deserted when British Second Army forces captured it May 3, 1945. Picture shows huge concrete ack-ack fortress with four-gun-position flak towers amid ruins.

Soviet flag is unfurled on Reichstag Building in Berlin. Germany's capital fell to the Russians on May 2, after ten days of bitter street fighting. More than 70,000 prisoners were taken, and Marshal Stalin announced the destruction of the German Ninth Army southeast of Berlin. The Baltic ports of Rostock and Warnemeunde were also won.

Tanks of the Tenth Armored Division enter Garmisch-Partenkirchen, scene of the 1936 Winter Olympic games. Americans thrust south from Oberammergau to seize the resort on April 30.

Italian prisoners of war wave at Brenner Pass sign as they are returned to Italy from Austria. The U.S. Seventh Army drove through the Brenner Pass to join the Fifth Army, May 4.

Hitler's mountain eyrie at Berchtesgaden is rest spot for war-weary Americans. On May 5 the Third Infantry Division, against light resistance, mopped up Berchtesgaden, taking over 2,000 prisoners. It was from this Eagle's Nest atop Obersalzberg Mountain in the Bavarian Alps that Hitler once ruled the greater part of Europe.

American infantrymen cling to medium tanks as they advance toward Linz, key communications center in Austria. On May 5 General Patton's forces swept through Linz into Czechoslovakia to a point only 50 miles from the Russians in the east. The Czechoslovak pocket was the last German redoubt still holding out at the end.

Civilian clad Nazi officers, emissaries of German general in Italy, sign unconditional surrender effective May 2, 1945, at secret meeting with Allied representatives at Caserta, April 30.

Admiral von Friedeburg, Commander in Chief of the German Navy, surrenders unconditionally to General Montgomery near Hamburg, May 4, yielding all Nazi troops in northern Germany.

Col. General Gustav Jodl, Nazi Chief of Staff, surrenders Germany to the Allies. Seated at right is Gen. Adm. Hans Georg Friedeburg and at left, an aide, who both watch as the Prussian representative of Grand Admiral Doenitz, Hitler's successor, affixes his signature to the unconditional surrender at Supreme Allied Headquarters at Rheims, France, May 7, 1945.

Map-lined room in Rheims schoolhouse is scene of German capitulation. Facing the Nazi delegates (backs to camera) are representatives of the United States, Britain, Russia, and France, who signed the four copies of the pact after General Jodl and made the surrender effective at exactly 2:41 A.M., May 7, 1945, French time (8:41 P.M., May 6, E.W.T.). Maj. Gen. Ivan Susloparoff here signs for the Union of Soviet Russia.

Field Marshal Wilhelm Keitel (with baton), Col. Gen. Paul Stumpf, and Gen. Adm. Friedeburg (behind Stumpf), commanders in chief of German Army, Air Force, and Navy, emerge from room at Soviet Headquarters in Berlin after ratifying surrender. Signing was completed at 12:01 A.M., May 9, Berlin time (6:01 P.M., May 8, E.W.T.), when cease-fire order became effective. Actually, German troops in Czechoslovakia continued to attack Prague and battled the Russians until May 12 before giving themselves up as prisoners of war.

President Truman and Prime Minister Churchill descend steps of the President's Berlin residence after their arrival in the capital on July 15 to meet with Premier Stalin.

New "Big Three" plan future Allied policy at Potsdam Conference, July 17–Aug. 2, 1945. Right to left are Stalin, Truman, and Attlee, Britain's Labor Prime Minister.

JAPANESE MEET DEFEAT

The Philippines Campaign—Conquest of Iwo Jima and Okinawa—Final Surrender

On Leyte U.S. forces landed behind enemy lines and secured Ormoc on December 10. By December 25 all organized resistance on Leyte had ceased. In the meantime, on December 15, the Americans invaded Mindoro Island. Luzon came next on January 9, 1945. General MacArthur moved his forces down the central Luzon plain and entered Manila on February 3. Americans freed the inmates of Cabanatuan prison camp on January 30, while entry into Manila opened the doors of Bilibid, Santo Tomas and other internment camps. On February 25, most of the city was liberated. By June 27 Luzon had been won. Corregidor fell to the Americans on March 1, and on March 10 U.S. troops landed at Zamboanga on Mindanao. Pushing on to Panay, Cebu, and Palawan, General MacArthur controlled all the Philippine Islands on July 4.

Superfortresses, meanwhile, were carrying the war to the Japanese. On October 25 they blasted Omura on Kyushu; on November 3 Rangoon was bombed; then Singapore and Sumatra. The middle of November saw the bombardment of Omura, Nanking, and Shanghai. On November 24 Tokyo was bombed by B-29's. During the remainder of 1944 and the early months of 1945, Superfortresses in ever-increasing numbers continued to blast Japan.

The next stepping-stone to Tokyo was Iwo Jima. On February 19 U.S. Marines hit the beaches of the small volcanic island. They established a beachhead on the east coast and by February 23 gained the crest of Mount Suribachi on the southern tip of the island. Organized resistance ended on March 16 after one of the most desperate struggles of the Corps' history. On April 1 American troops invaded Okinawa Island in the Ryuku chain. U.S. forces battled for 81 days before gaining control of the island on June 21, despite Japan's most effective use of *Kamikaze* or suicide planes.

Meanwhile, the atomic bomb was being produced at Oak Ridge, Tennessee. On August 6 the first bomb almost entirely wiped out Hiroshima. The second destroyed Nagasaki on August 9. Japan then sued for peace and on September 2, 1945 (Tokyo time), surrendered unconditionally aboard the U.S.S. *Missouri* in Tokyo Bay.

Ormoc, last Japanese supply port on Leyte, lies in ruins after being taken by American troops on Dec. 10, 1944. Halted temporarily, General MacArthur sent an amphibious force through Surigao Strait to land below Ormoc, December 7. Having split enemy forces and sealed off Ormoc Bay, U.S. soldiers won the port in three days and then proceeded to clamp a vise around the Japanese on Leyte's northwestern bulge. By December 25 the Americans had crushed all organized resistance on Leyte.

Mindoro-bound LST, struck by Japanese bombers during landing operations on December 15, is surrounded by small vessels which went to her aid. Machine gunner carefully scans the sky for enemy planes. The unexpected invasion of Mindoro Island met with little enemy opposition and put U.S. troops 155 miles south of Manila.

Luzon's beaches again become a battleground as U.S. troops swarm ashore in the Lingayen Gulf area, Jan. 9, 1945. Only token resistance was encountered, and General MacArthur was able to land 100,000 men in record time. While opposition stiffened as Americans drove toward Manila, the beachhead had been widened to almost fifty miles after one week of fighting, and capture of Lingayen Airfield the first day enabled our planes to support the advance. Also, our Navy roved the seas and prevented reinforcements from reaching the enemy.

First Ledo Road convoy moves across Salween River suspension bridge and along Kaolikung Mountain ranges on the 1,000-mile trek from Ledo, India, to Kunming, China. Wanting, the last objective in the Salween campaign, which was designed to open the China end of the Burma-Ledo road, was occupied on Jan. 20, 1945; the road was completed in late January.

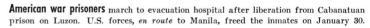

U.S. tanks cross burned bridge on way to Olongapo naval base and Bataan after landings on Zambales beachhead on Luzon, January 29. Olongapo was seized the following day.

American war prisoners march to evacuation hospital after liberation from Cabanatuan prison on Luzon. U.S. forces, *en route* to Manila, freed the inmates on January 30.

Santo Tomas Internment Camp, for three years the home of 3,000 American and British internees, revealed crowded living quarters when American troops entered Manila February 3 and freed inmates.

Japanese command car is destroyed by Philippine guerrillas in Manila. Two occupants were burned to death; others were shot down on the boulevard as they ran.

Manila burns as Japanese suicide troops make a stand in the old section of the city. Late in January U.S. infantry and paratroopers made new landings above and below Manila and with our forces advancing from Lingayen Gulf closed a pincers on the city from three directions. When American troops entered Manila on February 3, the enemy retired to the walled city south of the Pasig River. The Navy opened the final phase of the assault by bombarding the entrance to Manila Bay on February 13. Not until the second week in March was Manila cleared of the enemy.

Fujiyama, Japan's sacred mountain, is photographed through nose of a B-29. The picturesque volcano marked the course of Superfortresses on way to bomb war production centers in Tokyo.

Tokyo aircraft-engine factory, 15 miles from the Imperial Palace, burns after raid by U.S. Navy planes, February 16-17, 1945. Twelve hundred planes from 15 carriers participated. In a simultaneous attack, warships blasted Iwo Jima previous to invasion.

Corregidor's flagstaff again carries the American colors. Enemy opposition ended on Corregidor, March 1, 1945.

Landing craft churn toward Zamboanga on the southwestern tip of Mindanao, March 10, 1945, opening the battle for the second largest island in the Philippines. The city and its airfield were quickly captured, and eight days later the 40th Division moved into Panay. Cebu was invaded on March 26 and Negros on March 29, the Japanese putting up only scattered resistance.

Navy Task Force ships land Marines of the Fifth Amphibious Corps on Iwo Jima, Feb. 19, 1945. Bombs and shells from heavy pre-invasion bombardment were still bursting ashore as landing craft hit the beach. LCI(G)'s (Landing Craft Infantry Gunboats) had cleared the way for the Marines by moving into the beaches and firing into shore positions with small caliber guns. But the enemy's big guns, well camouflaged in reinforced caves, were not knocked out. As the Marines stormed ashore, the Japanese opened up, pouring shells from high ground onto our forces.

Marine dead and wrecked equipment line the beach at Iwo after initial assault. American casualties at the end of the 26-day struggle totaled 4,189 killed, 441 missing, 15,308 wounded.

Motomaya Airfield, Number One, in the shadow of Iwo's Suribachi Volcano, was taken on Feb. 20, 1945. Tiny Iwo Island was scene of one of the bloodiest battles in Marine history.

Fourth Division Marines shell Japanese on Iwo Jima after beachhead has been established under fire from Suribachi's guns. Iwo's conquest was necessitated by its location. Only 750 miles from Tokyo, and directly en route of the bombing B-29's from Saipan, it had served as a warning beacon for air defenses on the Japanese mainland. Moreover, capture of Iwo would enable our fighters to escort the big planes over Japan, and provide intermediate landing fields for the bombers in case of emergency.

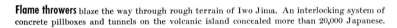

Flame throwers blaze the way through rough terrain of Iwo Jima. An interlocking system of concrete pillboxes and tunnels on the volcanic island concealed more than 20,000 Japanese.

Mt. Suribachi on Iwo is taken and the American flag is raised on its summit. On February 23 the Marines gained the crest of the extinct volcano on the southern tip of the island.

Crippled B-29, returning from raid on Japan, is forced to make landing on Motoyama Airfield, Number One, Iwo Jima. Marines flocked to the airport for a close-up of the Superfortress.

Okinawa is objective of Fifth Fleet warships. American forces invaded this key island in the Ryukyus, April 1, 1945, after a terrific air and naval bombardment had shattered defenses.

Rockets, spreading destruction, blast Okinawa beach preparatory to American landings. The Pacific bastion, 360 miles from the enemy's home islands, was last barrier to Japan's mainland.

Old Glory is raised over Okinawa as U.S. soldiers wade ashore, April 1, 1945. Initial opposition was slight, and the central third of the island was in American hands by the week-end.

American soldiers plod inland on Okinawa, while, in the background, the materiel of war is brought ashore to supply the combat forces. By April 10 they had overrun half of Motobu.

Japanese destroyer escort keels over under attack by B-25 bombers of the 345th U.S. Air Group near Amoy, China, on April 6, 1945. Panic-stricken sailors sprawl on the side of the sinking ship or cling to wreckage in the sea. The enemy frigate had exploded from direct hit amidships. Attacking planes, known as the Air Apaches, sank a second frigate in the same action.

LST's unload invasion vehicles at Tarakan, Borneo, on May 1, 1945, a few hours after Australian infantrymen made the initial assault on the island. Using tanks and flame-throwers to reduce pillbox and tunnel strongpoints, Allied troops captured Tarakan City and the island's airfield on May 5.

Empty brass shells at Yonabaru are gathered for salvage. American forces entered Yonabaru, Okinawa's fifth city and the eastern anchor of the Japanese line, on May 23, 1945. Finding the city reduced to rubble, they moved on to take heights dominating Rioi and Itarashiku to the south.

Seventh Infantry Division cleans enemy forces out of volcanic caves on Okinawa. During the 81-day battle, 103,000 Japanese of a garrison of over 110,000 were killed, the rest captured.

Aged Okinawans smoke American cigarettes. The problem of dispossessed civilians on Okinawa was complicated by the helplessness of native refugees worn down by Japanese rule.

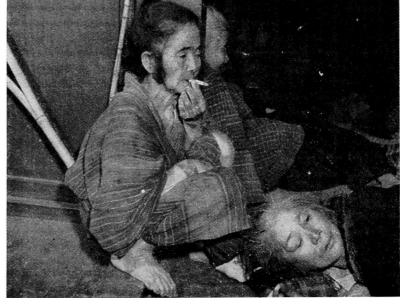

Aircraft carrier U.S.S. Franklin lists to starboard after being struck by two 500-pound bombs from a Japanese dive-bomber while operating against enemy fleet units in the Inland Sea, only 60 miles from the coast of Japan. The hits, scored on March 19, 1945, caused 1,000 casualties and forced the *Franklin* to return to New York.

Fire-fighters saturate the flight deck of the U.S.S. *Enterprise* with chemicals when an anti-aircraft shell from another ship in the fleet goes astray and strikes "Big E" during an attack on the Japanese coast, March 20, 1945. The *Enterprise,* "sunk" six times according to enemy claims, had successfully fought off four Japanese *Kamikaze* planes before the accident.

Wreckage crowds aft main deck of U.S.S. *Nevada* following Japanese *Kamikaze* attack off Okinawa, March 27, 1945. Commissioned in 1916, the *Nevada* earned an enviable record during World War II. Although badly damaged at Pearl Harbor, she was rebuilt and saw action off Normandy, the Aleutians, and the Ryukyu Islands.

Kamikaze planes strike the destroyer *Hazelwood* and leave its superstructure a shambles during action off the northeast coast of Okinawa, April 29, 1945. The pilots of *Kamikaze* planes were locked in their cockpits and committed to suicide missions. Introduced during the Leyte campaign, the *Kamikazes* reached full effectiveness off the Okinawa coast.

Gaping hole in her flight deck shows the results of a *Kamikaze* attack on the U.S.S. *Bunker Hill* on May 11, 1945. The carrier's crew fought for hours to control the fire which started in the pilots' ready room and threatened to destroy the ship. Ranked as one of the war's major surviving casualties, the *Bunker Hill* was returned to a west coast shipyard for repairs.

Cruiser Wilkesbarre stands by and pours water into the burning *Bunker Hill*. Damaged herself when she came alongside, the *Wilkesbarre* played an important role in saving the carrier. The *Bunker Hill* lost 373 of her crew. *Kamikazes* were named after the "Divine Wind" which once protected Japan.

Japanese battleship Haruna (*right*) is badly damaged while at anchor near Kure, July 28, 1945. Despite adverse weather, Third Fleet aircraft took a heavy toll of enemy shipping and aviation strength in a three-day strike on Japan's Kobe-Kure area.

Third Fleet planes fly over Japanese coastline on way inland in Toyko area, July 10, 1945. Sailing close to enemy shores with 1,000 planes on a mission to destroy or neutralize Japanese air power, Admiral Halsey's forces achieved a complete tactical surprise.

Toyama, Japanese industrial city, burns during B-29 night incendiary attack on August 2, 1945. More than ninety per cent of the Honshu Island city was utterly devastated by raging fires. The Superfortress blow also seared cities of Hachioji, Mito, and Nagaoka.

U.S. warships (*left*) shell Japan's shore installations for the first time, July 14–15, 1945, blasting area 275 miles north of Tokyo. Some of the most powerful ships of the Third Fleet trained their guns on northern Honshu and Hokkaido in two-day unopposed assault.

Oak Ridge, Tennessee, was site of one of three giant plants for the manufacture of the new atomic bomb. Possessing more power than 20,000 tons of TNT and a destructive force equal to the load of 2,000 B-29's, the weapon was developed in absolute secrecy. The release of atomic energy on Hiroshima and Nagasaki brought complete destruction.

Atomic bomb refugees, packed into freight cars, leave ghost city of Hiroshima. The first atomic bomb, dropped on Hiroshima Aug. 6, 1945, killed more than 60,000 persons.

Second atomic bomb explodes over Nagasaki, port and industrial center, on August 9. Smoke and dust billowed up to 20,000 feet as blazing fires almost obliterated the city.

Japanese surrender delegates arrive at Ie Shima from Tokyo, Aug. 19, 1945. Japan's offer to surrender was made on August 10 and accepted August 11. The delegation, headed by Gen. Kawabe Takashiro (second from left), was flown from Ie to Manila to receive instructions from General MacArthur's staff.

First American occupation forces of the 11th Airborne Division are loaded into trucks after landing at Atsugi Airfield, 20 miles from Tokyo, on August 30. These troops were immediately sent to secure the Yokohama area. Two days before, advance officers and technicians had landed to prepare the airfield for our huge transports.

General MacArthur arrives at Atsugi Airfield, Aug. 30, 1945, and leaves his plane, appropriately named *Bataan,* to step for the first time on Japanese soil. Simultaneously with Allied acceptance of the Japanese surrender on August 11, General MacArthur had been appointed Supreme Allied Commander in charge of Japanese capitulation.

Japanese destroyer, covered by guns of the U.S.S. *Nicholas*, brings officers and harbor pilots to a conference aboard the U.S.S. *Missouri* in Sagami Bay, August 26. The Japanese gave us data on channels of Tokyo Bay.

55,000-ton Missouri, flanked by destroyer, steams into Tokyo Bay, August 28, after waiting two days in Sagami Bay for demining of the upper waters.

Representatives of Japanese Government, headed by Foreign Minister Mamoru Shigemitsu, arrive aboard the *Missouri* at 8:55 A.M., September 2, Tokyo time, to sign final articles of surrender. Formal garb of the civilian delegates and the medal-bedecked and booted Japanese military were in sharp contrast to American officers in their neat but tieless regulation Pacific uniforms.

INSTRUMENT OF SURRENDER

General Yoshijiro Umezu signs surrender on behalf of Japanese Imperial General Headquarters at ceremonies on the *Missouri*, Sept. 2, 1945 (Tokyo Time). At left, General MacArthur; center, Lieut. General Sutherland, MacArthur's Chief of Staff.

This historic surrender document, signed aboard the *Missouri* in Tokyo Bay, ended World War II. First signature, for the Japanese Government, was that of Japan's Foreign Minister on behalf of the Emperor. General Umezu signed for Japan's military forces. Then General MacArthur and Allied representatives affixed their names, accepting the surrender.

General Douglas MacArthur, as Supreme Allied Commander, signs Japanese surrender document aboard the battleship *Missouri* in Tokyo Bay. Behind him are Lieut. General Jonathan Wainwright, left, and British Lieut. General Arthur E. Percival. both just liberated from Japanese prison camp. They witnessed Japan's surrender by special invitation of General MacArthur.